PRAISE F(

Frazzlebrain

"In a stressful time, *Frazzlebrain* stands as a beacon of calm and kindness, a book that combines experience and common sense, research, and remarkably helpful advice for improving the way we live our lives today."

—Deborah Blum, Pulitzer-Prize winning journalist and author of
Love at Goon Park: Harry Harlow and the Science of Affection

"Dr. Simmons Schneider has a talent for making complex terms easy to understand. Her book *Frazzlebrain* is a user-friendly, step-by-step guide of self-improvement skills. She has created a not-to-be-missed model for creating wholeness and happiness in life."

—Cathy Scott, *Los Angeles Times* bestselling author of
The Killing of Tupac Shakur and *Murder of a Mafia Daughter*

"*Frazzlebrain* is destined to become the go-to book for people experiencing anxiety, anger, and stress in their lives. It should also serve as a referring guidebook for clinicians, life coaches, instructors, stress management trainers, and others who seek to give their clients, patients, and students a pathway to move from helpless and hopeless to thriving and resilient."

—Dr. Steve Albrecht, HR trainer, security consultant, and employee coach

"Gina Simmons Schneider translates the mind-boggling advances in neuropsychology into beautifully described practical methods and skills for making your body a newfound friend and for calming long-standing patterns in your mind."

—Doug Braun-Harvey, LMFT, CGP, CST, author of
Treating Out of Control Sexual Behavior: Rethinking Sex Addiction

"In her gentle and very informative book, Dr. Simmons Schneider teaches us how to find our internal wisdom and to increase our abilities to face painful emotions, such as anxiety, anger, and frustration. This book is a much-needed resource for anyone who has ever struggled with stress and anxiety, as it teaches the readers about how to meet even our toughest emotions with ease and kindness."

—**Dr. Janina Scarlet,** award-winning author of *Superhero Therapy*

"Whether chapter-by-chapter or as a whole, *Frazzlebrain* offers a guidepost to greater inner and interpersonal peace on every page. Prepare to be defrazzled and dazzled by *Frazzlebrain*."

—**Brian H. Spitzberg, PhD, CTM™,** Senate Distinguished Professor,
School of Communication, San Diego State University

"Everyone occasionally needs tools to ensure that negative emotions do not erode mental or physical health. As tensions keep mounting in society today, the timing is ideal for the arrival of *Frazzlebrain*. Gina Simmons Schneider's offering is a must read for anyone wishing to calm the mind, tune the body, and unleash the healing power of play and imagination."

—**Terry Marks-Tarlow, PhD,** Adjunct Professor, Pacifica Graduate Institute, California Institute
of Integral Studies, and author of *Clinical Intuition in Psychotherapy, Awakening Clinical Intuition,
Psyche's Veil, A Fractal Epistemology for a Scientific Psychology,* and *Mythic Imagination Today*

"*Frazzlebrain* connects the dots where most of the topics addressed you'd only find in separate resources. It's a holistic viewpoint, connecting it all together for you. The stories are true, relatable, and realistic. Gina's writing and overall tone is comforting, heart-full, and compassionate. I will be referencing this work in my coaching and presentations going forward! Truly well-done!"

—**Sheryl Roush,** CEO, Sparkle Presentations, Inc, international speaker, and author

"Intelligently written with compassion and insight, Dr. Simmons Schneider's *Frazzlebrain* is filled with case studies, scientific research, personal stories, and lots of practical advice. This book is a welcome addition to the literature that will benefit professionals and non-professionals alike."

—**Wayne Regina, PsyD,** author of *Applying Family Systems Theory
to Mediation: A Practitioner's Guide*

Frazzlebrain

Gina Simmons Schneider

Frazzlebrain

BREAK FREE

from Anxiety, Anger, and Stress
Using Advanced Discoveries in Neuropsychology

CENTRAL RECOVERY PRESS

Las Vegas

Central Recovery Press (CRP) is committed to publishing exceptional materials addressing addiction treatment, recovery, and behavioral healthcare topics.

For more information, visit www.centralrecoverypress.com.

Publisher: Central Recovery Press
3321 N. Buffalo Drive
Las Vegas, NV 89129

26 25 24 23 22   1 2 3 4 5

Library of Congress Cataloging-in-Publication Data

Names: Schneider, Gina Simmons, author.
Title: Frazzlebrain : break free from anxiety, anger, and stress using
   advanced discoveries in neuropsychology / Gina Simmons Schneider, Ph.D.
Identifiers: LCCN 2021044541 (print) | LCCN 2021044542 (ebook) | ISBN
   9781949481624 (paperback) | ISBN 9781949481631 (ebook)
Subjects: LCSH: Stress (Psychology) | Neuropsychology. |
   Anxiety--Prevention. | Anger--Prevention.
Classification: LCC BF575.S75 S53 2022 (print) | LCC BF575.S75 (ebook) |
   DDC 155.9/042--dc23/eng/20211104
LC record available at https://lccn.loc.gov/2021044541
LC ebook record available at https://lccn.loc.gov/2021044542

Every attempt has been made to contact copyright holders. If copyright holders have not been properly acknowledged please contact us. Central Recovery Press will be happy to rectify the omission in future printings of this book.

Photo of Gina Simmons Schneider courtesy of Emily Rathburn Photography.

Publisher's Note
Our books represent the experiences and opinions of their authors only. The information contained herein is not medical advice. This book is not an alternative to medical advice from your doctor or other professional healthcare provider.

Every effort has been made to ensure that events, institutions, and statistics presented in our books as facts are accurate and up-to-date. To protect their privacy, the names of some of the people, places, and institutions in this book may have been changed.

Cover design and interior by Marisa Jackson.

For Jay, Brandon, Daniel, and Chloe,
my heart and raison d'etre,

and Nola, who paved the way.

To my clients and class participants,
thank you for sharing your precious stories with me.
I admire the healing wisdom within you.

Contents

Chapter Ten: *CalmBrain* for Life

- *Track your transformation*
- *Maintain your progress*
- *Stay connected and strong*

- *How do you know if you need professional help?*
- *Which type of therapy works the best?*
- *How do you find a therapist?*
- *Should you consider medication?*

FOREWORD

I n January 2021, a "Stress in America" survey reported that adults in the United States confronted a bitter election, political unrest and violence, questions about the economy, and a return to whatever normal would be called, all on top of a mounting death toll due to COVID-19. Stress is one of those evergreen topics—subjects journalists feel do not exactly go away. It will find its way back to all of us.

Prior to becoming a mental health therapist, I worked as a freelance journalist, writing instructor, and author of publishing, work-at-home, and travel reference books. Stress became a frequent topic in my magazine and newspaper work in addition to book research. Penning both *Surviving Separation and Divorce* and *The Angry Child,* which I co-authored as a journalist, inspired me to begin a midlife master's degree in clinical counseling. Of course, I had to keep working while I did so. Temporary stress, I guess you could say, in order to alleviate stress for others someday.

Thus, for twenty years, beginning in 1985, I taught hundreds of aspiring writers and guided many professionals on how to bring their academic, work, and life experience to the published page.

Gina Simmons Schneider and I met in one such class online in 2005 where we got to know one another, literally across the country. Dr. Schneider continued her private practice, begun decades before in San Diego, California, while I completed my degree at Johns Hopkins University. She served as an enthusiastic cheerleader and sounding board for my start in this field. The sharp ideas I recognized in her fifteen years ago are ever more insightful ones that I find in our collegial relationship today.

Over the years, we shared many thoughts about psychology references. I always appreciated her client referrals to my relationship-based books, including the 2005 release of *Overcoming Passive-Aggression: How to Stop Hidden Anger from Spoiling Your Relationships, Career, and Happiness*. When I drafted the 2016 update, I combed through dozens of new academic studies, news reports, and helpful materials. I found the ideal adjunct to therapy in *Manage Anger Daily Meditation*, which Dr. Gina Schneider and her husband, Jay Schneider, LCSW, developed on audio CD as well as MP3 download. Not only did I list this as a resource then, but I currently recommend it on my private practice site.

Like many mental health providers, particularly as a global pandemic drove demand for our services, I'm just as time challenged. Finding a few spare moments stands as an impasse between a handy book idea and its ultimate outcome in published form. Thus, when Dr. Schneider confided that she got up earlier each morning to craft chapter after chapter of *Frazzlebrain*, the book you now enjoy, my first human reactions were in this order: *Wow! I need to take whatever vitamin regimen she's on*. And, *Way to go*, because my excitement soars for her and for her readers.

Finally, we can benefit from the passion Gina Simmons Schneider, PhD, has for neuroscience and from her knowledge of and pathways out of anxiety, anger, and stress, which she aptly dubs in this book the three-headed monster. We can trust in the extensive research she has done to bring us the best minds and ideas, all within a writing style that's succinctly erudite yet appropriately detailed. Trust me, that's not always easy to accomplish, but she has delivered.

Frazzlebrain deserves to be on our bookshelves because we all get mired in frustration and overwhelm that, left unchecked, allows cynicism to emerge. Dr. Schneider's expertise and explanations afford us strategies to cap the erupting anxiety and overflowing angst. This can happen with or without the passive aggression or hidden anger that I researched. Without this *Frazzlebrain* resource, we may have more, not less, frazzle in our lives.

There's a quiz you must not miss and solid research on the not-so-obvious takeaways—on how shame activates pain receptors, gut microbiome affecting serotonin, pets and how they increase our oxytocin, mindfulness and blue spaces that soothe our brains. More than twenty different Frazzle Hacks teach skills and challenge new behavior. Who knew that rewriting your frazzled life story from the opposite, optimistic perspective could turn the day around or that extending small acts of Intentional Kindness offers a similar advantage?

Affirmations may not be a new concept, yet Dr. Schneider provides exact phrasing so that readers can increase their self-care and self-compassion and lower the arousal in their nervous systems. I've always been a fan of "the ask," the action where you ask for the interview when sending your resume, the assignment when submitting a proposal, or in this case, when you label your problem, remain open to a new approach, and ask for assistance. Dr. Schneider created Hope Generators for this very purpose. You can read more about these on your own because I recommend that you try this hack.

The writer in me loved the hack on Strengthening Curiosity as well as the general discussion of Flexible Curiosity. As a mental health colleague, personal and/or writing coach, this book inspires me to expand my metaphors into Compelling Fantasy (another hack) and to have my own clients identify which fictional characters they believe to be superheroes to inspire them in therapy.

Let's face it: the world as we know it has changed. We witness a more polarized society that often doesn't bring out the best of the human condition. Thus, there's pent-up frustration, a lack of understanding, or sheer misinformation that generates cumulative anxiety and stress.

We also now work quite differently. Our expectations have shifted. We look out for things we didn't used to and take fewer things we enjoy for granted. Most people have stepped up to face insurmountable challenges, using science, technology, compassion, and empathy to help each other along, especially because of the unanticipated pandemic we have shared.

Indeed, we celebrate joy precisely because we've had moments, or sadly long stretches, submerged in burdens, sometimes tragedies, feeling hassled and worn out.

Be frazzled no more! Highlighter in one hand, this book in the other, get ready to kick back and flex your open mind to the de-stressing opportunities that await you when you explore the pages ahead.

–Loriann Oberlin, MS, LCPC
www.loriannoberlin.com

How to Be Calm in a Frazzled World

For fast-acting relief try slowing down.

LILY TOMLIN

If you have picked up this book, you must know what it feels like to be frazzled. It might feel like a pressured sense of worry and irritability. You may feel some restless fatigue too. Racing between the demands of work, health, family, and friends, you feel stretched thin and foggy-headed. That's *frazzlebrain*.

If you feel frazzled, you dwell in good company. A recent survey from the American Psychological Association found that 84 percent of Americans feel some stress. Nearly half (47 percent) reported that their stress had increased in the last year. Another quarter said they suffered extreme stress (APA, Stress in America survey, 2021). The top five stressors include:

1. **Money**
2. **Work**
3. **Family responsibilities**
4. **Personal health**
5. **Health of a family member**

All this pressure can lead you to feel anxious and worried. You might notice symptoms like insomnia, racing heart, irritability, negativity, and nervousness. The pressure of stress and anxiety sometimes leads to angry outbursts.

Anger can disrupt our relationships at home and at work. Relationship conflicts can make us feel even more stressed. Add to that complex life events, like a financial setback or a move, and life can seem out of control. The good news is that you can learn to control your response to those events and circumstances. You can transform from *frazzlebrain* to *CalmBrain* by simply aiming your thoughts, behaviors, and experiences differently.

What is *CalmBrain?* It is a state of serene awareness. You're absorbed in the present moment. You breathe deeply, slowly, and effortlessly. Your heart rate slows, and your blood pressure lowers. Your muscles loosen and relax. You feel an easy stillness. Your mind is alert and flexible.

Calm is not merely the absence of stress but the powerful presence of peace.

The English poet John Dryden wrote, "We first make our habits, and then our habits make us." When you change your frazzled, habitual response to stress, space opens in your mind for calmness to emerge.

Advances in neuropsychology—how the brain interacts with feelings, behaviors, and experiences—demonstrate how your remarkable brain can help you cope better and feel happier. Your thoughts and behaviors directly impact the structure and chemistry of your brain. When you learn to steer your thoughts, behaviors, and experiences optimally, you'll feel calmer and happier.

I wrote this book to show you how to grab ahold of your brain's ability to calm, heal, and soothe itself. While other books focus on stress management, anger control, or anxiety relief, this book takes a radically different approach. It shows how anxiety, anger, and stress connect within your body's complex nervous system.

Imagine for a moment that there are two parts inside of you in a tug of war. You may feel pulled at one end of the rope by your anger, irritation, fury, and at the other end, anxiety, fear, worry. Above you is a giant magnifying glass, representing stressors such as unexpected traffic, plumbing leaks, or relationship conflicts. This magnifying glass of stress heats the tension, causing anger and anxiety to intensify.

Neuropsychologists have discovered a link between anger and anxiety. You can find this connection in the fight, flight, or freeze stress response. If you tend to worry a lot, you might avoid or flee stressful situations. Or perhaps you freeze up and feel a bit helpless to change a challenging problem. You might choose to avoid talking with your bullying boss. Or you feel hesitant to speak up when challenged.

If you are quick to anger, you might display more of the fight response. You might challenge others with expressions of irritability or outrage. Acting angry can make you feel bad later if you have offended a coworker or your spouse.

Whether you express more of an anxious/worried response or an irritable/angry response, the nervous system performs its intricate ballet. Neurotransmitters, chemical messengers in the brain, activate. Your body releases hormones that control bodily functions. These chemical reactions mobilize your body's defenses.

I have worked as a psychotherapist, conflict and anger management specialist, and executive coach for more than twenty-five years. Many of my clients struggled with unexpressed worries. Even though they came to me for help with anger, underlying worries troubled them. I also noticed that the people I treated for anxiety symptoms (intense worry) also harbored hidden anger. Stressful life events, like illness, or a relationship loss, made them seek psychotherapy.

Stress magnifies anxiety and anger. Our nervous system often responds to stress, creating symptoms that cause suffering. Your nervous system is composed of the brain, spinal cord, and a complex web of nerves. When your nerves feel frazzled, you might notice physical symptoms like headaches or gut discomfort. Signs of emotional distress, like insomnia, irritability, and sadness, can trouble you even more. These symptoms might prompt you to see a doctor or do something to help yourself feel better.

Anger and anxiety can seem like two sides of the same coin. In Roman mythology, the two-faced god Janus illustrates this point. Janus, the god of war and peace, future and past, presided over the beginning and end of conflicts. One face looked to the future; the other face looked to the past. Like Janus, anxiety and anger play a role in most human conflicts. If you suffer from anxiety, you might spend much of your mental energy concerned about the future. Perhaps you worry about job security, your child's schooling, or future health concerns.

When you feel angry, you might stew over past resentments. Suppose you put the two-faced Janus head onto a coin and flipped it. On any given day, the angry hothead might present with nervous anxiety, and the mild-mannered anxiety sufferer might tremble with smoldering rage.

4

Anger and anxiety might focus your mind on the past or the future. Present-moment stresses, like your car breaking down, magnify your emotions. Sometimes stress can take you to the breaking point. You need practical tools to help you cope better. This book will help you cultivate self-soothing thoughts, behaviors, and experiences. These tools will strengthen your resilience to stress and expand your capacity for happiness.

You can harness your own nervous system to increase your happiness and well-being.

Neuroscientists and psychology researchers have identified how thoughts, behaviors, and experiences can lower stress, anger, and anxiety. We know how happier brains operate and how to generate the brain's self-healing properties. You will learn how to use your brain and body to *defrazzle* and cultivate happiness. I am delighted to share these discoveries with you so that you can heal your frazzled brain. Let's start with Andrew's story.

How Andrew Changed His Response to Stress and Got the Girl

Andrew, a thirty-two-year-old regional sales manager, came to my office seeking help to manage stress. Andrew had met a woman he felt he might one day marry. His job required a lot of travel. He felt his overwhelming travel schedule interfered with his ability to spend time with his girlfriend. "I'm successful financially, but I cannot lead the lifestyle I really want. I don't eat right. It's hard to exercise. I have money but no life," he said. His father had passed away from a heart attack the previous year at sixty, leaving his mother alone.

On top of that, his mother had recently learned that she had breast cancer. "I feel like my mother needs me to spend time with her as well. Our family is still grieving. I'm worried about my mom, and I'm constantly on the road. I don't want to die young like my dad."

Andrew felt embarrassed about recent episodes of road rage. He would find himself yelling and cursing at people who committed driving errors on the road. Andrew knew that his reactions were extreme. He didn't know how to cope with his enormous stress and worry. "I feel frazzled all the time," Andrew said. "I don't want this feeling to ruin my relationship. If I quit my job, I don't know what I could do to support myself. But if I stay in this life, I could lose my girlfriend and my health. I'm trapped."

Andrew's story illustrates the many pressures of modern life. Andrew has *frazzlebrain*.

My research reveals that you do not need to perform an extreme life makeover to feel happier and healthier. I told Andrew that he didn't need to change his job or go back to school or make any significant changes to feel less stress. This was a radical concept for Andrew. He didn't believe that he could harness the power of his own brain to heal the stress he experienced.

I asked him to try a few things "as a scientific experiment." Andrew was astonished to learn that the key to his happiness and well-being resided within his own mind. Andrew learned that much of his frazzled worry stemmed from trying to solve all his problems at once. He even worried about future issues that might not ever happen. He started to see the connection between worrying about the future and his present stress. Andrew needed to change his habitual thoughts. He learned to stop future thinking and instead pay attention to the present moment.

We tried some exercises in my office to help him focus his mind on the present moment. He expressed surprise that he could calm down that quickly. I suggested that when he started to feel overwhelmed, he should gently redirect his mind to the immediate task in front of him. He found it calming. I explained that mindfulness—focusing on the present moment, on purpose, without judgment—changes the brain's chemistry. Andrew could meditate on airplanes and feel refreshed.

Andrew began to cultivate thoughts of gratitude toward his job. It provided him a good living. He stopped dwelling on what he could not do for his mother and girlfriend. Instead, he developed enjoyable ways to stay connected to them while on the road. As he better managed his anxiety and stress, he found ways to gather support for his mother. He pledged to help her through her surgery and support her recovery.

Andrew arrived for a therapy appointment after his mother's cancer went into remission. He said that his mother had expressed gratitude that he had been taking good care of himself. That freed her to focus on her own health and not worry so much about him. She told him that his frequent calls made her feel connected. When he found caregivers to help her recover from surgery, she felt loved and cared for even when he was out of town.

Andrew learned how he could eat a heart-healthy diet and get some exercise while on the road. We explored how he could make his travel time more fun. Experiences that connected him to life, nature, and fun offered opportunities for joy. On each trip, he would try to find a way to commune with nature. He learned that he could make sales calls on the phone while walking in a local park. He liked listening to music and audiobooks. He began to feel better about his personal and professional growth. Andrew strengthened his ability to cope with grief and stress. That impressed his girlfriend. I'm happy to report that they are now married.

Andrew transformed his frazzled brain chemistry with small, simple changes. Using *focused thoughts, intentional behaviors*, and *healing experiences*, Andrew became calmer. He had learned how to soothe his mind, care for his body, and stay connected to the people he loved. He began to feel sharper, younger, happier.

—*mm*—

Many people like Andrew have sought my help for symptoms of anger, anxiety, and stress. Distress drove them to seek the help of a professional psychotherapist.

Struggling parents learn how to slow down in the morning. Mornings are no longer an angry, irritated race to get to school on time but instead a time for connection with their children.

Couples who are suffering from the weight of competitive responsibilities learn to *defrazzle* their lives. Courageous people battling anxiety, anger, and stress learn how to face life in all its crazy frazzled majesty.

Years ago, I began a search for cutting-edge research to better help my frazzled clients. I devoured neuroscience research. It revealed how you could change your brain chemistry at will. I talked with neuroscience researchers who shared their latest findings.

You will learn how my clients used these techniques to improve their lives. I attended brain-based psychotherapy workshops led by neuropsychologists, psychologists, and physicians. They taught me how your adaptable brain can heal, calm, and soothe itself. I collected the most powerful and practical tools to share with you in this book. I want you to benefit from all that I've learned so that you can *defrazzle* and feel happier too.

Take a moment to answer the following questions based on how you have felt in the last seven days:

How Frazzled Are You?

To determine your level of *frazzlebrain*, answer yes or no to the following questions:

1. Do you feel like there are not enough hours in the day to do what you need to do?
2. Has a doctor diagnosed you with any stress-related conditions like gastrointestinal issues, migraine headaches, insomnia, or anxiety?
3. Do you find yourself feeling impatient and irritable too often?
4. Do you frequently worry about things you have no control over, like weather patterns, the global economy, or terrorism?
5. Do you rarely spend time with friends or engage in hobbies or fun activities?
6. Do you find it difficult to tolerate the mistakes of others?
7. Do you often feel tired, drained, unmotivated, or depressed?
8. Have friends, coworkers, or family advised you to calm down, slow down, or relax?
9. Do you startle easily?
10. Do you frequently find it challenging to motivate yourself to get your work done?

RESULTS

Yes to three or fewer: Good job! You actively try to take good care of yourself. You may occasionally feel frazzled and could benefit from the exercises in this book.

Yes to four to six: Your score shows a moderate level of *frazzlebrain*. You will notice significant benefits to your mood, health, and well-being when you incorporate the exercises at the included in each chapter.

Yes to seven or more: Your severe level of *frazzlebrain* may already cause you significant distress. You may feel unhappy with physical or psychological symptoms. You will notice the strongest benefit from incorporating the strategies recommended in this book.

What did you notice after taking this quiz? Did the results surprise you? Check in with yourself from time to time and retake this quiz. See if your score changes after you practice some of the techniques in this book. The exercises will help you strengthen your brain's ability to recover more quickly from the challenges of life.

What You Will Learn in This Book

Frazzlebrain is divided into three parts. **Part I: Focused Thoughts**, shows you how to focus your mind to calm and energize yourself. **Part II: Intentional Behaviors**, teaches you what specific actions will help you feel more serenity. **Part III: Healing Experiences**, shows you what experiences retrain your brain to respond to stress more calmly. Each chapter presents a unique way to lower anger, anxiety, and stress while improving your overall health and resilience.

You will get the chance to practice stress-relieving techniques or *frazzle hacks* throughout the book. These exercises help you strengthen your brain muscles to make you more resilient. It's a good idea to keep a journal next to you while you read this book. Use the journal to practice the *frazzle hacks*, record your feelings, and honor your progress.

Empower Your Brain's Self-Healing Properties

For decades, scientists believed that the brain could never heal or repair itself once it suffered damage or neuron loss. However, exciting neuroscience research reveals that the brain is *neuroplastic*. Psychiatrist and author Norman Doidge, MD, explains: "Neuroplasticity is the property of the brain that enables it to change its own structure and functioning in response to activity and mental experience" (Doidge 2015). Suppose you can change the structure and functioning of your brain by intentionally choosing healthier thoughts, behaviors, and experiences. Dr. Rick Hanson, the author of *Just One Thing*, writes, "There's a traditional saying that the mind takes the shape it rests upon; the modern update is that the brain takes the shape the mind rests upon" (Hanson 2011).

What we repeatedly think and do influences how our brain functions. Our thoughts and actions influence the brain's structure, chemistry, and electrical activity.

Life experiences can also change the structure and function of the brain. The trauma of witnessing a violent crime, for example, can change your brain. These changes cause stress reactions to memory triggers. However, when you cultivate positive experiences in your life, such as the experience of awe and wonder you might feel after hiking to a mountaintop, your brain recovers. Positive experiences help the traumatized brain heal. This book will share tools to help you change your frazzled responses and generate a calm happiness within you.

In **Part I: Focused Thoughts**, you will learn how to focus your thoughts on what you want to feel. Learning how to soften your stress response can strengthen your brain's self-healing properties.

As you read, you will learn why your brain gets frazzled and how to cultivate a more patient attitude. You will receive six quick and easy tools you can use to help you support and soothe yourself. You will discover how to use the power of your imagination to change your stress response. I will share with you how to visualize to calm your mind.

Learning to reduce cynical and hostile attitudes can help you create a happier, calm, unfrazzled life. I will show you how to refrain from harsh criticism of yourself and others. You will learn why excessive critical thinking proves to be harmful and what to think about instead.

The human imagination has the power to change brain chemistry. It can even create physical changes in your body. You will learn about the extraordinary breadth of both the placebo effect (how positive expectations create positive results) and the nocebo effect (how negative expectations create adverse effects). Your expectations can often determine the outcome of treatment. It helps to point your imagination in the direction you want your life to go. Positive mental rehearsal packs as powerful a punch as an actual rehearsal to enhance performance.

Positive imagery influences your mood and helps you generate more creative ideas. It also allows you to reduce anxiety and stress. You will learn why worrying can be so seductive. Yet worry wastes imagination power. When you gently redirect thoughts away from worry, your mood and performance improve.

In **Part II: Intentional Behaviors**, you will learn how your actions shape your emotional brain. Your brain and your gut interact to produce hormones and chemical messengers that can either heat up stress or cool it down. I will share easy ways to cool down your anxiety, anger, and stress, which can help keep your gut healthy. You will learn what behaviors help you tame anxiety, anger, and stress.

You can also change your brain chemistry by cultivating a kind brain. Neuroscience research shows that when you act with kindness toward others, something in your brain changes. Kindness helps you feel more capable no matter what your circumstances. When you tend to your relationships with caring, you feel happier.

Expanding kindness into a purpose greater than yourself allows you to feel a part of something significant. Expressing caring toward a greater community of people reduces loneliness and makes you feel supported. When you find meaning beyond yourself, you feel more resilient, happier, and less frazzled.

I share a questionnaire in Chapter Six to help you find your greater purpose. Striving to help others causes positive changes in your neurochemistry. It enables you to cultivate a feeling of competence and connection. You will learn why your relationship with yourself also matters. When you tend to yourself first, you develop a more peaceful state of mind. When you treat yourself well, you feel more capable and generous toward others. If you establish good self-care habits, you have more energy reserves to draw upon during tough times.

You can also reduce *frazzlebrain* by taking time to commune with nature. The human brain and body need time outside. You will learn about the natural antidepressant effects of a walk in the forest. The Japanese call it "forest bathing." Gardening can help prevent infections, create feelings of happiness, and lower stress. In modern life, we use a lot of dead things like computers, televisions, and smartphones. You feel happier when you interact with living things in real life. Planting flowers, playing with a dog, climbing a tree, or swimming in the ocean or a lake can help you feel calmer. Nature time can restore balance, reducing the tendency to worry.

In **Part III: Healing Experiences**, you will learn why some forms of anxiety can only be repaired by experience. For some anxiety sufferers, changing thoughts and behaviors is not enough for symptom relief. The amygdala, the threat-sensing part of the brain, only learns from experience. To reduce nervous system arousal, you need healing experiences. Healing experiences retrain your brain to respond calmly.

Relationships change your brain in significant ways. Good relationships lower our anxiety, anger, and stress and help us cope better when life gets challenging. When we cultivate strong, healthy, and rewarding relationships throughout life and grow a nurturing support system of reliable people, the brain heals. Choosing uplifting influences helps your brain maintain a healthy balance of chemicals. You strengthen that balance when you turn your mind toward uplifting thoughts, actions, and experiences.

Sometimes you get so caught up in the struggles of daily life that you forget how to create positive emotions. Positive emotions like joy, hope, gratitude, and serenity provide significant health benefits. When positive emotions increase, that frazzled feeling decreases. You might think that positive things must happen to you before you can feel good. You do not need to wait for something wonderful to happen to feel better. Create your own positive emotions through play and other activities that challenge you a little. When you take better care of yourself, positive emotions bubble up spontaneously within you.

I will share scientific research on the power of play. Playfulness helps your brain recover from stress and promotes happiness. The great playwright George Bernard Shaw wrote, "We don't stop playing because we grow old; we grow old because we stop playing." You will learn why you should make play a priority in your adult life and how it can help you feel younger.

Cultivating experiences of awe and wonder, like one might enjoy while visiting Niagara Falls, helps the brain recover from stress. When you learn how to allow joyful moments to occur effortlessly, you expand your resilience to stress.

Mindfulness (the practice of paying attention to the present moment without judgment) trains your brain to respond with calm strength to stressful life events. Mindfulness meditation works to broaden your brain's ability to manage anxiety, anger, and stress. I provide easy steps to get you started that won't cost any money and take very little time.

You will learn the value of self-compassion and how to cultivate it within yourself. Compassion research reveals that empathic concern for yourself and others is the key to mental and physical well-being. When you attend with compassion to yourself and others, you can help create a more peaceful community.

The final chapter provides a way to measure and track your progress. Tracking your progress will help you stay focused on improving your thoughts, behaviors, and experiences. In the appendix, you will learn how to decide whether you should seek professional help. I provide helpful tips on finding the right therapist for you and whether you should consider medication.

Each chapter features *frazzle hack* exercises to help you practice brain healing techniques. Every activity invites you to try something different to help you achieve a calmer, happier, healthier lifestyle. These techniques stem from over twenty-five years' experience as a licensed psychotherapist. I have coached executives managing challenging work conflicts and provided training for Fortune 500 companies striving to improve morale. I share real case examples after changing identifying factors, and some cases are composites to preserve the privacy of my clients.

The recommendations in this book stem from scientific research and my personal and professional practice. Each chapter offers tools and exercises to help you feel happier, reduce stress, and improve your functioning at work and home.

I invite you to take the challenge to reduce your anxiety, anger, and stress. Begin where you can. Try one thing at a time. Use the *frazzle hacks*, worksheets, and self-improvement skills provided. Pay special attention to those exercises and methods that give you the most relief and support. These techniques work. To get the most out of this book, use a journal to record your *frazzle hack* exercises, keep track of your changes, and measure your progress. Writing about your efforts strengthens the lessons learned and helps you speed up the process of change.

Changing how you think and behave, habits that may have become ingrained, can feel challenging. With this book's tools, you'll be well on your way to a happier, calmer, more resilient you. Those who have used these strategies report remarkable quality-of-life improvements. Now grab a pen or pencil, your *frazzle hack* journal, and get started!

Focused Thoughts

PART I

ONE

How to Cool Down and Self-Soothe

It is not stress that kills us, it is our reaction to it.

HANS SELYE

There is an old Swedish proverb, "Worry gives a small thing a big shadow." Worrisome, anxious thoughts and feelings can magnify and cast a giant shadow over your life. Anger, anxiety, and stress interact, causing changes in your brain chemistry and physiology. Much of the time, anger gets its fuel from underlying anxiety, worries, fear, and pain. Those with anxiety often harbor suppressed, unexpressed anger. Sometimes you feel stress and may not realize that you're angry until you lose your temper out of the blue.

This combination of anxiety, anger, and stress floods your body with stress chemicals. These chemicals create tension, discomfort, and fog your ability to concentrate. This is *frazzlebrain,* a psychophysiological state caused by unmanaged stress, anxiety, and anger.

In this chapter, you'll learn how to activate the *cooling system* of your brain, taking you from *frazzlebrain* to *CalmBrain*. When you think self-calming thoughts, you find relief from anxiety, anger, and stress. When you feel frazzled, you may spend time thinking of ways to get even with those who have hurt you. It is vital to resist the urge for revenge when someone makes you angry. It activates the *hot system* of your brain that wants immediate gratification. The desire for revenge can keep you agitated, impatient, and angry for far longer. Attitudes, like the need to win at all costs, can fuel anger and distress. This book will provide calming strategies to help you *defrazzle* and cope better.

If we live long enough, we will all experience something difficult. You can find comfort in self-soothing thoughts, behaviors, and experiences. You will learn why hope is healthy. You can cultivate optimism and hopefulness to counteract *frazzlebrain*. But first, it helps to understand how *frazzlebrain* develops.

Recently I observed a confrontation between an older woman and a young male cashier at a grocery store. The cashier would not redeem the woman's coupon. She raised her voice in anger, and the cashier tried to calm her down, explaining why he could not honor the coupon. I watched this unfold and noticed that the woman spoke with a thick accent. She struggled a little to understand the fine print on the coupon. Maybe she worried about money because she needed to stretch every dollar.

Hidden anxiety often gets expressed as some form of anger. Anger can range from mild annoyance to homicidal rage. Anxiety presents as a softer emotion, covered up by anger's hard exterior. Anxiety often stems from internal conflicts or arguments with the self. Here are some examples of internal conflicts:

- You need to find a better-paying job, but most opportunities require moving to another state.
- You need a raise but feel uncomfortable asking your boss because you recently took sick time.
- You want to spend the holidays with your parents this year but feel guilty. Your husband has not seen his family in more than a year, and he wants to celebrate with them.
- Your doctor says you are at risk for diabetes, and you need to exercise more. But your child has a learning disability and requires more time to help her with her homework.
- You have been taking care of your sick mother, and you feel tired and need a break. It makes you feel resentful and guilty.

In the last example, you find that you feel tired and resentful caring for your sick mother. Perhaps you worry that the pace of caring for your mother might break you. You want your mother to get the care she needs, but you doubt your own stamina and ability to rise to the challenge. These inner conflicts might make you irritable with your mother. You might also feel irritable with any other people in your life who want something from you.

These underlying anxieties can trigger anger, irritability, and distress. If you come home to find out that your house has flooded, that stress magnifies the worry and anger you already feel. Now you're suffering from *frazzlebrain*. Underlying anxiety causes a constant drip of tension that fuels anger outbursts (Murphy and Oberlin 2016).

How Stress Magnifies Difficult Emotions

Stress acts like a magnifier for difficult emotions. The three-headed monster of anxiety, anger, and stress can upset us all. *Frazzlebrain* triggers racing heart rate, shallow breathing, worrisome thoughts, and pressure to find a solution to every imagined negative outcome. During times like these, we feel a profound urge to act but feel frazzled and cloudy-headed.

Frazzlebrain does not help us make good decisions or solve complicated problems. In fact, it can make us more accident-prone, distracted, and less focused. When frazzled, you may find yourself racing around yet accomplishing little. You feel a pressured sense of urgency, impatience, and irritability.

To combat *frazzlebrain*, first pause, slow down, and quiet your nervous system. When you feel pressure, slowing down requires a bit of patience. It may surprise you that you can teach yourself to practice patience.

Cultivating Patience

"I don't have patience. If I had patience, I wouldn't have this anger problem!" said Mark, a forty-year-old electrical engineer. Mark's employer had referred him to me for conflict management coaching. Mark felt frustrated at the notion that he could learn patience. He believed patience was a natural talent that he did not possess. Feeling justified in his anger, he blamed incompetent managers for his workplace problems. Instead of addressing Mark's concerns, the boss focused on Mark's anger problem. Mark's angry behavior did not work for him. It didn't make anything better at work. It made things worse for him. Mark needed to learn patience.

HeartMath Institute Founder Doc Childre calls patience "the art of intelligent waiting." Patience requires the capacity to sit with disturbing feelings without acting on them. Instead of giving in to a hostile urge, patience allows you to consider your best option. Patience has many advantages. It allows you time to think about what course of action might prove most helpful. Patience is the capacity to wait, to endure through pain. In effect, patience requires great courage. Patience requires us to face our feelings of helplessness. Helplessness feels very painful. That's why it takes courage to acknowledge that pain. Patience does not mean you push down, deny, repress, or avoid negative feelings. Patience requires that you pause while uncomfortable feelings bubble up inside of you.

Patience requires delaying the satisfaction of yelling at a reckless driver or a disrespectful teen. The angry animal within wants to growl, scream, kick, and bite. Yet those behaviors will not get you a raise, a promotion, the respect of your peers, your teenager, or your spouse. Acting out in anger does release tension and, in the moment, reduces the pressure you might feel in your body. Yet angry outbursts won't inspire the long-term cooperation you want from others. Learning to delay gratification in the short term can help you reap big rewards in the long run.

Lessons from the Marshmallow Test

You may have seen amusing YouTube videos of the famous marshmallow experiments done with children in the 1960s and early 1970s. In this series of experiments, Stanford University researchers Walter Mischel and Ebbe B. Ebbesen wanted to see if there were differences between children who could delay gratification and those who could not. They told preschool children (ages four to six) that they could either eat a marshmallow now or wait and get two marshmallows later. The researcher left the child alone in a room with a marshmallow for about fifteen minutes, and sometimes longer (Mischel and Ebbesen 1970).

Some of the children would gobble the marshmallow immediately. Others would squirm and avoid looking at it. Some children picked it up, smelled it, and appeared tormented by the long delay. When they returned, if the child had not yet eaten the treat, the experimenter would give the child two. Mischel and Ebbesen followed these children over many years to see how they fared in life.

Those children who could wait seemed to perform better in life and earned higher SAT scores. By age thirty, they had a healthier BMI (body mass index). They showed better self-worth and coped better with stress and frustration (Mischel 2014). A later study using fMRI scans found differences in brain structures between those who could wait and those who could not. They found that the part of the brain related to motivation and self-control (frontostriatal network) was more active in those who could wait. The part related to emotions, desires, and addiction (ventral striatum) was more pronounced in those less likely to wait (Luerssen, et al. 2015).

The bottom line is that they found that you can stick with something difficult if you can delay gratification and tolerate frustration. Learning anything challenging, like playing piano, learning a new language, or memorizing equations, requires handling frustration. The capacity to stick with something hard requires patience.

Interestingly, it might be adaptive for some kids to eat the treat immediately and not wait for the later payoff. For example, some children grow up with untrustworthy caregivers. Those kids are better off eating the marshmallow now. Trusting that a delay in gratification will lead to a payoff later helps us wait. If you do not believe that hard work can help you master a skill, you will not be motivated to try. Instead, you might favor things that come easy to you. If you grew up in poverty, you might have learned to spend your money now because it may not be there for you later (Mischel 1961).

Mischel performed more marshmallow tests where the experimenter showed the kids their trustworthiness. They showed the children that they could summon the experimenter by ringing a bell. Children played with the researchers before the start of the experiment. The casual play with the experimenter helped the children became familiar and comfortable with them. The researchers found out what treats the children preferred. They substituted a favorite treat for the marshmallows. Even after those changes, researchers still saw differences between the two groups of children.

Successful delayers tried different strategies to reduce their discomfort while waiting. Some would squirm and fidget, push the bell and the treat as far away as they could. Some would doze off to sleep, while others made up little songs or games. Those kids who could delay found ways to comfort, amuse, or entertain themselves while they waited. Dr. Mischel calls this *activating the cooling system.*

Our brains are wired in the hot system to want gratification now. We have a bias for short-term payoffs and must learn how to cool that down to wait for a bigger payoff later. That requires some mental effort. Yet because our brain is malleable, we can train ourselves to delay gratification for something greater later.

You can learn to cope better with frustration, anxiety, and stress. If preschool children can find methods to comfort and soothe themselves, so can you. It's like any other skill. The capacity to tolerate the discomfort of anger, anxiety, and stress requires practice. You can activate and strengthen your brain's cooling system with the following three steps:

Three Steps to Activate Your Cooling System

1. **Recognize that you feel something uncomfortable.**
2. **Name that uncomfortable feeling**—for example, stress, anger, embarrassment, worry.
3. **Provide support, soothing, and comfort to yourself.**

Recognizing your feelings allows you to notice that something feels wrong. Like physical pain, emotional pain tells you that something needs your attention. If you do not notice your own discomfort, that can allow the pain to grow worse.

How to Recognize Discomfort

You might ask, "How do I know I am feeling something if I don't recognize the feeling in the first place?" It helps to notice when your behavior seems out of proportion to the situation. For example, perhaps you arrive home on most days, and your toddler's toys in the living room don't bother you. But on this day, you find the toys intolerable and begin to get angry at your spouse for not cleaning up the mess. When you find yourself irritated about things that usually don't bother you, ask yourself, "What am I feeling? What do I need?" Pay attention to your emotions so you can provide yourself some care. Other signs that your feelings might need attention include:

- **Compassion fatigue:** difficulty summoning concern for someone for whom you would usually care.
- **Accident proneness:** carelessness or a lack of awareness of your physical environment.
- **Physical discomfort:** headaches, body aches, fatigue, even after a good night of sleep.

- **Forgetfulness:** losing items, forgetting names, leaving your essential documents in the wrong place.
- **Bitterness:** persistent brooding feelings of anger, annoyance, or irritation.

When you care for yourself, you have room for compassion. Perhaps a coworker recently received a diagnosis of cancer. If you feel more irritation than compassion, you need to give yourself some care.

Forgetting essential things shows some interfering distraction that may need your attention. Clumsiness, accident proneness, and forgetfulness suggest that you need to slow down. It helps to pay closer attention to yourself as you move through your life.

If you feel persistently bitter, irritated, or annoyed, it suggests unmet needs. When you provide some attention to those needs, you will feel better.

Why Naming Your Feelings Matters

Naming the feeling helps you understand it, face it, and see it as separate from yourself. You *have* the feeling; you are not one with the feeling. For example, one night, driving home from work, I started feeling irritated. I paid attention to that restless, uncomfortable feeling. Then I asked myself, "What is this emotion?" I called this feeling *irritation*. "What irritates me right now? What is the irritation about?" I asked. I remembered I needed to stop at the grocery store. I noticed I felt hungry and tired, and I just wanted to go straight home and prepare dinner. I named the irritation. "I am tired and hungry, and I want to eat and rest," I said to myself.

After noticing and naming the feelings, I offered myself some support and comfort. "Since I'm hungry, I could buy and eat a healthy snack at the market to help me feel better and finish my chores." I told myself, "You'll feel better after eating a snack." As simple as this sounds, many people do not name or notice their feelings at all. For some, self-neglect is almost a badge of honor.

Some parents, trying to toughen up their kids, encourage them not to talk about discomfort. Many parents punish their children for expressing their feelings. When those children grow up, they often feel shame and neglect themselves when they feel bad.

At any age, you can pivot away from the harsh shame and self-neglect learned in childhood. Anxiety, anger, and stress ease when you begin to support and soothe yourself.

How to Support and Soothe Yourself

At the first sign of discomfort, take these three steps:

1. **Notice discomfort.**
2. **Name the feeling.**
3. **Apply self-soothing.**

Many people do not know where to start to soothe themselves. Sometimes people reach for a pill, a beer, or another drug for a feel-good experience. Drug dependency doesn't help you develop your self-soothing muscle. Depending on drugs for self-soothing often leads to substance abuse and addiction. Instead, it is helpful to cultivate a wide range of soothing behaviors.

Self-soothing begins with your five senses: seeing, hearing, smelling, tasting, and touching. Find an activity that would pleasantly activate one or more of your five senses. Try to focus your mind on the sensory signals you're receiving and nothing else. When you pay attention to sensory details in the present moment, your thoughts and mental chatter fade into the background. Your nervous system settles down. It makes room for positive feelings to bubble up within you.

Five Senses Soothing

- **Seeing:** Arrange flowers in a vase. Take a walk in a beautiful setting. Visit an art museum. Look at a fun magazine. Watch animals at play.
- **Hearing:** Listen to music. Enjoy the sounds of nature. Watch videos of children laughing. Play a musical instrument. Compliment yourself. Talk to a dear friend. Enjoy a quiet moment.
- **Smelling:** Stop and smell the roses. Bake something delicious. Use an infuser with your favorite fragrance. Light a scented candle.
- **Tasting:** Slow down when you eat. Savor each bite. Sip on a comforting tea or flavored coffee. Stop and savor three meals per day.
- **Touching:** Massage your body with scented lotion. Take a hot bath or Jacuzzi. Go for a swim. Hug a friend. Make love.

When you take time out of each day to comfort yourself, you feel less frazzled and happier. When you practice self-soothing daily, you become more skilled at calming yourself. You handle life stresses better. It works even when faced with aggravating and worrying situations, like a bullying boss or a hostile neighbor.

Frazzle Hack: Self-Soothing

Take a moment to sit in a comfortable chair with your feet on the floor. Take five slow and deep breaths. Notice where in your body you may be feeling discomfort, tension, or pain. Let yourself take several deeper breaths. Tell the tense parts of your body that it is okay to release the tension. Turn your attention to your sense of touch. Gently massage the parts of your body that feel discomfort. Use your hands or a massage tool. Next, draw your attention to the parts of your body that feel no pain, tension, or discomfort. Breathe deeply. Allow your mind to notice that many parts of your body feel relaxed, free from pain, and comfortable. Notice how it feels to draw your attention to the parts of your body that feel comfortable. Wrap your arms around yourself. Hold yourself in this moment. Record your impressions in your frazzle hack journal.

Why Revenge Feels Sweet but Leaves You Bitter

Sometimes things make us feel bitter, angry, and worried. Maybe your boss gave you an unfavorable review. It might make you puff up with righteous indignation; maybe you feel a little powerless or victimized. Thoughts of revenge or quitting or telling off the boss might flood your mind. How many of us dream of getting back at the office bully, the disloyal friend, or the sadistic professor?

A client discovered that her husband was having an affair. She followed him in her car one night. While he engaged in a tryst with his girlfriend, she took his computer from his car, deleted the hard drive, and replaced it in his trunk. Some of you reading this story might be thinking, "You go, girl!" You might feel a little charge, a sense of justice, empathizing with my client who got her revenge. Some of you might sympathize with the husband. You would not want your computer sabotaged.

When harmed, most of us feel motivated to punish the responsible individual. This motivation to punish resides in a part of the brain called the dorsal striatum. Located toward the top of the brain behind the eyes and in front of the ears, the dorsal striatum becomes active when we anticipate pleasure, like eating a good meal. This brain region also plays a vital role in addiction and obesity, as it holds dopamine receptors associated with intense pleasure. We can get a sense of satisfaction from feeling like someone got what they deserved. It makes things feel fairer, and for a moment, we feel better (Balleine and Hikosaka 2007).

Revenge Makes You Unhappy

While fantasies about getting even can feel sweet, research shows that we end up feeling worse if we act on that fantasy. Social psychologist Kevin Carlsmith, PhD, and his colleagues performed a study that allowed participants to punish someone who cheated them. Participants *allowed* to punish the cheater felt worse than those who did *not* punish the cheater. When we take the path of revenge, we continue to obsess about our injury, making us feel unhappy. Those people who were not given the opportunity to retaliate felt happier. They moved on from the slight and recovered faster (Carlsmith, Wilson, and Gilbert 2008).

Some people have a tougher time letting go of anger and revenge. Social psychologist Ian McKee of Australia found that the most vengeful people have two social attitudes: right-wing authoritarianism and social dominance. "People who are more vengeful tend to be those who are motivated by power, by authority, and by the desire for status," says Dr. McKee. "They don't want to lose face" (McKee and Feather 2008). They choose pride and dominance over happiness and social connection.

Social neuroscientist Tania Singer found that men and women differ in how they process revenge in the brain. In this study, subjects played an economics game while their brains were monitored with fMRI scans. Subjects observed some people who played unfairly receive an electric shock punishment. Both male and female subjects showed empathy for players who received punishments (with activation in the fronto-insular and anterior cingulate cortices). But men showed significantly less empathy for the unfair players. When the cheating players were punished, men showed activation in the pleasure/reward centers of the brain (nucleus accumbens). Women, however, showed empathy for the suffering of both fair players and unfair players.

Dr. Singer suggests that men may see themselves as more dominant. Perhaps they feel responsible for monitoring the behavior of others so that social justice prevails. In contrast, women seem to feel empathy for both fair and unfair players, which may help maintain social connections. Social connections help preserve the social glue of society. This tendency to punish others appears more common in tribal cultures or gangs and criminal organizations, where a legal justice system does not exist (Singer, et al. 2006).

Sometimes families can behave like tribal gang cultures, with threats of punishment and struggles for dominance. These families foster a tense climate that can lead to anger, anxiety, and stress. In many of these families, saving face, winning, or establishing dominance, is more important than cultivating a feeling of safety and trust.

Saving Face vs. Cultivating Trust

For many years, I worked with families seeking help for their angry, unmanageable teenagers. One family—I'll call them the Coopers—brought their fifteen-year-old son Josh to my office for treatment for disobedient, angry, disrespectful behavior. Josh initially refused to come into my office and remained in the car. His desperate parents looked frazzled, embarrassed, and angry, describing their son's defiance. "We've grounded him, taken away his phone, his computer, his television, his ability to see his friends, and still, he refuses to do what we tell him to do. He has no respect."

"What did you say to your son about this appointment?" I asked.

"We knew he wouldn't come, so we just picked him up from school and brought him here, and now he won't get out of the car," said Josh's dad.

I was still quite curious and asked, "So, what did you tell him?"

"Well, we told him we were taking him to the mall to use his birthday gift cards and instead brought him here. When we got here, we told him that he would not get to use his gift cards because of his bad behavior but would have to go to counseling instead. He just flipped out and refused to come in," the mom said.

After further exploring the history of bad behavior and punishment, it became clear that the parents used punishment to establish dominance and frustrate their son to get back at him for his disrespectful behavior. They described the many punishments they inflicted on Josh with vengeful glee as if they were defeating an enemy. When Josh misbehaved, they responded with more punishment and humiliation.

Josh had lost trust in his parents, and they had lost trust in him. The parents did not realize that their focus on dominance and respect over love, trust, and connection, created a hostile atmosphere in their home. Using punishment as a power play rather than a teaching opportunity caused their son to learn to use power and control in retaliation.

Josh's parents gave me permission to go down to the car and talk to him in the parking lot, alone. Josh seemed respectful, sad, and angry.

"I don't need counseling. They can't make me go," Josh told me, with tears in his eyes. "They just keep making me do things and don't even care about what's going on in my life."

I stood outside the car and saw a lonely, unhappy teen trying to save face.

"Would you like me to see if I can help you and your parents get along better?" I asked.

"I don't know if anything can help," Josh replied. Eventually, he agreed to talk with me without his parents present.

Josh, his parents, and I agreed on some basic ground rules of counseling. Honesty, mutual consent, and consideration of the schedules of both Josh and his parents were necessary before we scheduled each appointment. Eventually, the parents cultivated some essential trust and made some mutual agreements with Josh, reducing the pattern of cruel punishment and retaliation in their home.

Families that suffer from problem anger most commonly complain about a "lack of respect." Hostility, revenge, and retaliation stream forth to establish dominance, obedience, and respect. Saving face becomes more important than fostering love, trust, joy, connection, and community. People who grow up in families like this learn that they cannot trust, feel safe, and relax in relationships because a battle is always underway. When you maintain a constant readiness for self-defense, you will feel more frazzled than the average person.

Neuropsychology researchers found differences in the brains of those who value dominance and respect over community and connection. Those with a Social Dominance Orientation (SDO) believe that some social groups are better than others. They value dominance hierarchies such as ranks, scores, net worth, or other forms of power. These folks feel comfortable with social inequalities. They believe that the rich deserve their wealth because they earned it while the poor will remain so due to their laziness. They identify others based on social rank, status, and merit rather than individuals with unique qualities worthy of respect. A high social dominance orientation allows one to narrow the groups of people worthy of concern and justify the value of one's own group over other groups. High SDO scorers are more likely to believe:

- *Males should dominate, and females should submit.*
- *Authority figures deserve obedience without question.*
- *Some racial groups are better than other groups.*
- *Their country is better than any other country.*

Researchers discovered two key brain regions that showed sensitivity to social ranks. Those with a high score on the SDO scale showed increased activation of these two brain regions (dorsolateral prefrontal cortex and superior temporal sulcus). The SDO scale can even predict political attitudes and behaviors associated with a preference for dominance and hierarchies. High SDO attitudes can often trigger anger and frazzled reactions toward those who disagree or push for progressive changes to the established order. High SDO people find it difficult to feel compassion for those in other groups who might be suffering (Romain, Girard, and Dreher 2017).

In contrast, people with a low SDO score possess more egalitarian values such as, "All men are created equal" or, "We are all god's children." These folks value the universal rights of humanity and see diversity in organizations as a strength rather than a problem. Lower SDO scorers display higher levels of empathy and compassion for the suffering of others, regardless of their social standing. They can feel empathy for those outside of their identity group (Pratto, et al. 1994). Low SDO scorers are more likely to believe the following:

- *Women's rights are human rights.*
- *Everyone deserves an equal opportunity to pursue what makes them happy.*
- *One should judge another by the content of their character and not by their race.*
- *Those who have the means should help those who are less fortunate.*

The greater empathy that low SDO people feel can help them buffer some of the stresses of life. Those with high levels of empathy are rated as more likable (Marcus 1980). Empathetic individuals cultivate better collaboration and cooperation with others (Radzvilavicius, Stewart, and Plotkin 2019).

Look at your attitudes and observe how some of your angry, frazzled feelings may link to social dominance beliefs and attitudes. Ask yourself if you could soften the desire for dominance, winning, or getting your way, and instead imagine leading with caring and compassion. Just imagining a little empathy and understanding can help you feel less angry.

Frazzle Hack: Empathy

Take a moment to close your eyes, settle yourself down a bit. Take five deep breaths. Slowly inhale through your nose, and slowly exhale through your mouth. Notice your breathing as it gets deeper, slower, more prolonged. Think about someone you know who may be going through a difficult struggle right now. Imagine that person in front of you. What are they wearing? What expression is on his/her/their face? Then imagine yourself saying the following to that person: "I hope that you can find peace right now. I hope that you can live with ease through your current struggle. May you feel contentment and happiness. May you be healthy."

Sit quietly for a few moments. Notice what you feel after imagining compassion for another. Do you feel more relaxed? Write down what you noticed in your frazzle hack journal.

Some people were taught that the best way to deal with anger was to "let it out" or discharge the pressure by yelling, hitting something, or blowing up at someone. In the early days of marital therapy, psychologists encouraged angry couples to hit each other with soft foam-covered bats to "let out" their anger. Subsequent research showed that "letting out" your anger in that way doesn't work.

Why "Letting Out Anger" Doesn't Work

Brad Bushman of Iowa State University published a study showing that the more we release our anger on a punching bag or a person, the angrier we remain (Bushman 2002). If you want to feel better after someone harms you, it's best to stop focusing on the injury and do something positive for yourself.

One client found that she felt significantly better when she stopped revenge fantasies and passive-aggressive behavior toward her bully boss. Instead, whenever she experienced a difficult day at work, she imagined making a delicious dinner and enjoying it with her loving husband. An avid cook, she looked up recipes and focused on stimulating her brain's pleasure centers. Eventually, whenever her boss "went on a rampage," she smiled, licked her lips, and thought, "We're going to eat good tonight."

The modern American workplace provides fertile ground for frequent acts of revenge. Rude to a fast-food worker? Better check your hamburger before you bite. Insult your colleague in a meeting? Count on some negative comments about you from that department. In the book, *Getting Even: The Truth About Workplace Revenge—And How to Stop It,* authors Tripp and Bies found that non-violent acts of revenge are common in the workplace (Tripp and Bies 2009).

If workers respond to perceived slights, insults, or emotional injuries with some form of retaliation, it's not surprising that conflicts in the workplace are so common. Middle managers spend 25 percent of their time dealing with workplace conflict. CEOs spend an average of 26 percent of their time managing conflict. If every negative feeling in the workplace produced a retaliatory action, conflicts remain a self-fueling problem for managers. That leaves everyone frazzled.

Six Tips and Tricks to Help You Feel Better Fast

You can improve your mood and recover from angry, vengeful feelings by finding healthy ways to make your own life happier.

When you realize that you can create experiences in your own life that can change your brain chemistry, you feel empowered. First, you must decide between stewing in anger at the memory of the terrible injustice you sustained or trying to feel better. Ask yourself, "Do I want to stay angry, or do I want to feel better?" Behaviors that make you feel comforted and supported directly address the source of your suffering.

You can even improve your mood by imagining or planning pleasurable activities. Your thoughts, what you dwell upon mentally, your behaviors, habits, and life experiences can change your mindset and brain chemistry. You feel happier when you intentionally shift the focus of your thoughts away from anger and pain to uplifting ideas. The next time you want to mentally rehearse one hundred ways to tell off your nasty coworker, instead:

1. **Buy yourself a present.** Thinking about something you would like to get for yourself can boost your mood, even if you have not purchased a thing. When you dream about buying yourself something enjoyable, you distract yourself from ruminating on your anger. If it's in your budget to buy yourself a gift, even something as simple as a magazine or a new fishing lure can boost your mood with a little of the neurotransmitter dopamine.

2. **Enjoy a hobby.** My husband and I play guitar together. Sometimes I use this brain hack and lookup songs I would like to learn. Music, sports, cooking, woodworking, art, sewing are a few hobbies that allow self-expression, creativity, and fun. It is hard to stay mad when you're having fun. Engaging in hobbies exercises the brain and builds competencies while reducing the tendency to obsess about the negative. It can also lower the stress chemical cortisol.

3. **Socialize.** Just thinking about doing fun activities with friends can instantly change your mood. Plan a fun picnic. Organize a game night. Go to a movie with your spouse. Social activities distract us from the frustrating routines of everyday life and support us. Socializing can increase the output of the hormone oxytocin, which creates a warm feeling of bonding and connection.

4. **Plan a trip.** Plan a trip abroad or play tourist in your hometown. Getting away from the familiar gives us perspective on our lives and helps us see things in a new way. Just planning a trip moves your mind away from the source of distress and toward something pleasurable. Pointing your attention to pleasant thoughts helps reduce the number of negative thoughts that lead to feeling frazzled.

5. **Focus on self-improvement.** When we do something to make our own life better, rather than trying to make the life of another worse, we can enjoy the sweeter taste of success. One client had always wanted to read the complete works of George Bernard Shaw. Another chose to train to compete in bodybuilding. Self-improvement activities boost your mood, help you feel a sense of control over your life, and distract the mind from its negative thought bias. It can also help you grow new neural connections that add to your happiness and emotional resilience (Begley 2008).

6. **Explore the spiritual.** Engage in meaningful religious or spiritual rituals. Read inspirational texts. Perform volunteer work. Keep a gratitude journal. Spend time in nature or stargaze. Download and use mindfulness meditations or happiness applications on your computer or smartphone. These activities refocus your mind on meaning, awe, beauty, and goodness—values that nourish joy and reduce *frazzlebrain*.

These hacks work even if you just imagine performing them and don't take any action at all. When you imagine buying yourself a present, your mind no longer ruminates on the hostile, negative thoughts that fuel *frazzlebrain*. If you window shop at the mall with a friend or check out the specifications of the latest new cars online, your mind focuses on thoughts that can provide some enjoyment, even if you never purchase a thing. You can achieve the same delight by looking at pictures of exotic locations you might like to visit someday or anticipating a party you would like to plan with friends.

While the desire for revenge resides in every human brain, you have the free will to choose a different response. The response you choose can determine whether you feel better or worse, empowered or helpless.

Final Takeaway

Anxiety and anger are linked and magnified by stress. That frazzled feeling interferes with effective coping. You can calm yourself and become more resilient by activating the cooling system of your brain. First, identify your discomfort. Then name the feeling. Finally, provide yourself some soothing and comfort.

You learned that revenge could feel sweet now but leaves you feeling bitter later. When you maintain attitudes of social dominance, you feel less empathetic and more frazzled. You also learned that letting out anger doesn't help you feel better in the long run. It's best to engage in self-soothing behaviors and focus on making yourself feel better. Soothing behaviors stimulate the five senses. When you engage in soothing activities that stimulate your senses each day, you feel less frazzled and more resilient.

In the next chapter, you will learn why hostility and cynicism hurt you. Hopefulness is a healthy antidote to *frazzlebrain*. Hope counteracts the negative impact of cynical hostility. You will receive helpful hope generators to aim your mind toward optimism and resilience. But first, it helps to understand how *frazzlebrain* develops.

TWO

From Hostility to Hope

You are full of unshaped dreams . . . you are laden with beginnings . . . there is hope in you.

LOLA RIDGE

When things don't happen the way we think they should, we can get yelping mad. Perhaps you did not get that well-deserved promotion at work. Or maybe your spouse failed to follow through on a promise. Your anger and frustration can leak out in mean comments and hostile behavior. Anger progresses along a continuum from occasional irritability to frequent rage. When anger flares up, it alerts you that something is wrong.

We vulnerable humans need anger to recognize threats and muster the physical energy to defend ourselves. Sometimes our anger is unnecessary and serves no self-protective function. For example, I once worked with a married couple who raged at one another over which way the toilet paper roll should go. Another family spent weeks fighting about who should take the trash bin to the street. If your anger serves no actual self-protective function, psychotherapists call that unnecessary anger.

This chapter will help you learn how to reduce unnecessary anger and hostility. One powerful way to reduce anger is to increase feelings of hopefulness. Hope is the desire for something good and the belief that it is attainable. Hope activates a different part of the brain than hostility. Hopefulness can counteract random, anxious thoughts that fuel anger (Gallagher and Lopez 2018).

Hope and optimism calm the nervous system and broaden our ability to consider options. When you foster hope that things can get better, it inspires more productive action. Most of us do not intend to generate anger or hostility on purpose. Feelings seem to flare up involuntarily. You can train your brain to move from hostility to hope flexibly. I'll share more about how to generate hope and reap its many benefits later in this chapter. But first, it helps to understand what causes us to flare up over small things.

What Causes Unnecessary Anger?

Cynical attitudes can fuel unnecessary anger. Cynicism is the belief that people are fundamentally selfish. Cynicism primes you to feel angry and threatened by most people because you assume the worst of them. You might distrust the motives of someone even when they do something nice for you. When you distrust others most of the time, you can develop chronic anger. Chronic anger can become cemented into your personality. Without knowing quite how it happens, you might find yourself feeling angry much of the time. Psychologists call this personality trait *cynical hostility*.

Cynical hostility is a personality style that causes you to distrust and become antagonistic toward others. You might feel more guarded, suspicious, and nervous around people you don't know. I once counseled a bright, attractive, but lonely sixty-five-year-old woman named Ellen. She had lived alone for many years after a traumatic breakup. She sought help for her angry outbursts at coworkers. "This isn't like me. I don't know why I've become such an angry person," she lamented. Ellen feared her social isolation would only increase if she continued feeling distrust and anger toward others.

I taught Ellen how to generate hopefulness to counteract her cynicism. In addition, she learned how to foster compassion for herself and others. As Ellen aimed her thoughts in a hopeful and compassionate direction, she noticed her anger decrease. With less anger and cynicism, she felt more motivated to socialize. As a result, she felt happier and less lonely.

Psychologists have studied the effects of the cynical hostility personality style on everything from relationships to physical health. Chronic anger and cynicism contribute to *frazzlebrain* by keeping your nervous system on alert for constant threat. It's hard to relax if you remain on vigilant alert to protect and defend yourself. Cynical hostility maintains a steady drip of stress chemicals pumping through your body. Those chemicals can make it difficult for you to trust and feel safe. That lack of trust and safety keeps you frazzled for no reason.

How Does Cynical Hostility Develop?

Some people were taught cynical beliefs from early childhood. Thoughts like "People just want to use you" or "Everyone just cares about themselves" can prime you to feel more tense and hostile. Some studies show a genetic component to chronic anger and cynical hostility (Cates, et al. 1993). You can inherit this tendency from your parents, and you can learn it from other early childhood influences.

Cynical hostility tends to cluster in neighborhoods. Living in noisy areas near airports, for example, can increase your risk of developing cynical hostility. Exposure to the stress of noisy, unsafe neighborhoods can also make it more likely that you will develop this trait (King 2012). Combat veterans can develop cynical hostility from their trauma sustained during battle (Kubany, et al. 1994).

My late beloved father-in-law, wounded in the battle of Okinawa during World War II, embraced the family nickname "Senior Grumpa" with good humor. His grumpy curmudgeon personality appeared to stem from his life-threatening experiences in combat. When he became irritable over small matters, one of his grandchildren would say something like, "Oh, that's Senior Grumpa." He would laugh and soften a bit. On his headstone, along with his war hero emblem, it reads, "Loving son, husband, father, grandfather, great-grandfather and our beloved Sr. Grumpa."

Yes, good and loving people can succumb to cynicism and suffer from higher rates of anxiety and anger.

Cynicism Is on the Rise

If you feel cynical, you are not alone. In several recent studies, rates of cynicism appear to be on the rise among young people. Google searches for the word *cynicism* have doubled since 2004. Young people report a greater distrust of each other and institutions than ever before. Cynical attitudes appear in the writings of some of our most celebrated authors. The ancient Greek philosopher, Diogenes, was called "Diogenes the Cynic." He once told a man on the street if he had any wish for him at all, it would be for him to hang himself. Science fiction author W. H. Mitchell quipped, "Everyone is awful in their own special way." The playwright George Bernard Shaw called cynicism "the power of accurate observation."

When talented thinkers support cynical attitudes, it takes some convincing to challenge those beliefs. Comedic actor and television host Steven Colbert said that cynicism "is a self-imposed blindness, a rejection of the world because we are afraid it will hurt us or disappoint us. Cynics always say 'no.' But saying 'yes' begins things. Saying 'yes' is how things grow. Saying 'yes' leads to knowledge" (Colbert 2006).

Cynicism and anger can close us off to new ideas, growth, and knowledge. The fear of getting hurt or suffering humiliation can cause us to avoid people and experiences. This avoidance blocks the growth that stems from new, potentially healing experiences.

Sometimes cynicism develops as a defense against disappointment. We say *no* because we fear negative consequences. Yet, the best way to protect yourself from hurt is to learn how to generate positive emotions inside yourself. You can learn how to feel hopeful and optimistic by saying *yes* to some of the tools I share with you later in this chapter. When you know how to help yourself feel more hopeful and optimistic, you see positive changes in your relationships. Psychologists have discovered that when we manage chronic anger and cynicism, our relationships get better. Better relationships make us happier. Let me illustrate with an example from my work with angry families.

Years ago, I provided therapy groups for angry teens and their parents. These parents felt extremely frazzled trying to cope with out-of-control teenagers with big, bad, scary tempers. I noticed that most of these teens and their parents exhibited highly cynical attitudes and hostile behavior. They used a lot of mean and hateful language. Malicious comments such as "I hate you," "You're lazy," and "You're nuts" were frequently blasted by both parents and teens. Parents made negative comments about their teens, like, "He's just trying to manipulate you to get out of doing chores," or "She only cares about herself."

Cynicism, or deep distrust, blocked these families from resolving painful conflicts. They got better at resolving disputes when they learned to challenge the negative and cynical thoughts that fueled their anger. These parents of angry children had trouble noticing that their teenagers felt a lot of stress and emotional pain. The teens experienced their parents as hostile, punishing people who wanted to take away all their fun. These children could not see that their parents loved and cared about them but struggled to cope with their teens' anger.

When we see others in a cynical or hostile way, we make ourselves suffer more. It keeps us angry and tense. When we assume that other people wish to harm us, it makes us guarded, suspicious, and uncomfortable. The negative emotions narrow our thinking and distort our perception.

Cynical attitudes interfere with the ability to feel hopeful and optimistic. Hopefulness helps us better buffer the hardships of life. When we feel hopeful, we are more likely to experience positive emotions. Hope can help you reduce cynicism and hostility. But the seductive lure of negative thinking can sometimes prove hard to resist.

Before showing you how to reduce cynical hostility, I invite you to take this Cynical Hostility Checkup. Look at the following list of situations. In this checkup, you will read the description of a common problem. Read the statement that follows the problem. Make a checkmark by that statement if you're likely to think something similar. This checkup is for your eyes only. I applaud you for saying yes to the opportunity to take an honest look at your cynical attitudes.

Cynical Hostility Checkup

1. **Your car breaks down on the freeway, and many people pass without stopping. You think:**
   Those drivers only care about themselves.

2. **Your close friend admits that she has been leaving work early but cheating on her time reports to her boss. You think:**
   A lot of people would cheat on their time if they knew they could get away with it.

3. **A car salesman tells you the price of a new car you are considering purchasing. You think:**
   Most salespeople lie to manipulate and make more money.

4. **You lose your wallet at a restaurant. Upon returning to look for it you think:**
   I can't trust people to turn in a wallet when they find it.

5. **You stayed late at your job to cover for a coworker who called in sick. You think:**
   That coworker does not appreciate what I do for them.

6. **Your neighbor keeps coming over to borrow your tools. You think:**
   That neighbor is taking unfair advantage of me.

7. **A close member of your family recently passed away. Not many people have called to offer sympathy. You think:**
   Those people are just selfish and do not care about me.

8. **A friend was belligerent and aggressive to you while drunk at a party. After the party, the friend entered an alcohol rehabilitation treatment program. You think:**
   People who have a drinking problem will never change.

9. **A homeless person outside your office asks you for money for food. You think:**
   Homeless people are lazy and not trustworthy.

10. **You learn from your boss that one of your coworkers falsely accused you of wrongdoing. You think:**
    Anyone who falsely accuses me should be punished.

11. **An acquaintance invites you to join a social club. You think:**
    Most people are not worth my time and attention.

12. **A waitress provides warm, cheerful, and fast service to your party at a restaurant. You think:**
    She is nice only because she wants a good tip.

SCORING

If you checked 0 to 2: You show a low level of cynical hostility. This low level may help you enjoy better relationships. You may also benefit from better health than those with more cynicism and hostility. If you checked one or two items, the Cynical Hostility Tamer in the next section might help you feel calmer and happier.

If you checked 3 to 5: You have a moderate level of cynical hostility. You may approach others with suspicion. Suspicious, cynical, and hostile attitudes arouse the nervous system. That arousal releases low levels of stress chemicals in your body. Those chemicals can harm your health over time. You can benefit from the Cynical Hostility Tamer in the next section.

If you checked six or more: You demonstrate a high level of cynical hostility. You may already have some physical symptoms of stress. Your relationships and sense of happiness likely suffer as well. You will benefit the most from the Cynical Hostility Tamer provided later in this chapter.

Cynical Hostility Can Hurt You

Cynical and hostile attitudes have long been associated with many negative health outcomes. Cynics have higher rates of early death from coronary artery disease, are more likely to suffer dementia, and heal less quickly from illness and surgery (Brydon, et al. 2012). Cynical hostility is also associated with lower income and more difficult interpersonal relationships (Stavrova and Ehlebracht 2016). Cynical hostility even serves as a predictor of mortality from all causes (Miller, et al. 1996).

The good news is that your brain can recover and heal itself. When you learn how to redirect your automatic cynical thoughts, you increase hopefulness. You can receive health benefits as well. You may feel skeptical about the value of challenging your negative attitudes. Sometimes suspicion of others can seem wise.

Isn't It Smart to Be Cynical?

Many people from my training and counseling programs will ask, "But what if people really do want to hurt you?" Perhaps a shady salesperson cheated you out of your hard-earned money. Some of us have endured the betrayal of people we once trusted. If you belong to a minority group, you may have suffered from the hateful behavior of strangers. Maybe you have been a victim of violent crime after assuming the best of someone.

Some have suffered from traumatic events in childhood. Childhood abuse and trauma can cause changes in your brain that make you more prone to cynical hostility. Those changes include enlargement of the threat-sensing part of the brain, the amygdala. Changes in the hippocampus, where emotional memories are stored, can prime you to feel more threatened under stress (Young, et al. 2019).

You may not want to give up your cynical hostility. It is normal to want to protect yourself from emotional, physical, or financial harm. You do not want to act like a fool. Cynicism can seem like an intelligent and competent way to think.

A recent study published in the *Personality and Social Psychology Bulletin* set out to see if cynical individuals were more competent. Looking at several studies with over 200,000 subjects from thirty countries, these researchers found that the most cynical generally did worse on cognitive ability and academic competency tests. Those who scored the highest in competency chose a cynical belief only under specific conditions. Those who scored lowest in competency tended to pick the cynical position across most situations unconditionally. If you think more flexibly and not just cynically, you increase your competency (Stravrova and Ehlebracht 2018).

The Value of Flexible Curiosity

A healthy curiosity about the honesty and motives of a salesperson can help you make better financial decisions. A skeptical interest might encourage you to double-check the fine print on a contract. It is prudent to look for other evidence besides a person's word before spending your hard-earned money. Skepticism, or the ability to suspend judgment until you get good evidence, provides a more emotionally neutral way to deal with people we do not know. It allows you to remain curious, open to new information, and withhold judgment.

Approaching someone with curiosity, as opposed to cynicism, allows you to notice more. When you see more, you will likely make better, more competent decisions. Instead of an automatic negative bias about someone, a skeptical and curious approach allows you to relax a bit. You can relax and still protect yourself.

Sometimes you might find your cynical hostility directed inward toward yourself. Harsh self-criticism can cause brain changes that make you feel just as frazzled and unhappy as cynical hostility toward others. Too much self-criticism can hurt you.

But What if You're Mad at Yourself?

Severe self-criticism, self-loathing, and negative self-perceptions contribute to anger, anxiety, and depression. For example, Megan, a twenty-eight-year-old office manager, sought my help after a breakup with a boyfriend. Megan told me how much she hated her body. In the first session, she recited a long list of things she hated about her appearance. She felt she was too fat, had "huge thighs, back fat, and bad skin." When I looked at Megan, I saw a well-groomed and attractive woman of average weight, with a pretty smile.

Her boyfriend ended the relationship after she yelled at him in anger when he put his arm around her. She felt so self-conscious about her perceived "back fat" that she could not stand to be touched there. Megan assumed that her boyfriend loathed her body as much as she did. She often snapped at him when he complimented her appearance because any attention to her body, including positive attention, triggered anxiety, anger, and stress for her. Megan's self-criticism and self-loathing caused her so much distress that it destroyed her relationship. It also prevented her from enjoying physical affection and love from a caring partner.

Self-criticism shows up in the lateral prefrontal cortex (located at the side and toward the front) and the dorsal anterior cingulate regions of the brain (toward the top and middle part of the brain). These brain structures signal us to stop when we are making a mistake. Critical thinking isn't all flawed. It helps us stay safe, accomplish tasks effectively, and avoid regrettable actions. However, if we lack self-compassion (processed in the ventral lateral prefrontal cortex), we can develop anxiety and depression.

How to Remedy Toxic Self-Criticism

Megan's anxiety about her appearance interfered with her ability to love and connect with men fully. Her hostility toward herself and her appearance leaked out in hostility toward others. She wanted my help to change that unhealthy pattern. We started by changing her inner story about her attractiveness.

I asked her if she only dated crazy, psychotic men who were delusional.

"No," she said.

So, I asked, "Did the men you date compliment your appearance or tell you that they found you attractive?"

"Yes," she said.

"So, these men weren't crazy, and they found you attractive?"

"Yes," she answered.

We worked together on a list of attributes that made her attractive to many men. We spent a lot of time including a combination of strengths that make a person lovable. Only some of those qualities included appearance. She identified that her sense of humor, singing talent, thoughtfulness, and loyalty were endearing qualities that others admired about her.

Megan learned to stop thinking about herself as a combination of body parts in an imaginary beauty contest. Instead, she focused her thoughts on specific attributes that made her a lovable person. I recommended that Megan make a list of these qualities and keep it handy. Every time she started to criticize her body, she would take out the list and read it. In this way, she retrained her brain to stop the toxic self-criticism.

Many people feel nervous anxiety when required to speak in front of a large group. The more severe your self-criticism, the more likely you will suffer from nervous tension and discomfort. However, when you shift your thinking away from imagined mistakes and toward reassuring self-talk, you will manage your nervous tension and perform better. Reassuring self-talk like, "I am well prepared," or "Nerves are normal and give me energy" acts as a pep talk to help you through a stressful situation. When you use reassuring self-talk, you shift your mental energy from one part of your brain to another, from frazzled to focused.

If you feel uncomfortable meeting new people, you probably imagine a lot of self-critical thoughts. "I will feel awkward. People will think I'm stupid, unattractive, boring." Your self-critical thoughts keep you stuck worrying about making a mistake or appearing foolish. In a sense, you are mentally rehearsing a worst-case scenario.

In contrast, self-reassuring thoughts such as "I'm a kind person" and "I am a good listener" can help shift your brain activity to the ventral lateral prefrontal cortex. This part of the brain opens your options. It allows you to try new behaviors like asking questions, sharing stories, or telling jokes. The more options that you generate, the more flexible and effective you will feel in social situations. One part of the brain says, "Stop. Don't move. You will make a mistake." The other part of your brain says, "I have options. I can try a lot of new things to help me reach my goals."

Self-Criticism and Achievement

You might believe that self-criticism helps you strive for excellence. If you fail to scold yourself, you worry that you will settle for mediocrity or fail to achieve your full potential. To improve any behavior, whether it is playing a musical instrument or completing a report for work, you need to think critically, or the finished product will suffer. However, psychologists who study excellence in performance know that practice does make perfect. We are less likely to practice if practice makes us feel miserable and worthless. The more joy, pleasure, and interest we feel in the activity, the more likely we will continue to spend hours practicing that activity.

Suppose you want to lose weight and work out; criticizing yourself for being fat while at the gym will make you want to avoid going to the gym. Instead, praise yourself for the effort while making it pleasurable. That will increase your adherence to an exercise program. We need self-reassuring, encouraging, and self-calming thoughts to keep us going. Otherwise, our natural tendency to avoid pain will make us stop. We all want to avoid the uncomfortable feelings generated by our inner critical, judgmental, and negative thoughts.

Self-criticism is not all harmful. If your self-criticism aims to improve your performance or recognize mistakes, it serves a valuable purpose. After spotting an error in your writing, self-criticism helps you create a better paper. If, on the other hand, you tell yourself, "I can't write," the criticism stings more.

Thoughts like "I can't" make you want to stop trying. Global statements of self-criticism like, "I'm ugly, stupid, and I can't do anything right," lead to exaggerated emotional reactions and stop you from feeling motivated to try harder. Healthy self-criticism causes less pain and encourages self-improvement. Healthy self-criticism provides you with a specific way to improve. For example:

"You interrupt others too often in meetings. Try to let people finish their thoughts before you speak." In this example, you're focused on specific actions you can do to improve. This self-criticism highlights where you're less effective and offers suggestions to help you perform better next time.

The kind of self-criticism that can lead to *frazzlebrain* tends to exaggerate the importance or meaning of your mistakes or awkwardness. Soon, you find yourself so absorbed in negative self-talk that you stop noticing the broader world around you. It can make you hyper-focused on yourself. Everything can feel like pressure, a threat, or walking-on-nails uncomfortable. When you focus on specific behaviors you wish to improve, it becomes easier to imagine yourself improving.

When you believe you can make something better, we call that *hope*. Hope helps you generate more options and reduce *frazzlebrain*. The following table demonstrates the difference between self-criticism that can prove toxic to your serenity and healthy self-criticism that can help you improve your performance.

TOXIC SELF-CRITICISM	HEALTHY SELF-CRITICISM
I am a terrible friend.	*I made an insensitive remark. I need to apologize.*
I am a coward.	*I feel guilty about not defending my coworker in that meeting. I will next time.*
I am unlovable.	*If I show more kindness and caring toward others, I will likely cultivate strong relationships.*
I will always be alone.	*If I stop avoiding social activities, I will likely find companionship.*
I am a failure.	*I lost my job. If I keep looking, I can find another one.*

When you shift your thinking from toxic self-criticism to healthy self-criticism, you feel more motivated and happier. Your nervous system tension eases. You feel more patient and resilient.

In the next section, you will learn how to reduce cynical hostility toward yourself and others. I will show you how to tame cynical hostility with compassion for others and yourself. You will learn why hope is healthy. You will receive hope generators to help you feel happier, more motivated, and resilient.

Shift Expectations to Soften Cynicism

Exaggerated expectations, whether optimistic or cynical, can set you up for disappointment. An old *New Yorker* cartoon showed a waiter taking an order from a couple at a fine restaurant. He says, "I think I can recommend the veal, but at the same time, I feel I must caution you against unrealistically high expectations." Unrealistically high expectations may harden our response to disappointment.

Sometimes we find ourselves hardened and cynical when something other than what we expect happens. Our birthday comes, and we don't get a call from our closest friends. We do not get the raise we deserve. The disappointment leaves us feeling wounded, and our thoughts lean toward the hostile and cynical. You might remember your friends' birthdays and assume that they will return the favor.

When you perform exceptionally well at work, you expect to get recognized in your compensation. We want the world to work according to our expectations, to what we believe is right, fair, proper, and reasonable. Yet, we live in a far more complex world. At these times, it helps to reset our expectations to reality, not to what we wish would happen. When you adapt to reality, instead of clinging to what reality "should" be, you cope better with what life throws your way.

I will share a personal story to illustrate how resetting expectations can turn disappointment into something extraordinary. It all began with the planning of my mother's eightieth birthday celebration. My mother did not want a big party. Instead, she said she wanted an intimate weekend in Los Angeles with close family. She wanted to spend a day at the world-famous Getty Museum and then see a live theater production.

My husband and I planned the weekend with hotel accommodations, theater tickets, and dinner reservations. We rented a large van to accommodate our party. The ride up to Los Angeles from San Diego delighted us all as my mother regaled us with stories from her childhood summers riding horses in Wyoming. We spent all day Saturday enjoying the inspiring Getty Museum on a beautiful, sunny October day. The special birthday dinner that night felt perfect as we savored the excellent meal and stimulating warm family conversation.

The following day, we awoke in our hotel room. My husband got the tickets out for the matinee performance and immediately panicked. The tickets we had purchased for our entire party were for the previous day. You know that moment when you wish you could go back in time, get a do-over? He let me know, and I felt sick too. We wanted my mother to enjoy the perfect weekend with her family, and we had screwed it up. My husband went to the hotel computer to see if he could salvage the day. No tickets were available for anything that day for a party our size. Now we had to tell everyone that we had utterly screwed up. My mother, wise, happy, and adept at rolling with the punches of life, said, "Oh, kids, I'm having the best time. Do you know what I want to do today? I want to go back to your house, watch the football game, and order pizza."

We then sat together in our hotel room and talked for about two hours. My mother asked us all to imagine ourselves at eighty, looking back on a life well-lived. What would we like to remember with fondness? What did we most value? Her grandchildren and children shared their hopes and dreams, feeling relaxed, unhurried, and happy. Then we piled into the van and drove home for an afternoon of football, pizza, and quality family time. As we look back on that weekend, the most memorable experience for all of us was those two hours we spent huddled together in the hotel room, talking about life.

Disappointments do not inevitably lead to anger or cynicism. We can choose to shift expectations and soften our cynical and self-critical judgments. The more quickly we reset our thinking to accept the present reality, the better we adapt. Sometimes that is hard to do when you're disappointed with yourself, as my husband and I were when we made a mistake with the theater tickets. While self-criticism and its evil cousin, self-loathing, feel mighty painful, you can learn to harness your brainpower away from self-criticism and toward self-compassion.

Tame Cynical Hostility with Compassion

If cynical and hostile attitudes tense your nervous system, what attitudes help relax your nervous system? Researchers have amassed a significant body of evidence demonstrating the health and well-being benefits of compassion. Compassion, or empathy, enables you to put yourself in another person's shoes. You notice their distress or suffering and wish for the relief of that suffering or pain. Compassion toward others inspires a feeling that you want to do something to help the other person suffer less.

When you cultivate compassion, you feel better inside. It feels better to care about others than to fear others. Caring about the well-being of others produces different physiological reactions in the body. Compassion also helps you notice more of the physical environment (Tarrasch, Margalit-Shalom, and Berger 2017). When you see more, you can better protect yourself from any danger. Perceiving situations more accurately can help you make better decisions.

What Is Compassion?

A *New Yorker* cartoon shows a couple walking on the beach where they spot a beached whale. The caption reads, "Damn, he's seen us. Now we'll have to act all compassionate." Sometimes it can seem like a lot of work to feel empathy for the suffering of others. Yet, when we exercise compassion, we reap many benefits. Dr. Paul Gilbert, the founder of the Compassionate Mind Foundation, defined the term as "a basic kindness, with a deep awareness of the suffering of oneself and of other living things, coupled with the wish and effort to relieve it." Compassion comes in three parts:

1. **A basic kindness toward all living things.**
2. **An awareness of the suffering of oneself and other living beings.**
3. **A wish and effort extended to relieve the suffering of oneself and others.**

Compassion packs a lot into one word. When we are on the receiving end of someone else's compassion, we feel less pain. When we make an effort to help others, they heal more quickly and suffer less. Cultivating compassion can transform your life and the life of every person you touch with it. You can learn how to develop compassion and reap its many benefits.

Why Cultivate Compassion?

Compassion is good for your brain. Dr. Richard J. Davidson, researcher, and professor of psychology and psychiatry at the University of Wisconsin-Madison, has performed pioneering research in compassion cultivation. In a series of experiments looking at how compassion meditation (focused attention on compassionate thoughts) affects the brain, he and his team found that compassion meditation:

- **Decreases feelings of personal distress** (decreased activation of the amygdala, the threat-sensing part of the brain.)
- **Increases goal-directed behaviors pointed toward helping others** (increased activation of the dorsolateral prefrontal cortex where problem-solving occurs.)
- **Increases connectivity in the brain** (between the prefrontal cortex, the insula, related to social emotions like empathy, and the nucleus accumbens, part of the reward system of the brain). This brain connectivity allows you to feel inspired to help rather than feel depressed by the suffering of others. Increased connectivity and integration of the brain are associated with feelings of well-being and mental health (Davidson and Begley 2012).

It may seem difficult to feel compassion for someone you believe has harmed you or caused you pain. Why should you care about another person when they do not care about you? One reason to cultivate compassion is that it makes you feel happier. Staying frustrated, cynical, and hostile keeps you on the alert for the next time someone will harm you.

Cynical hostility stresses your nervous system and fuels *frazzlebrain*. Compassion, in contrast, helps you feel calmer and more in control of your emotions. Compassion lowers anxiety and stress and increases your ability to experience positive emotions. It activates the stress-buffering systems of your body that reduce inflammation. Compassion can help reverse the harmful effects of stress on your body.

Self-compassion

It can be challenging to show compassion to others if you are not addressing your own needs. If you are stranded on the freeway, it's hard to have compassion for the people passing you by. At that moment, you need to get yourself and your car to a safe place. So compassion for others does not mean you neglect yourself; it helps to cultivate compassion for yourself as well.

Many people with cynical and hostile attitudes aim those nasty thoughts inward. Stranded in your car, you might think, "You idiot! Why didn't you take the car in for service?!" Using kinder, more compassionate language toward yourself can help you cope better with the situation. You will also suffer less.

Dr. Kristin Neff describes self-compassion as responding to ourselves as if we were "a dear friend in need." Rather than punishing ourselves with self-criticism, the kindness of compassion can help "soothe and calm our troubled minds" (Neff 2011). Dr. Neff, associate professor of Human Development at the University of Texas, Austin, is a pioneering researcher in self-compassion. She and her colleague, Dr. Chris Germer (a clinical psychologist and lecturer in psychiatry at Harvard Medical School), developed an eight-week course called Mindful Self-Compassion (MSC). This course provides mindfulness meditation strategies that focus on creating a compassionate attitude toward oneself and others.

I'm excited to share how you can benefit from intentionally cultivating thoughtful compassion in your daily life. But first,

I would like to share with you how compassion cultivation changed my life.

The Transformative Power of Compassion

I volunteered to participate in a research study on the effects of self-compassion training on helping professionals (Scarlet, et al. 2017). Professionals who help others—like doctors, nurses, and psychotherapists—constantly see people in physical and emotional pain. Because of that chronic exposure to suffering, we are subject to high rates of burnout or compassion fatigue.

After decades of helping people struggling with extreme life events, I felt exhausted. My children were grown and out of the house. I was mourning the empty nest and searching for something more to help me feel fulfilled. I still loved my work, but I felt deflated. My usual enthusiasm at the beginning of the day had dwindled to a memory. On one day, I met with a man who had just found out his wife was cheating on him with his good friend. The following client, a young woman, sobbed about the recent death of her infant child. Another man shook, recalling the trauma of barely surviving a stabbing attack. The next woman expressed terror waiting for the results of a breast biopsy.

The enormity of human suffering left me exhausted at the end of the day. Mixed in with the clients coping with pain were clients celebrating major promotions, wedding engagements, and thrilling trips abroad. I noticed I had trouble leaving the pain of one client behind as I entered the next session. My usual head-clearing strategies that had worked for years were not working anymore. Compassion training arrived for me at the perfect time.

Our training group included about twenty nurses, physicians, social workers, physical therapists, and psychotherapists. As we went around the room sharing our work and hopes for the training, I noticed one physician. He appeared coldly disengaged and mildly irritated. The rest of us shared something personal. His answers were vague and impersonal. I wondered if his patients felt that coldness too. Members of our group formed close bonds; we learned how to meditate and cultivate compassion for ourselves and each other.

At the end of the eight-week training, we each shared how compassion training impacted us personally. Our instructor, Dr. Janina Scarlet, asked, "Has anyone in your life commented on any changes that they have observed in you?" The physician, who had initially appeared cold and irritated, spoke first. "One of my patients asked me if I was 'in love,'" he said. We all laughed. He did have a warm glow about him. "It's not that I'm in love. I'm still happily married to my wife." We laughed again. "I just noticed, after becoming more mindful, that my habit of taking notes on the computer while my clients were talking with me made them feel that I didn't care. I changed how I talk to patients. Now I start each meeting face-to-face with my patient. I offer them my full attention and compassion. Then I tell them I will have to write things down in their record to take good care of their needs. This class has completely transformed the way I practice medicine."

For me, the transformation was more personal. I became aware that I had not recognized the pain I felt for my clients. I had not noticed that I needed to feel comforted from the secondary pain I experienced from exposure to their intense suffering. Even as I preached to my clients the importance of self-care, I had neglected to care for myself. Acknowledging to myself that my work could cause me pain strangely surprised me. Previously I told myself this was all a typical day's work and shut down awareness of my discomfort. I just felt tired, drained.

Dr. Neff and Dr. Germer define self-compassion as comprising three essential concepts:

1. **Self-kindness:** The wish for our own happiness, and the willingness to act on that wish.
2. **Common humanity:** The awareness that when we suffer, we share common feelings that connect us with others, rather than feeling isolated and alone in our suffering.
3. **Mindfulness:** The ability to remain aware of our own pain without ignoring it, magnifying it, or judging it.

Here are how these three components of compassion helped me recover:

1. **Self-kindness:** I had to acknowledge that my work was hard. I had been ignoring my own needs. Instead of self-criticism, I learned to say kinder things to myself, like, "You did a good job today. You helped your clients cope with a lot of suffering. You worked hard. Now take a well-deserved rest break tonight."
2. **Common humanity:** Other helping professionals and I share similar suffering when we come into intimate contact with the pain of others. It felt comforting to know that others experienced the same emotions. We share the burden of helping others navigate their worst days. I further felt a deeper connection to all humanity, a sense that no one need feel alone in their pain, including myself.
3. **Mindfulness:** I implemented mindfulness, deep breathing, and self-soothing strategies between sessions. I focused on paying deeper attention, not just to my clients but also to

my feelings within each session. If I felt tension, I focused on relaxing and shifting my posture for more comfort. As a result, I felt more effective with my clients and reinvigorated by the work.

Sometimes when we work on self-compassion, we can get some side benefits as well. I noticed my appreciation for small things, like the beauty of nature, had returned to me. I felt happier. Lighter. Calmer.

Below is a list of compassion phrases that you can apply to yourself and others. These phrases stem from Buddhist loving-kindness and compassion meditations. It helps to settle down a bit, slow the mind down with deep breathing, and focus on the present moment before you begin to use these phrases. It is not necessary to say these out loud. These phrases aim your thinking in a compassionate, open-hearted direction. Try focusing your attention on one or more of these phrases. Notice how your mind and body respond to this shift in thought.

- **May you be free from pain.**
- **May you feel at peace.**
- **May you live with ease.**
- **May you be safe.**
- **May you be healthy.**

As you might notice from the above phrases, they contain some concern for the suffering of another. When you think in a concerned way about yourself or another, you open your heart and mind. That opening can calm your nervous system. As your nervous system settles, you can bounce back from stress more quickly. It makes space for happier feelings to emerge.

To cultivate compassion for yourself, simply substitute the word "I" for the "you" in the above phrases. For example, *May I be healthy*, or *May I be safe*. If you prefer to talk to yourself as if you were speaking to a friend, you can use the word "you." Allow yourself to experiment with the language that you prefer. The most important goal is to aim your mind in the direction of compassion. To practice compassion for yourself and others, try the following *frazzle hack:*

Frazzle Hack: Cynical Hostility Tamer

Sit comfortably with your feet on the floor. Close your eyes. Take a few deep breaths. Breathe in through your nose and out slowly through your mouth to settle yourself down a bit. Focus on your breathing for a few moments, bringing your restless mind back to your breathing whenever it drifts away. Think about an interpersonal conflict or issue that has troubled you lately. Visualize that person struggling as you are with this conflict or problem. Open your eyes slowly. Pick one of the statements compassion phrases that you could say to this person without any resentment:

- *May you be free from pain.*
- *May you feel at peace.*
- *May you live with ease.*
- *May you be safe.*
- *May you be healthy.*

After you think the compassionate phrase, take a deep breath through your nose and exhale slowly through your mouth. Perform this process three times like this: May you be safe (inhale/exhale), May you be safe (inhale/exhale), May you be safe (inhale/exhale). With each breath, try to slow down your exhalation.

Next, imagine providing compassion to yourself. What phrase(s) do you need to hear the most right now? Perhaps you need to feel at ease. Then say to yourself, "May I live with ease." Perform this process three times as well like this: May I live with ease (inhale/exhale), May I live with ease (inhale/exhale), May I live with ease (inhale/exhale). Again, with each breath, try slowing the exhalations.

Find a compassion phrase to say for yourself and one for the person or persons with whom you have a conflict. If you feel it is appropriate, you can use the same phrase for yourself and the other person in the example. As your negative and hostile thoughts return (as they usually do), substitute the compassion phrase instead.

Compassion helps us think more flexibly. That flexibility allows us to cope better with the challenges we face. Cultivating compassion gets easier with practice. Note how you feel after challenging your cynical beliefs with compassionate thoughts. Record your impressions in your frazzle hack *journal.*

What if I Am Not Cynical, Just Judgmental?

Sometimes we find ourselves not so much hostile and cynical but, rather, more judgmental. We have high standards for our behavior and others too. It irritates us when people do not conform to our expectations. For example, I'm not too fond of it when people tell me they will do something and fail to follow through. When I am angry about this, I think, "Why did he bother telling me something to get me hopeful, just to let me down in the end? It's like she purposely wanted to hurt me for no reason." The astute reader has already spotted the cynicism in those thoughts. I proclaim that people should consistently deliver on what they promise. I can get myself all worked up if someone does not live up to my imperative. I might judge that person as "flaky" or "not trustworthy." I judge the offender to protect myself from future hurt feelings. I narrow my thinking to good/bad. I label that person as hurtful and separate myself from them in my mind.

Yet when I challenge my cynical and judgmental thoughts, I aim my mind in a different direction. I remind myself that the offender probably intended to follow through on the promise. Perhaps they did wish to please and not hurt me. Maybe he just forgot, or the circumstances changed and she could no longer deliver on the promise. If I think that way, I still might feel disappointed, but my resentment and negative feelings lessen. I might also remember times when I failed to deliver on something that I promised. I would like to feel forgiven for my imperfections. Applying compassion phrases like, May I live with ease, or May I feel peaceful, softens anger. I feel more empowered to make myself feel better. When I use compassionate thoughts, I feel calmer and more connected to others, and less angry and disconnected.

When life gets difficult, we all need encouragement to keep trying. Sometimes we don't get much encouragement from our employers, spouses, or friends. Yet, you can learn how to give yourself compassion and encouragement. Try the Compassionate Affirmations frazzle hack below, and notice how it feels to foster supportive, compassionate self-talk.

Frazzle Hack: Compassionate Affirmations

Take a moment and try to think about how your harsh, punishing thoughts might add to feelings of discouragement, defeat, despair, or hopelessness. Think about what type of compassion, encouragement, and support you would like to receive. You can deliver your own encouragement by substituting encouraging thoughts for self-critical or discouraging thoughts. Create your own positive message of self-encouragement or use some from the list below. Make a note of any statements that make you feel something. Sometimes statements that elicit the strongest reactions, both positive and negative, will prove the most helpful to you:

> *I can accept myself right now, just as I am.*
> *I can make mistakes, learn from them, and grow.*
> *I can talk to others without judging myself.*
> *My smile and presence comfort others.*
> *I can treat myself and others with kindness.*
> *I can relax and be myself.*
> *I can live in peace.*
> *I can breathe deeply and relax.*
> *I can feel safe and supported.*
> *I can give myself loving-kindness when I hurt.*

When you practice self-compassion, healthy self-criticism, and self-care, you can lower your nervous system arousal. As you feel calmer, you can think more flexibly, aiding your ability to cope with life's troubles.

The Healing Effects of Hope

In a study published in the *International Journal of Psychophysiology*, researchers found that those with an optimistic orientation showed a faster recovery of the stress chemical cortisol after exposure to stress than those with a pessimistic perspective. Optimism or hopefulness acts as a physiological buffer to stress and helps us recover faster (Puig-Perez, et al. 2015).

Hopefulness also helps you try harder to address your difficulties, as it provides motivation. Hopefulness benefits your health. It makes you more likely to follow through with necessary medical treatments and activities like exercise that keep you healthy. Hopefulness or optimism allows you to consider possibilities for problem-solving (Kress, Bristle, and Aue 2018). When you feel pessimistic or hopeless, you fail to explore solutions. It's as if you say to yourself, "What's the use? Why bother?" However, you can learn to cultivate hope. It starts with how you think about or describe your problems to yourself.

To illustrate how your thinking shapes how you face problems, I will share the stories of Bill and Robert. Both men faced a recent job loss. They each had a completely different way of thinking about their predicament.

Bill, age forty-five, lost his job at a tech company after a few bad encounters with a hostile manager. He came to my office, rumpled and unshaven, with a look of dour despair. "I could barely get out of bed today," he said. "What's the point? I'm an incompetent loser. No one will hire me. Why bother trying?"

He proceeded with a long list of reasons why he would never find another job. Age discrimination, the economy, his past failures all proved to Bill that he was unemployable. He believed there was nothing he could do to prevent the predictable cascade of failure from following. Bill expected that he would lose his house, family, self-respect, and ultimately his life because of this job loss. He believed that one failure, the loss of this job, would now ruin every other part of his life. Bill's exaggerated, global description of his unemployment problem caused him to magnify it to all areas of his life instead of focusing on the specific issue of finding a job.

In contrast, Robert, age fifty, lost his job when his company merged with another company, and he had a clash with the new management over the direction of his position. Robert came to me dressed for an interview, angry and stressed but determined to get another job as quickly as possible. He had arranged a lunch with a former colleague that day and had plans to contact recruiters in his field. Robert believed that he would find work. He attributed his current unemployment to a specific situation, namely, his last employer, rather than a global problem that "No one hires older workers," as Bill believed. Robert's hope mobilized his job-seeking behaviors. He scheduled lunches, called recruiters, attended interviews, and dressed in business attire to make a favorable impression on potential employers.

When you feel frazzled after a failure or setback, which response do you think more likely leads to success? Should you believe, like Bill, one sign of failure applies to all areas of your life, or would it be better to assume, like Robert, that you can find a solution to a specific problem?

Psychologists discovered that if you generate hopefulness as Robert mustered, you can think about a broader range of solutions. You will engage in actions that will increase your likelihood of success. Even if you naturally lean toward the pessimistic view, like Bill, you can learn to generate hope and optimism and reap its many rewards (Abramson 1978) .

How to Generate Hope

To turn your mind toward more hopeful, healthier thinking, try these hope generators:

- **Be specific:** Identify your problem in specific, measurable ways rather than in a general, global way. For example: *Specific*: "I need to make $300 more per month to pay my bills and save money." *General*: "I'm broke." When you define a problem in specific, measurable ways, you can begin to feel hopeful about a solution. When you make a general, nonspecific statement, like "I'm broke," it can leave you feeling overwhelmed. You will feel less frazzled, helpless, and anxious when defining your problem in measurable, precise terms.

- **Try something new:** When you try something new, you activate neural circuits that speed up learning and move mental energy away from hopelessness and into action. If you do the same thing repeatedly, you will probably remain stuck in the same situation. Trying something new allows you to see, experience, and think about your problem from a different perspective. For example, if you usually try to cope with public speaking nervousness by taking deep breaths, relaxing, and vigorous preparation, but you still feel overwhelmed, try adding something new and different. Try exercising in the morning before you speak in public. Exercise could help you release tension and feel more confident and relaxed.

- **Ask for help:** Sometimes, you can feel hopeless and all alone with a problem and see no way to resolve it yourself. Hiding problems and acting tough can wear you down and keep you feeling stuck. Ask for advice or help from a trusted friend, a professional therapist, or an expert. You will feel less alone with your problem. You gain new ideas that might help you fix it. For example, many people worried about financial issues never seek the help of a professional advisor. Asking for help from a professional can give you hope that you can solve your financial stress.

- **Comfort yourself:** Self-critical thoughts can make you feel overwhelmed. You can generate more hope when you provide yourself comfort and encouragement. Try to talk to yourself as if you were caring for a close friend. Substitute realistic, hopeful statements such as: "I can handle this. I can figure out how to solve this problem. I can learn to calm down and relax. I can ask for help." Apply compassion phrases like, "May I be peaceful, May I live with ease" to soothe and comfort yourself.

Generating hope can help you dust yourself off after a painful upset and keep trying. That is just what my client Alberta did, and it helped her get over a painful rejection and keep looking for the man she eventually married.

Alberta, a vibrant, heavyset woman of thirty-two, started using a dating website to find a husband. After a painful rejection by a man who said, "I don't date fat women," she told me, "Men don't like fat women. I'll never be able to get married and have a family." After we talked, I asked her to apply the hope generators. I asked Alberta to define her problem in more specific terms. Alberta said, "Okay, this specific guy did not want to date me. I can keep looking for someone who will want to date me." To try something new, I suggested she try a new way of dating where she could meet men personally, to avoid the problem of a man rejecting her for her appearance after the date had already commenced.

She already started one hope generator (ask for help) when she consulted me for therapy. I asked her if she had friends who could provide her with support and encouragement. Finally, I recommended that she mute her inner critic, the voice that told her she would never find a mate because of her weight.

I asked her if she knew other women who were married and overweight.

"Yes," she said.

"Then that thought that no one will marry you because of your weight isn't realistic or helpful," I said.

I asked Alberta to find a more realistic and hopeful message to think about while dating.

"How about, 'the right man for me will love me for who I am. If other overweight women can find husbands, then I can too,'" she declared.

I told her that sounded like a healthy and realistic statement of hope. Alberta kept those hope generators going, and two years later, she was engaged to be married. When faced with a problem, apply the hope generators to get you started and calm your frazzled brain.

Frazzle Hack: Hope Generators

Pick a personal problem you would like to solve. Choose something that currently makes you feel frazzled. Apply the four hope generators to your situation. Write your responses in your frazzle hack journal.

- *Define the problem in specific, measurable terms. (I need to find a job that pays $50,000 per year within the next six months.)*

- *Identify a new approach that you could take to address the problem. (Find unique places to network and share my resume.)*
- *Ask someone for help, advice, or consultation. (Seek out recruiters, a career coach, mentor, former employer.)*
- *Comfort yourself with a realistic and hopeful statement. (If I keep looking for an excellent job while trying new methods and asking for help, I will likely achieve success.)*

You will know if you feel more hopeful if you find yourself taking more action to address your problem. That is how you move forward. Moving forward demonstrates hopefulness. Note in your journal what you have tried and what you would like to continue.

Final Takeaway

Chronic anger and hostility can lead to a personality style called cynical hostility. Cynical attitudes fuel frazzled overreactions to life stress. You can reduce *frazzlebrain* by generating compassion and hopefulness. Hopefulness and compassion reduce the intensity and frequency of cynical and hostile thoughts.

Begin mindful compassion by focusing on deep breathing. Once you feel settled down a bit, use compassion phrases like:

- **May you live with ease**
- **May you be safe**
- **May you feel at peace**

If you suffer from toxic self-criticism, try using compassionate affirmations like:

- I can make mistakes, learn from them, and grow.
- I can accept myself right now, just as I am.
- I can give myself loving-kindness when I hurt.

To reduce cynicism and anger, apply the Hope Generators:

- Define the problem in specific terms
- Try something new
- Ask for help
- Comfort yourself

In the next chapter, you will get to explore the limitless world of your imagination. You will learn how mental imagery influences anger, anxiety, and stress. Tools to harness your imagination will help you create stronger life satisfaction and joy.

THREE

The Power of Imagination

Man's mind, once stretched by a new idea, never regains its original dimensions.

OLIVER WENDELL HOLMES

When you watch children at play, you can see the workings of imagination when a stick morphs into a sword, a magic wand, or a rifle. A blanket may transform into a tent, a cape, or wings. As we grow into adulthood, the freedom to imagine often gets replaced by the need for focused attention in the real world. Yet, the power of the mind to think about things that are not present possesses life-changing effects.

When you feel frazzled, your mind conjures potential negative outcomes and irritants. These worrisome thoughts trigger nervous system arousal as alarm bells go off in the brain. That "uh oh" feeling stems from chemical messengers that activate stress hormones. These physiological changes mobilize your body for action. Imagining some danger or worry can cause changes in the brain and body as if the risk existed in the present moment. Flooded with worry, you might feel trapped in your negative feelings and unsure how to help yourself feel better. This chapter will show you how to detach from worry and harness your imagination to reduce stress and feel happier.

Your brain is a go-anywhere tool that can make you feel good. When you learn to intentionally focus your imagination on things that make you feel good, you worry less. Using your brain's natural ability to imagine helps you control your emotional reactions.

Researchers from Oxford University and the University of California, Davis found that individuals who filled their minds with positive mental images could boost their mood and perform better on a test (Blackwell, et al. 2015). Somehow, just allowing ourselves to picture or visualize positive things can make us perform better in life and feel better. Your mind might find it very seductive to sink into sadness or worry. If that happens, assign yourself the task of imagining something delightful, positive, or enjoyable. Your mood will lift quite quickly and effortlessly.

It helps to begin by creating one compelling, delightful fantasy that you can use at any time to uplift your mood instantly.

The Compelling Fantasy

For decades I have worked as a psychotherapist helping people suffering from anxiety, anger, and stress. My clients needed a simple tool to use whenever they found themselves ruminating on their worries. They needed a reliable substitute for the worrisome thoughts that plagued them. I taught my clients a technique, the *compelling fantasy*, to help them immediately improve their mood, reduce worry, and stress, and increase mental flexibility. The compelling fantasy consists of four simple rules:

1. **When you think about this fantasy, it makes you feel good.**
2. **The fantasy has no angry, hostile, violent, or vengeful intention.**
3. **The fantasy compels you to keep going, filling in details that expand and build on one another.**
4. **The fantasy is not sexual.** (Sexual fantasies are fine for sexual pleasure, but the compelling fantasy works to lower nervous-system arousal. Because sexual fantasies arouse the nervous system and can sometimes leave one feeling agitated, it is best to avoid them for this exercise. The compelling fantasy stimulates the release of relaxing, pleasurable chemicals in your body that produce mild joy and contentment.)

How to Create Your Compelling Fantasy

Start with anything that gives you pleasure in your real life. Do you enjoy a hobby like woodworking, music, quilting, or art? Do you like to create business ideas? Does scientific exploration fascinate you? Do you love to travel? Do not limit your fantasy to what you would do in real life.

Part of what can keep us trapped in unhappiness is the need to limit our thinking to only what we deem practical and realistic. We often fail to dream big because of financial or physical limitations. Or you might resist imagining delightful things out of fear of disappointment when they do not come true. So, to protect yourself from disappointment, you continue the bias for negative thoughts that make you suffer.

The compelling fantasy allows your creative imagination to push beyond the limits you might usually impose on yourself. It gives you the freedom to expand your world of possibilities mentally. You can feel joy, wonder, fun, and excitement without ever taking that trip or having that adventure in real life. Here are a few examples of compelling fantasies my clients have found delightful and helpful:

- **The Ideal Vacation Fantasy:** Imagine you can take a trip anywhere for as long as you like. Where would you like to go? What celebrity would you like to chat with on the plane, train, automobile, ship, space shuttle? Who are your travel companions? Feel free to pick anyone from history. Or make it a solo trip. Remember, in fantasy, there are no limits to time, space, or resources. What activities, sights, adventures will you explore?

- **The Lone Explorer Fantasy:** You dream of hiking the Appalachian trail with only your backpack and walking stick as your companions. What would you pack? Where would you begin? Perhaps you enjoy sleeping under the stars, connecting the constellations. Imagine the photographs you might take.

- **The 100 Million Dollar Windfall Fantasy:** Through a fantastic twist of fate, you find yourself with a fortune. After you buy everything you dream of for yourself, friends, and family, how will you live your daily life? What charities or foundations will you support? Where would you like to live? What new things would you like to try?

- **The Design, Build, and Decorate Your Dream House Fantasy:** Will you design a villa in the south of France? A beach house? A castle? A modern high-rise apartment in New York City?

A mountain cabin? What colors, furnishings, art, landscaping will you use for your dream home?

- **The Rock Star Fantasy:** Who do you want in your band? What instrument(s) do you play? Where do you perform? What songs are on your playlist? What kind of costumes or outfits do you wear? Do you play large stadiums or classical venues like Carnegie Hall?

- **The Ideal Dinner Party:** Who will you invite to this memorable party? What food will you serve? How will you seat everyone? What subjects will your guests talk about? Does your party have a theme? Imagine all the details from the early preparation to the end of the evening clean-up.

Feel free to practice your fantasy while on your commute to work, engaging in tedious tasks, or when you feel stressed or blue. The goal of the compelling fantasy is to create mild contentment and increase mental flexibility, a sign of mental health. As you practice, you get better at it. I suggest that you exercise your fantasy imagination daily. That way, your skill improves, helping you to shift your thoughts to something pleasant.

My Story

I stumbled upon the power of fantasy, like many people do, by necessity. I grew up poor. We frequently moved to ever-smaller rental units. My parents suffered the indignity of repossessed cars, furniture, and bankruptcy. There was no money for toys, games, birthday parties, or bicycles. Yet my younger sister and I could turn bamboo into a native hut, yarn into dolls, and boards into tree houses with our imaginations. In some ways, the absence of toys may have helped shape our minds to enjoy creativity. We could sail through the trees on a rope like Tarzan, make rainbows out of sun-melted crayons, and soar into space while gazing at the night sky.

As I grew, my imagination turned to music, songwriting, poetry, and big dreams. With no money for college, I worked and attended a community college. The fees were low, and I could schedule classes around my restaurant and housecleaning jobs. I dreamed of making a career as a singer-songwriter. I took courses in music, drama, dance, and the usual general education requirements. I auditioned for a working band and got my first steady professional singing job.

Soon the imagined thrill of singing in front of an audience dimmed after several harrowing encounters with drunken men. One included a stalker who left threatening notes on my car, and another repeatedly called the nightclub to leave lewd and threatening messages for me. My imagined life as a singer-songwriter appeared far more glamourous than reality.

I kept attending college, as I loved reading and learning. Yet I had reached a career crisis point. What if you get to do what you always wanted to do and find out you hate it? In despair, one day, I took a walk. I saw a green flyer on a wall. It said, "Volunteers needed for a suicide crisis hotline. No experience necessary. Will train." My favorite classes in college, besides music and writing, were the psychology classes. I loved helping people. But I needed a paying job. Volunteer work did not make a lot of sense. I took the number anyway.

After a screening interview, a forty-hour training program, and supervision with live calls, I was a hotline volunteer. For more than a year, I worked every Sunday helping people in suicidal despair and giving low-income families food from our pantry. I even helped rescue a woman from her homicidal husband. I felt happier than I ever had performing music.

My hotline experience led to one vivid, compelling fantasy: I saw myself as a psychotherapist working in a red brick building with a courtyard fountain. On the door of my office was a black-and-white sign displaying my name with a PhD after it. The fantasy seemed so farfetched yet so compelling. More details spilled out in daydreams during workday commutes. Somehow, I would find a way to get advanced degrees in psychology and become a psychotherapist. The dream of a career helping others kept me going even as I often grew discouraged. Poverty can crush hopes and dreams. Yet that one compelling fantasy propelled me out of poverty and into the professional class.

I obtained a Master of Arts and doctorate in psychology, completed internships, passed the licensing exam, and opened my private practice. The office I leased provided a convenient location but no red brick or water fountain. Eventually, the owners remodeled the building. To my great delight and surprise, they added a red brick courtyard with a water fountain. My vivid, compelling fantasy had come to life.

When you focus the power of your imagination, you gain the energy and motivation to overcome any obstacle. Some people tell me, "I don't have much of an imagination. I can't do this because I'm not creative." Yet when I ask them to describe something that happened to them, they use images and metaphors that show a vivid imagination at work.

Manage Your Metaphors

According to psychologists who study these things, you may not realize it, but you already use fantasy or imagery about six times per minute. We think in images, symbols, and metaphors all the time (Landau, Meier, and Keefer 2010). We create these images to help us understand and communicate our feelings and experiences. If

I am mad at someone, I might say, "Get off my back!" When you dislike your job, you might think, "I feel trapped in this cubicle." We describe someone who irritates us as "a pain in the neck." We do not actually have an enemy hanging on our back, the cubicle at work is not a prison, and a person does not exist in our neck, causing it pain. Yet, these metaphors help us express why we feel burdened, trapped, or distressed.

You've probably heard many of these commonly used metaphors for various levels of anger: blow a gasket or a fuse, erupt like a volcano, spit nails, flip your lid, powder keg, pressure cooker, pissed-off, rubbed me the wrong way, wound up, got on my nerves, fit to be tied, steamed up, stormy, pain in the butt, hot-blooded, blood boiling, seeing red, fuming, fly off the handle, foaming at the mouth, champing at the bit, burning up, bitter taste.

Metaphors paint mental pictures or fantasies that can produce pleasurable or painful feelings and sensations. These conceptual metaphors shape our thoughts and attitudes (Landau, Meier, and Keefer 2010). You can magnify your suffering if you tell yourself, "My kids drive me crazy," or "my partner holds me back." Changing the metaphor, imagery, or fantasy can change how you feel. Perhaps your child's behavior proves challenging and demanding, but you do not need a stay in a mental hospital. Your partner might object to some of the things you wish to do, but your partner is hopefully not physically restraining you.

Negative metaphors and fantasies can trigger the release of stress chemicals, like cortisol, that cause us to feel anxiety. Over time those chemicals can make us sick. Changing those stories and metaphors can change our brain chemistry and make us healthier and more resilient.

Finding Your Superpower

Empowering images energize and create hope. While battling a serious illness that required a bone marrow transplant to stay alive, a friend adopted the nickname "Turbo Man," after an Arnold Schwarzenegger action figure and movie. In his red Turbo Man shirt and hospital oxygen mask, he resembles a superhero. Family and friends join in the fun. We declare, "You've got this Turbo Man!" As "Turbo Man," he faces this medical ordeal with strength, good humor, and a sense of personal power.

Dr. Janina Scarlet, author of *Superhero Therapy: A Hero's Journey Through Acceptance and Commitment Therapy*, uses identification with superheroes to help people find the strength they never knew they possessed. She helps people who struggle with trauma, depression, and anxiety. Dr. Scarlet guides them to explore the superhero inside themselves. She points out how every superhero in movies and comic books starts with a tragic beginning. Each also possesses a weakness or vulnerability that causes them suffering. Still, we admire these figures as they fight for something worthy.

Dr. Scarlet is a slender, petite woman with superhero-red hair and a penetrating gaze. She was exposed to radiation poisoning as a small child after the Chernobyl nuclear disaster in Russia. She suffered weather-related debilitating migraines, seizures, and chronic pain. At age twelve, she and her family came to the United States. Her classmates treated her like she was contaminated, called her "radioactive," and bullied her mercilessly. She felt depressed, lonely, and full of self-loathing.

One day she saw the film *Super Mutants*. These characters had all suffered some genetic mutation, as she had. Her favorite character was Thunder because she could control the weather. Dr. Scarlet writes, "It was after seeing this film that I first became fascinated with the idea of using fictional characters, like superheroes, to help myself and others overcome difficult emotional experiences." Her compelling fantasy of superhero powers helped her become a successful psychologist, author, and meditation teacher.

The stories that shaped my compelling fantasy stemmed from Shirley Temple movies. The young actress often played an impoverished and abandoned child. She inspired those around her to be more courageous through sheer optimism and goodness. The solid relationships she built with tap-dancing friends or caregivers made it possible to conquer cruel enemies. I tap-danced to her routines in early childhood and imagined conquering bullies with artistic excellence and optimism. I summoned inspiration from Shirley Temple when I gave food to needy families as a volunteer. It didn't matter that I was scraping by as a college student. No matter how little you have, like Shirley Temple, you can always help someone. Exercise your compelling fantasy; it might just lift your mood and increase your motivation to accomplish goals.

What stories, fictional characters, or true stories inspire you? Take a moment to write in your *frazzle hack* journal about the characters and stories that inspire you.

Looking Through an Optimistic Lens

Once you cultivate your compelling fantasy and practice exercising your imagination, allow yourself to take the leap and find your superpower story. You may not realize this, but we think in stories as well as metaphors. Our memories consist of stories that we weave together to make sense of the world. Sometimes our stories are pessimistic, reflecting pain and trauma; sometimes they are optimistic stories of victory and success, reflecting positive emotions. Positive psychologists like Dr. Martin Seligman researched the benefits of optimism.

Optimism, the tendency to expect positive future events, enhances well-being and encourages us to try harder. Pessimism, the propensity to expect adverse future events, reduces hope and discourages problem-solving activity. When you write your life story through an optimistic lens rather than a pessimistic lens, you reap many benefits. Optimism:

- **Reduces anxiety and anger.**
- **Strengthens ability to cope with stress.**
- **Protects from depression.**
- **Improves problem-solving ability and flexibility.**
- **Improves blood pressure and cardiovascular health**
  (Seligman 2006) (Conversano, et al. 2010).

Too much optimism, like too much chocolate, might not be good for you. Too much optimism could encourage high-risk behaviors, such as smoking, drinking, gambling, and other vices, without ever considering the downside of those behaviors. In contrast, too much pessimism might prevent you from trying new things, taking a career risk, or pursuing a dream because of the expectation of failure.

It helps to shoot for an optimal amount of optimism that considers realistic risks. If you suffer from anxiety, anger, and stress, then you probably lean more toward pessimism. Trying the *frazzle hacks* in this chapter can help you correct that negative bias.

I know many of you have suffered trauma in your life. Abuse, abandonment, neglect, violence, health problems, and many other concerns can make you feel anxious and hopeless. The novelist Tom Robbins penned one of my favorite lines:

It's never too late to have a happy childhood.

If you have suffered a lot in childhood, you can reinvent yourself in adulthood and find happiness. One way to capture that happy childhood is to write your life story through an optimistic lens.

Studies of optimists and pessimists reveal that optimists do not look exceedingly long at distressing visual images but will look longer at positive images. Pessimists do the opposite. They will look at the distressing pictures for much longer. There is an element of choice when we spotlight the adverse events in our lives but fail to pay much attention to those things that have gone well for us (Kress, Bristle, and Aue 2018).

In another study of optimism, subjects were asked to think about their best possible self (BPS) for five minutes per day for two weeks. They were told to think about their BPS in three domains: personal life, relationships, and professional life. Subjects showed a significant improvement in overall optimism and well-being after only one day. The positive effects lingered after two weeks (Carrillo, et al. 2019).

No matter what has happened to you, you can still tell the story from a positive perspective. When you do, your feelings about yourself begin to shift. Optimism can sneak in and offer many benefits. Here is an example of how you can tell your life story from an optimistic or a pessimistic perspective. The same person wrote the following two paragraphs. One story takes the pessimistic perspective; the other takes an optimistic view. All the facts are accurate:

Pessimistic Life Story

I grew up with two young, uneducated parents who did not have much money. At times we lacked decent clothes. People from the church had to bring us food. I was bullied at school because I could not attend parties, did not wear nice clothes, and was from a religious family. My parents fought a lot about money.

My dad could not hold a stable job. He attempted many get-rich-quick schemes that were doomed to fail. My father abandoned us and left us in more abject poverty. My mother struggled to make ends meet, forcing my sibling and me to work to help support the household at a young age. I had to work several jobs to pay my way through school to get out of poverty. I missed out on a lot of college and extracurricular activities because I had to work. My social life suffered because I had little time for friends or recreation. As a result, I had to postpone marriage and children until later in life.

Optimistic Life Story

I grew up with parents who loved music, socializing, nature, the arts, and creativity. My sister and I were encouraged to express ourselves creatively, so we learned to play musical instruments. We enjoyed informal gatherings at our home with singing, dancing, and joke-telling. My father included us in his many business ventures, so we learned how to do many things at a young age. We learned to fish, refinish furniture, pan for gold, sing in front of an audience, and edit films for movies. After our parents' divorce, my mother's job provided for most of our basic needs. My sibling and I were resourceful and earned money providing babysitting, office work, and sales for local businesses. By the time I got to college, I had already obtained ample work experience and never had trouble finding jobs that allowed me to support myself. My mother eventually remarried. She and my stepfather encouraged me and helped me pay for tuition at a university. As a result, I could get educated, obtain a professional career, find a loving husband, and have a fascinating family.

Yes, these stories are mine, as you may have guessed. I feel better when I linger on all the rewarding life events, without pretending the painful moments never happened. I find it empowers me. Try the exercise for yourself and see how you feel after.

Frazzle Hack: Happy Life Story

Write the story of your life from an optimistic perspective. Share the happy times, good fortune, loving relationships, moments of awe, beauty and wonder, fun. Tell the truth, but linger on the positive events, people, experiences, and wonders of your life so far. Take as much space as you need to write your happy life story.

How does it feel when you ponder the more optimistic version of your life story? How do you think you might include this optimistic perspective in your everyday life? Write your impressions in your frazzle hack journal.

Positive Imagery Can Relieve Worry

You might think that you cannot feel better until your issues and worries get resolved. I hear frazzled working parents say, "I can't relax until the kids are in bed, the dishes are done, and I've put everything neatly away." Every time you say to yourself, "I can't relax until . . ." you imagine that relaxation can only happen when conditions reach perfection. You picture a long list of prerequisites before you allow yourself to feel relaxed. That image serves as a form of self-hypnosis. Imagine a stage hypnotist putting you into a trance, saying, "You are getting sleepy; when you see messes, you cannot relax."

It serves no useful purpose to correlate daily household chores with stress. What if you pictured yourself feeling happy and relaxed while making dinner with your children while washing dishes while folding laundry while performing the functions of your job? If you imagine that you could feel comfortable and unfrazzled, even while engaging in the everyday activities of life, you open a door in your mind to that possibility. You change the self-hypnotic suggestion.

Author and positive-thinking guru Esther Hicks said, "Worry is using your imagination to create something you don't want." Some of us become accustomed to worried, frazzled thinking as the necessary cost of a busy life. We expect disasters and brace ourselves for catastrophe, rarely taking a moment to point the mind intentionally in the direction we wish it would go. When you practice thinking about things that make you feel happy, interested, excited, and delighted, your mind gets a rest, a chance to stretch. Your brain then releases soothing chemical messengers into the body.

To help your brain release the calming chemical messengers, it helps to visualize what you want. What feeling do you want to strengthen in your body? Do you wish to feel more at ease? More relaxed? Happier? How would that feel, look, sound, and even smell?

Researchers found that imagining positive outcomes helped relieve anxiety and improve mood and performance even more than just using verbal phrases like, "you can do it." Uplifting self-talk is helpful, but imagery has a more substantial impact on the positive mood that you wish to create.

You, Too, Can Hike the Tropics

Angie, a thirty-five-year-old project manager, reported feeling overwhelmed and frazzled at work. She often felt so tense that she came home every day with significant pain in her neck and shoulders. Her demanding job triggered so much anxiety that she considered going out on stress disability from work.

I asked her to tell me about times in her recent past when she felt relaxed and good. She described a fantastic vacation to the jungle island of Kauai. With her husband, she spent several days hiking, snorkeling, swimming, and boating. I asked if she had pictures. She took out her phone and showed me a few.

In my office, I then asked her to visualize hiking on Kauai, including what she wore, what flowers she smelled, what it felt like under her feet. After about five minutes of imagining herself on Kauai, I asked her how she felt.

"Great!" she replied.

"So, in five minutes of telling me about your vacation, while vividly picturing it in your mind, you changed your mood from anxious to great," I observed.

"Maybe I could do this at work," she said.

"Yes, and maybe having a picture reminder on your computer screen or in your office might help you generate those same feelings while you work," I suggested.

Angie worked for several more sessions on strengthening her imagination muscle to delight herself rather than torment herself. She kept improving each week until one day; she said, "I think I'm ready to graduate from therapy." I agreed. She had mastered the ability to make herself happier by using her imagination. It did not solve every problem in her life, but it gave her the strength to believe she could solve those problems on her own with calm poise.

Frazzle Hack: Imagine Calm

Take a few moments to settle yourself with your eyes closed. Take five deep breaths. Breathe in through your nose and release your breath slowly through your mouth. Notice the differences between the five breaths. One inhalation breath might be faster, another deeper, an exhalation slower. As your mind wanders, gently draw your attention back to noticing your breathing. Continue for a few more breaths. Next, picture yourself as you might look, feeling confident, calm, focused, and relaxed. Let your muscles go slack. Imagine yourself with a slight smile on your face, feeling warm, peaceful, and safe. When negative thoughts intrude, notice those thoughts, metaphors, and images. Let them pass on as you reimagine images and sensations of comfort, ease, confidence, and emotional safety. If it seems difficult to imagine yourself calm, try to remember when you last felt peaceful and relaxed. Picture the gentle rocking of a swing, the lapping of water on a boat, the easy comfort of clouds drifting on a warm day. Take images from that memory and magnify them. Add comforting details from your imagination. Say to yourself: "I allow myself to feel effortless peace, confidence, and safety." After a few minutes, open your eyes and record your thoughts and impressions in your frazzle hack journal.

When you take the time to visualize, using the compelling fantasy and the calming exercise above, you will notice a quiet sense of empowerment. Your mood improves, and your mind feels more limber. From this happier, more flexible perspective, your mental clarity and mood improve.

I work with many frazzled clients who report feeling a sense of threat, dread, or worry. That feeling of dread shapes how they interpret the actions of others. I worked with a thirty-five-year-old man named Frank, who suffered from stress and anxiety. He became angry after a colleague invited him to a party. "He knows I'm swamped and stressed. Why would he torture me like this?" The invitation gave rise to a tension in his gut and a sense of dread. Those stress sensations caused Frank to interpret an invitation to a party as a hostile act.

After calming his nervous system with deep breathing and meditation, Frank recognized that a party invitation did not constitute "torture." He had to feel safe before he could accurately interpret the meaning of a party invitation. After learning how to manage his physiological reactions, he trained his brain to experience a party invitation as a more emotionally neutral event.

While you might dismiss Frank's story as extreme, we all construct our interpretations of reality based on how we feel emotionally and physically. If I am in a hurry, I might interpret my talkative neighbor as an annoyance. If I feel relaxed and unpressured, my chatty neighbor seems friendly and interesting. Same person, different interpretation based on how I am feeling. The writer Anaïs Nin once said, "We don't see things as they are; we see things as we are."

It helps if we view our perceptions of others with gentle flexibility rather than as a fixed, concrete reality. That allows us to shift our perception when we receive new and contradictory information. Instead of feeling like a passive victim of your negative thoughts, you can point your mind in the direction you wish to go. Harnessing the power of your imagination can significantly improve your mood and your health.

Placebos and Nocebos

One example of the power of the mind that confounds drug researchers is called the placebo effect. When scientists create a study to examine the effects of a new drug, they must determine if the effects of the drug outperform the effects of a placebo or fake pill. Somehow, many people get better when they believe that they obtained treatment, even when they received a pill made from sugar or cornstarch.

Ted Kaptchuk, research professor at Harvard medical school, co-founded the Program in Placebo Studies and the Therapeutic Encounter (PiPS), at Beth Israel Deaconess Medical Center. Kaptchuk and his associates created an interesting placebo study of patients suffering from irritable bowel syndrome (IBS). They compared a group of patients on a waiting list with a group that received fake acupuncture (no real needles or skin puncturing.) A third group received sham acupuncture with a warm and caring treatment provider. Results showed that 28 percent of those on the waiting list reported symptom improvement, 44 percent of those receiving sham acupuncture alone reported progress, and a whopping 62 percent of patients who received sham acupuncture from a warm and caring provider reported significant improvement.

Researchers were surprised that combining a caring provider with a placebo treatment produced just as much improvement as the group that received actual IBS drugs in clinical drug trials (Kaptchuk, Kelley, et al. 2008).

But does the placebo effect work when people know they are getting the fake treatment? In one experiment, Kaptchuk told another group of patients suffering from IBS that they would receive a placebo. They took pills from bottles labeled "placebo." A separate group of IBS sufferers received no treatment. The researchers were shocked to find that the IBS sufferers who knowingly received the placebo reported symptom improvement almost as much as those who received real IBS drugs (Kaptchuk, Friedlander, et al. 2010). Something seemed to happen in the mind of the IBS sufferers that helped them improve.

Some patients experience negative results from placebos. Researchers call these "nocebo effects" from the Latin meaning "I shall harm." The word *placebo* means, "I shall please." A research team measured placebo and nocebo effects in the brain using functional magnetic resonance imaging (fMRI). They found that placebo and nocebo treatments affect areas of the brain responsible for pain reception. Nocebo effects differ from placebo effects in that they also activate the hippocampus, the part of the brain responsible for emotional memories and anxiety (J. Kong, R. Gollub, et al. 2006a) (J. Kong, R. L. Gollub, et al. 2008).

About a quarter of patients assigned to placebos in drug trials report a range of symptoms like headaches, pain, and nausea. Something quite different seems to be happening in the brains of those who experience pain from a placebo compared to those who experience relief. Somehow, those who imagine adverse outcomes seem to suffer even when they have received no treatment. In contrast, those who hope for improvement, who imagine feeling better, often experience relief from the fake treatment.

Dr. Ellen J. Langer, Harvard psychologist, looked at all kinds of placebo effects, not just the famous fake sugar pill given in drug trials, but placebo treatments, conditions, or ideas, that produce fascinating outcomes. In one experiment, Langer and her associates worked with hotel maids. The maids reported that they did not get enough exercise. One group of maids received the instruction that their job met the requirement for a vigorous exercise regimen recommended by the surgeon general. The other group of maids was given no such instruction. Before and after the experiment, researchers measured weight, body mass index, and waist-to-hip ratio. One month later, the maids who believed that their job required enough physical activity for good health lost weight, body mass, and inches compared to the other group doing the same job (Crum and Langer 2007). It seems that our expectations, beliefs, mindset, and imagination produce measurable outcomes in our bodies.

Imagination and Aging

In a 1979 study, Langer brought two groups of older men to a monastery in New Hampshire that replicated the world of 1959, when they were all much younger men. One group was instructed to imagine themselves living in that time and mentioned that they would feel as well as they did in 1959. The other group was told to just talk about 1959 and that "you may feel as well as you did." The total immersion group received coaching in the slang used in the 1950s. They watched movies, read magazines, and played games that were popular in 1959. The other group was not advised to immerse themselves in that period fully.

Both groups showed a reduction in signs of aging, with the most significant change in the immersion group. The experimental group showed improvements after only five days on tests of manual dexterity, memory, posture, weight, intelligence, and even hearing and eyesight. She calls this effect "counterclockwise" in her book *Counterclockwise: Mindful Health and the Power of Possibility* (Langer 2010).

Dr. Langer's research suggests that we can turn back the clock on aging a bit when we change our expectations about growing older. One group was primed to expect that they would feel better; the other group was told that they might feel better. Expectations, the mental picture of what we believe will happen, changed their body chemistry after only five days.

In one of Langer's early studies, she found that the expected cognitive decline from aging could be reversed if the elderly had a reason to remember. When older people were given small gifts in exchange for remembering things, their memory improved. In another study, nursing home residents who were given a plant to take care of and a choice about where to eat lunch or greet guests showed significant memory improvement. Remarkably, after a year and a half, fewer of them had died. If we feel that we have a reason to perform, produce, remember, somehow the body responds, and our abilities improve (Langer 2009). Engaging our imagination also can improve our performance of complex tasks.

Imagination and Performance

We have all heard that "practice makes perfect." Peak performers learn that mental practice makes perfect performance far more likely. It seems that mental practice, or imaginary practice, produces changes in the brain comparable to actual physical practice.

Dr. Alvaro Pascual-Leone, a Spanish physician and physiologist, wanted to study how thoughts change the brain. He was inspired by the Nobel laureate, Santiago Ramón y Cajal, who proposed in 1894 that the brain could change and adapt with focused mental exercise. Pascual-Leone used Transcranial Magnetic Stimulation (TMS) to map changes in the brains of novice piano players. In this study, he wanted to see if imaginary piano practice produced changes in the brain compared to real piano practice (Doidge 2007).

He taught two groups of people a piece of music, showing them exactly where to put their fingers and how the notes sounded. Then he divided them into two groups. One group mentally practiced the music in front of an electric keyboard for two hours a day for five days. They were told to imagine playing the music and hearing the notes. The other group physically practiced the music for two hours per day for five days. He mapped the brains of both groups before, during, and after.

At the end of five days, both groups performed the piece. A computer recorded the accuracy of their playing. The physical practice group, after ten hours of physical practice, played the piece more accurately than the imaginary practice group. They also showed enlargement of the cortical motor areas of the brain targeting the specific finger muscles used in their practice. However, when the imaginary practice group performed after only two hours of practice, they performed just as well as the physical practice group. Imagination can improve our performance on complex tasks even with minimal physical training (Pascual-Leone, et al. 1995).

Professional athletes learn to cope with anxiety by seeing it as a friend providing energy and motivation rather than an enemy creating fear and misery. The adrenalin rush an athlete feels right before a big competition can generate just the perfect amount of energy for an excellent performance. Researchers have demonstrated measurable performance improvements when athletes use imagery and mental practice (Weinberg 2008).

Imagined exercise can even increase your muscular strength, almost as much as physically performing the activity itself. In a study of finger strength, researchers Guang Yue and Kelly Cole found that muscular strength increased by 30 percent in the group that physically performed the exercise required by the study. Those who only imagined performing the exercise improved their muscle strength by 22 percent. It appears that you can strengthen your muscles with mental exercise alone, although not quite as much as physically performing the activity (Yue and Cole 1992). Not only does imagery help athletes manage anxiety, but it can also improve self-confidence and motivation to stick to practice and improve.

Neurophysiologists found that positive imagery produces positive performance effects, and negative imagery produces negative effects on performance. Like the nocebo effect, it appears that imagining adverse outcomes leads to negative results. The body follows where the mind goes.

Sometimes your mind might experience an argument between positive and negative thoughts. You can still help yourself perform better, even if your mind is conflicted, by allowing the positive imagery to dominate over the negative. Here's an example of how this works.

Not the experienced mountain biker, I found myself on my first long-haul ride gaining speed on a steep, gravelly hill that ended in a blind, sharp curve. I knew that a high-speed fall on slippery gravel could pose danger and I could not slow my speed. On one side of me was a cliff, on the other a mountain. As I sped downhill, a childhood bike accident haunted me. In that memory my bike toppled at high speed on a gravel road, leaving my left leg chewed up and bloody. That image battled with my positive intention to ride down the hill.

Knowing the effects of positive imagery, I ordered my mind to picture myself riding down the hill, upright, without falling. I started saying out loud, "Just ride down the hill!" I made it down the mountain, navigated the blind curve at high speed, and brought my bike to a stop. My legs shook so much that I fell over. Uninjured, I laughed at my victory over the two versions of that ride that battled it out in my head.

The goal of this chapter is not to eliminate all negative thoughts or images. We need to consider the downside as well as the upside in all our decisions. The *frazzle hacks* in this chapter help you create mental flexibility. When you refocus your mind on positive images, experiences, and metaphors, you lower stress, improve your mood, and feel happier.

Final Takeaway

You can use your imagination to decrease anxiety, anger, and stress while improving mental flexibility. Create your *compelling fantasy*, such as "the ideal vacation fantasy," to help you cultivate positive emotions.

Think about the language or metaphors that you use to describe events and feelings. Substitute metaphors and language that are neutral or positive to help you feel better. When you rewrite your life story through an optimistic lens, you savor the positive events in your life more fully. That optimistic view can help strengthen your ability to cope with stress and even improve your heart health. It helps to imagine positive outcomes. Positive imagery can help you feel better, age better, and perform better.

In Chapter Four, "Care for Your Gut, the Second Brain," you will learn why a healthy gut is essential for calming *frazzlebrain*. Mindful eating helps you tune in to your body's music. Establishing healthier habits improves your mental and physical health to strengthen your resilience.

Intentional

Behaviors

In Part I, you learned how to aim your thoughts to self-soothe, generate hope, and ignite your imagination to foster joy. While our thoughts are powerful, our actions influence brain chemistry as well. That is why in Part II, you will learn what behaviors can stimulate the self-soothing parts of your brain to make you feel happier and healthier.

FOUR

Care for Your Gut, the Second Brain

Habit is stronger than reason.

GEORGE SANTAYANA

Have you noticed that symptoms like stomachache, headache, gassy belly, or muscle pain might co-occur on days when you feel more frazzled? Like when you wake up with a mild headache, physical discomfort can set you up for a day of impatience, irritability, and overall *frazzlebrain*. It can feel and sound as if your body were a discordant instrument of noisy discomfort. Recent research reveals a significant connection between anxiety and stress, your brain chemistry, and your gut or gastrointestinal tract. You can boost your mood and decrease *frazzlebrain* by maintaining healthy habits that balance your gut. (Konturek 2011). This chapter will show you how to create internal harmony by properly caring for your belly, the second brain.

Here's a little gross-ology for you. We are composed mostly of single-celled organisms. Our cells are outnumbered ten to one by these organisms, primarily bacteria residing in our gut. Called the microbiome, our gut bacteria transmit from the placenta and amniotic fluid in our mother's womb. If your mother experienced severe stress during pregnancy, you might show a decrease of Bifidobacterium associated with proneness to inflammation (Clapp, et al. 2017).

Research with adult subjects has shown that those with a rich diversity of gut bacteria have better immune system health. Those with a less diverse microbiome are prone to pro-inflammatory bacteria. Inflammation in the gut can put you at risk for irritable bowel disease and other disorders (Rhee, Pothoulakis, and Mayer 2009); (Eckburg 2005). "The road to health is paved with good intestines," Dr. Sherry A. Rogers quipped. That road to good health begins at birth.

Babies born vaginally and breastfed babies show a richer diversity of gut bacteria (Gritz and Bhandari 2015). Hope is not lost if you or your children missed out on these early natural benefits. The microbiome differences between babies born by c-section or vaginal delivery tend to even out over time as babies adapt to a solid food diet (Backhed, Roswall, and Peng 2015). Good early nutrition from birth to age three helps babies develop a healthier microbiome.

It is heartening to note that your microbiome adapts to your environment and diet throughout your whole lifespan. Changes in gut bacteria can occur in as little as twenty-four hours after a change in diet (Clapp, et al. 2017). When you foster a more diverse bacterial climate, you obtain many health benefits, including:

- Strengthened immune system.
- Improved intestinal functioning and balance.
- Improved absorption of nutrients.
- A healthy metabolism.
- Lowered risk of gastrointestinal diseases.
- Lowered risk of other diseases later in life
  (Clapp et al. 2017).

You can reduce stress with well-balanced nutrition that includes a variety of fruits and vegetables every day (Radavelli-Bagatini, et al. 2021).

Good nutrition not only helps your physical health, but it benefits your mental health as well.

Gut Bacteria and Mental Health

The balance of your gut bacteria can alter your brain chemistry, making you either more anxious or bolder. Inflammation and bacterial imbalance of the gut have been shown to cause mental illnesses like anxiety and depression (Appleton 2018). Exciting new research shows that wholesome nutrition combined with stress management can heal or improve some mental illnesses. To illustrate, let me share the story of Billy, a fourteen-year-old boy brought to me for anxiety and anger management counseling.

The Boy Who Craved Fast-Food

Billy's parents reported that their once sweet, mild-mannered son was now raging, disrespectful, and fearful. Initially, I thought Billy's anger stemmed from the typical friction in families when a young teenager becomes irritable, and parents overreact. The family had suffered no significant trauma, no history of mental illness, or financial stresses.

Billy's mom reported normal labor and delivery and had breastfed him during his first year. The family attended church on Sundays, where they enjoyed a rich friendship network. Billy loved his church group friends and sang in the youth choir. Like his parents, Billy appeared overweight and pale. Polite and timid, he cried in the session with me. "I feel terrible, but I can't control my temper. I love my mom and dad. They try to help me, but I just get mad all the time!" He could not link his anger to any current frustrations, traumas, losses, or changes. Then I started asking about sleep, diet, and exercise.

"Billy sleeps great, but we don't get enough exercise," Billy's dad said sheepishly.

"I know we should, but we just don't seem to make it happen." Billy's mom said, "Every morning Billy has to have breakfast at McDonald's, or he will throw a fit!"

For the past year, Billy and his parents had started eating fast food every morning because it seemed to make Billy happy. I asked the parents about their health. Both were overdue for their annual physical exams. Both parents took medication for hypertension, and both had gastrointestinal issues as well. Billy had not seen his doctor in over a year. I shared my hypothesis: Billy's behavioral issues might stem from poor nutrition, lack of exercise, and lack of sunlight.

Though I explained that medical advice and nutrition were not my expertise, I knew the research and urged the family to schedule physical exams with their family doctor as well as a nutritionist.

"You seem to be a very loving family, and Billy is a wonderful boy," I said. "Sometimes psychological issues can stem from medical problems. We need to rule out medical issues before we proceed with counseling," I said. I asked Billy if he would try something new that might help him feel less angry. He said sure, he'd try.

We agreed to meet after they received physical exams and had seen a nutritionist for guidance on how to improve their diet. A few weeks later, Billy and his family returned.

"Well, you were right," Billy's dad said. "All of us had vitamin deficiencies. Vitamin D especially. We couldn't believe that we could be overweight and still not be getting enough nutrients."

The nutritionist helped them introduce healthier foods that they liked. They stopped their morning McDonald's visits.

"Your faces all have a warm, happy glow!" I observed.

"We go for a walk together every morning for thirty minutes now," Billy's mom said proudly. "I love the talks we have, and the sun feels really good too. Our vitamin D levels have gone up, and Billy hasn't had one meltdown!"

I asked Billy how he felt.

"I feel like myself again. I still get mad, but I don't feel so out of control like before." While it was hard for Billy and his family to believe that simple changes in their diet and behavior could improve Billy's mood, the evidence proved undeniable.

Gut Bacteria Can Improve Mental Health

Gut bacteria manufacture about 95 percent of the body's supply of serotonin. Serotonin is a neurotransmitter or chemical messenger released by a nerve cell. Serotonin is essential in the treatment of depression and anxiety. It also plays a role in the normal operations of most of our brain functions, including regulation of mood, appetite, sexual functioning, memory, and sleep. Deficits of serotonin lead to increased irritability, anxiety, depression, and anger.

In some promising studies with mice, researchers found that anxious mice given water laced with probiotics (helpful bacteria) were less likely to give up during a physical challenge and produced less stress hormone, corticosterone (showing a reduction of symptoms of depression and anxiety). A study with human subjects showed a significant decrease in anxiety and depression after only a thirty-day course of probiotics (Michaël Messaoudi 2011).

A growing body of research demonstrates that a healthy mix of bacteria in the gut can improve our physical and mental health. To better understand how this works, let us start with a basic understanding of digestion.

Digestion begins in the mouth. As you chew that crispy McIntosh apple, saliva starts to break down the nutrients. The action of chewing sends a message to your stomach to release digestive enzymes to break down the nutrients further. Muscles and mucosa continue breaking down the foods we eat as they move through our digestive tract (mouth, esophagus, stomach, small and large intestine, rectum, and anus).

When we race through the day, multitasking while shoving food into our mouths, we add stress to the work of digestion. Stress can cause the esophagus to spasm. It can also cause indigestion. Indigestion increases the environment for the growth of unhealthy bacteria in the gut. Harmful bacteria trigger a discordant cascade of unpleasant symptoms. Over time, chronic, unmanaged stress can lead to inflammatory responses and disease. You can decrease and even eliminate these toxic effects with a daily stress management practice, like the practices offered in this book. When you learn to generate a feeling of internal peace and harmony, your body responds and soothes itself.

A *New Yorker* cartoon shows a couple at a table. One is reading a science magazine. The caption reads, "It turns out it wasn't the giant asteroid that killed the dinosaurs. It was stress about the giant asteroid that killed the dinosaurs." While we cannot control all the asteroid disasters in life, we can manage our reactions to those stressors. Your body is built to withstand periodic stressful events without suffering long-term damage. The natural calming mechanisms of the body reset the nervous system once the stressor has passed. Practicing intentional behaviors that activate those natural calming mechanisms will strengthen your resilience.

You can think of the relationship between the brain and the gut as a conversation or a musical duet. Like a musical duet, sometimes one person sings, then the other, and then they sing together. Managing stress effectively requires harmonizing the musical conversation between your brain and your gut:

- **Top-down (Brain to gut):** Your thoughts and actions can decrease stress by activating positive coping strategies that lower the discharge of cortisol and other messengers that cause the stress response.
- **Bottom-up (Gut to brain):** Gut bacteria, inflammation, and other physiological changes affect brain chemistry, mood, and stress responses. Strengthening the diversity of the gut biome improves overall health and well-being.

It is best to use both top-down and bottom-up remedies to reduce anxiety and stress and improve physical and mental health.

One way to manage the top-down conversation involves strengthening thoughts and behaviors that help you cope. Cognitive Behavioral Therapy (CBT) encourages thoughts and behaviors that improve mood, reduce stress, and help you master your emotional reactions. In a study looking at gut bacteria composition before and after CBT, the CBT treatment improved the gut microbiome of subjects (Mayer 2018). This study shows a top-down effect. Your gut bacteria favorably responds when you improve your ability to cope with stress. It is not just the microbes in your gut from the bottom up that impact your mood. Your brain plays a significant part (K. Weir 2018).

While it is tempting to think of the gut-brain connection as a simple duet, it more accurately resembles a complex musical orchestra.

Attune to Your Body's Music

The brain-gut connection is like a musical conversation between the four different sections of an orchestra. Everyone has a unique mixture of gut bacteria. Each person's gut/brain orchestra has four main sections or ways of communicating.

1. **String Section (Neurologic Pathway):** Like the violins and violas of an orchestra, this pathway includes the vagus nerve that wanders from the brain through most organs of the body. It also includes the nerves spread throughout the gastrointestinal tract (GI), called the enteric nervous system (ENS). These strings vibrate in harmony with the central nervous system (CNS), made up of the brain and spinal cord, to aid in the work of digestion. This orchestra section includes neurotransmitters, or chemical messengers within the GI tract like GABA, serotonin, and melatonin, that perform vital physical and mental health functions (Breit, et al. 2018).

2. **Percussion Section (Endocrine Pathway):** These fancy drums and cymbals of the body influence neuropeptides or proteins that can impact our sleep/wake cycle, mood, and blood pressure. This section activates hormones and other chemical messengers that trigger the release of cortisol and norepinephrine, the stress chemicals that prompt our fight/flight response (Rabot, et al. 2016).

3. **Woodwinds Section (Humoral/Metabolic Pathway):** The flutes, oboes, and bassoons of the body form bacterial metabolites when the carbohydrates we eat ferment in our gut. Specifically, short-chain fatty acids (SCFA) influence immune system activity, assist in brain development, and impact the brain's overall health (C. H. Kim 2018) (Rogers, et al. 2016) (Sochocka, Donskow-Lysoniewska, and Diniz 2019). Disruption of this musical section has been linked to the development of autism (Dinan and Cryan 2017).

4. **Brass Section (Immune Pathway):** Like the trumpets, trombones, and tubas of an orchestra, you can feel the pain in your gut when this pathway is disrupted. Inflammation of the gut caused by bacterial imbalance triggers immune responses. This can lead to uncomfortable noise as our gut tries to wrestle with intestinal disruptions and gut pain sensitivity (Toribio-Mateas 2018).

You are the conductor of your orchestra. Each section of the brain/gut connection plays its part. Your diet and lifestyle choices direct how your body responds. If you listen carefully, you can correct the sour notes and make your own unique, beautiful song.

Attunement to your body's music begins when you pay attention to the signals your body sends.

Frazzle Hack: Mind–Body Attunement

This exercise helps you listen to your body to understand what it needs. Find a comfortable place to sit, ideally where your head is supported. Begin with five deep relaxing breaths. Inhale deeply through your nose and slowly release each breath through your mouth. Draw your attention to your breathing. If your mind wanders away, gently bring attention back to your breathing. Next, take a few regular breaths. Notice the difference between the five deep breaths and how you breathe normally. When you feel settled down a bit, draw your attention to your head. Let the muscles of your face go slack. Notice any sensations in your head.

Try to notice without any judgments. If you observe evaluations, criticisms, or worries, try to observe those thoughts briefly. Then let them pass by refocusing on your body sensations. Feel free to adjust your position or provide yourself comfort by massaging or stretching if that helps your body feel a bit better. From your head, next, go down to your neck and shoulders. After you attend to each body part, take a deep breath before moving on to the next part. Notice temperature, tension, relaxation, discomfort, comfort. Allow the muscles to go slack.

Continue this slow scan of your body, proceeding with each body part down to your feet. Notice the wisdom as your body tells you how it feels and what it needs. Take a couple of minutes to notice your whole body. Gently open your eyes, and with a deep breath, observe your mind/body attunement. Record your impressions in your frazzle hack journal.

How to Balance Your Gut

You can harmonize your gut health and soften your stress response by making simple improvements in nutrition and lifestyle.

- **Eat Mindfully:** When you eat, just eat. Do not combine the meal with television, books, driving, etc. Let yourself get a little bored. Boredom can free your mind to notice how and what you eat. Mindful eating can help you pay attention to how you feel. When you notice the foods you eat, the way you consume, you can make minor adjustments that will help you feel better. Awareness can help you stop eating when you feel full. Mindful eating fosters more savoring of your food and more enjoyment of meals.

- **Slow Down:** Give yourself moments where you do not rush, but instead savor a meal, a moment of laughter, a stroll. Slowing down settles your nervous system and helps you preserve and replenish energy. When you slow down while eating, you tend to chew your food better, which aids digestion and assimilation of healthy nutrients. It also sends a message to your brain that you can relax a bit. If slowing down is difficult for you, try putting your fork down after every bite.

- **Reduce Sugar:** Refined sugars, like that in a typical soda, give your unhealthy gut bacteria a thanksgiving feast. Many foods that come in a package or box, such as crackers, cereals, and chips, contain hidden sugar. It helps to substitute fruit, a natural sugar that provides energy, and many other healthy nutrients and fibers that strengthen the gut biome.

- **Eat Real Food:** Humorist Fran Lebowitz said, "Food is an important part of a balanced diet." Unfortunately, a lot of what we eat is not real food. Processed and packaged, stripped of nutrition, we eat lots of calories, but not enough real food. A plant-based diet consisting of a wide variety of fruits, vegetables, beans, and nuts fosters a rich diversity of gut bacteria. Those who eat more fruits and vegetables report less stress (Radavelli-Bagatini, S. et al., 2021). Foods that help balance the gut include those rich in tryptophan, a key chemical in the formation of serotonin. Tryptophan-rich foods include our favorite Thanksgiving turkey, bananas, beans, cheese, soy, chicken, eggs, and fish. Other foods rich in serotonin include walnuts, plums, pineapples, kiwis, and tomatoes.

- **Natural Probiotics:** Healthy bacteria live in the gut naturally and are necessary to restore balance. Valuable natural sources of healthy bacteria are yogurt (choose those with labels that read "contains live cultures"), sauerkraut, lactobacillus milk, kefir, kimchi, tempeh, kombucha, some cheeses (e.g., cheddar, mozzarella, gouda), and other fermented foods.

- **Drink Water:** Regular, frequent intake of water helps the gut function and can prevent constipation. Aim for at least eight glasses of water daily. Drink more when you exercise or feel thirsty. Tea, coffee, and alcohol take water from the body. Drink plain water to help your gut function smoothly (Jequier, E. et al., 2009).

A research review of several studies performed by the National Institute of Health did not find a significant change when healthy people took packaged probiotics. The science so far does not show that expensive probiotic supplements improve your health in any meaningful way if you are already healthy. A balanced diet that includes natural probiotics, like those listed above, does contribute to healthy gut functioning (Carpenter 2012). There is compelling new evidence supporting probiotic treatment for mental health disorders.

Psychobiotics, a New Frontier

Psychobiotics are specific probiotics that stimulate the production of neurotransmitters, hormones, anti-inflammatories, and short-chain fatty acids (SCFA). New research shows these psychobiotics deliver mental health benefits. Psychobiotics can improve mood and help you recover from stress. In scientific laboratories, researchers control the specific types of bacteria given and the dosage. Many commercial probiotics make outlandish health claims, and that concerns researchers. These supplements lack the vigorous regulation required of other products and medicines available. Immunocompromised patients could suffer harm from these products (Sharma, et al. 2021). Consumers cannot be sure that these probiotics offer the correct dosage or the right bacterial combination for their needs.

It is essential to consult with a doctor and nutritionist before taking supplements to treat any health condition. Do not fall victim to the marketing of these products on the internet. As Mark Twain wrote, "You may die of a misprint." Advertisers can make mighty claims and yet provide the wrong bacteria for you. Your doctor may be able to recommend specific products formulated to treat your needs. Check these trustworthy internet sites for science-based information:

- **Pubmed:** From the US National Library of Medicine, this site helps you search for published health and medical articles by topic, author, or journal. *https://www.ncbi.nlm.nih.gov/pubmed.*
- **The Cochrane Collaboration:** Based in the United Kingdom, this nonprofit organization reviews research on diseases and provides review reports. Primarily based in universities and hospitals, over 10,000 individuals independently check research. *www.cochrane.org.*

- **Quackwatch:** This independent international organization aims to debunk health-related fraud, pseudoscience, and misconduct. *www.quackwatch.org.*
- **US Government health sites:** These sites publish scientific articles based on government-funded research. You can recognize one of these sites by the .gov at the end of its URL. *www.nih.gov, https://usda.gov, www.nccih.nih.gov.*
- **ConsumerLab.com:** Consumer Lab tests dietary vitamins and supplements and give ratings on these products. You can find lots of free information on the website about products. If you want their complete reports, they charge a membership fee.
- **Labdoor.com:** An independent company that buys products off the shelf and sends them to laboratories to test their ingredients and look for potentially harmful contaminants. Products receive quality scores. As of this writing, this site provides information for free.

Pay close attention to your gut feelings. Those uncomfortable pangs can motivate you to take better care of yourself. View your discomfort as a form of disharmony. Minor tune-ups like healthy nutrition and regular stress management can help you feel more in harmony with the rhythms of your life. You might find yourself feeling happier too.

Stress and Your Gut

Three important endocrine glands (glands that secrete hormones) regulate our body's response to stress. The hypothalamus, pituitary, and adrenal glands, called the HPA axis, play an essential part in gut-brain communication. Our gut microbes are critical to the development and functioning of the HPA axis (Cani and Knauf

2016). The HPA axis in concert with the bacteria in our gut regulates several vital functions:

- **Energy balance**
- **Immune response**
- **Digestion**
- **Emotional state**
- **Stress reactions** (Mohajeri, et al. 2018) (Bonaz, Bazin, and Pellissier 2018) (Carpenter 2012).

When you practice daily stress management, you help the HPA axis regulate hormones and other chemical messengers to keep you feeling balanced. Learning the self-calming strategies in this book can help you activate top-down and bottom-up mechanisms for optimal health. In addition, try these proven strategies to reduce stress and maintain a healthy mind and gut:

1. **Exercise:** Moderate physical exercise increases serotonin levels as well as tryptophan, a chemical precursor to serotonin. This increase persists long after you have finished exercising. Physical activity builds resilience and improves your mood. Exercise reduces psychological stress, improves circulation, and lessens pain. Try for 150 minutes a week of mild to moderate activity. Make it easy. Take a thirty-minute walk, five days a week. Or try three fifty-minute workouts per week or some combination of the two. It is best to spread the exercise out rather than doing all 150 minutes in one day.

2. **Light:** Daily exposure to bright light increases serotonin levels and improves mood. Exposure to sunlight has been shown to help anxiety sufferers, those with mild to moderate depression, premenstrual dysphoric disorder, and pregnant

women suffering from depression. Vitamin D deficiency, implicated in a host of health problems, can be treated with moderate exposure to sunlight (S. N. Young 2007).

3. **Sleep:** A regular sleep/wake schedule helps foster a healthy gut. Chronic poor sleep patterns contribute to the development of obesity, diabetes, and infectious diseases. When our sleep is disrupted by late-night eating, shift work, and irregular sleeping patterns, it also disrupts our gut microbiome. If you can, try to go to sleep and wake up about the same time every day. Practice relaxing rituals before bedtime, such as a warm bath, soothing music, a comforting cup of tea, or a good book. Keep your bedroom cool and minimize late-night eating and drinking.

Pain in the Brain, Pain in the Gut

Growing up in a family with a lot of stress, perhaps neglect, abandonment, abuse, alcoholism, or conflict, can predispose one to gut sensitivity. Many people learn to cope with stressful environments by becoming sensitized to anger and the foul moods of others. The good news is your heightened sensitivity provides a superpower you can use to help influence a healthier gut.

"Following your inner guidance in the direction of comfort and safety is the first step toward healing," says licensed psychotherapist Nicola Ranson. A talented author with a soothing British accent, she has lived with ulcerative colitis, a painful inflammatory bowel disease (IBD). Colitis symptoms come and go, often flaring up during times of stress. "I saw how much stress impacted my health and was determined to understand how this worked and find the practices that helped me," Ranson says.

She is also a cancer survivor who helps others struggling with trauma and pain. She says that mind/body awareness "can help us make sense of how our own nervous systems bridge the fictitious divide between body and mind, providing the basis for more effective tools that draw from the body's self-healing properties."

You can use your physical and emotional pain awareness to aim your behavior toward a healthier brain-gut balance.

Emotional states, like anger, anxiety, and depression, often exacerbate physical disorders such as irritable bowel syndrome (IBS), inflammatory bowel disease (IBD), peptic ulcers, gastro-esophageal reflux disease (GERD), and adverse reactions to food allergies (Konturek 2011). These physical symptoms can increase anxiety leading to an unhealthy feedback loop between the brain and the gut. "Healing is more complex than learning to focus on feeling good and relaxing (although that definitely helps). It is also important to constructively address fear," says Ranson.

How to Cope with Fear

Fear of pain, physical harm, loss, and death mixed with daily stresses and anxieties can feel overwhelming. It helps to distinguish between pain (the physical sensations sent from body to brain) and suffering (our emotional interpretations of the painful sensations).

When my daughter was a toddler, she bloodied her knee for the first time. As I comforted her, she looked at me with terror in her eyes: "Is all my blood going to fall out?" Her interpretation amplified the sting of the bloody knee, causing her to believe that something far worse was happening. I explained, "No, honey, you just have a skinned knee. Your knee will stop bleeding, and you will be fine. A bloody knee just means you've been having fun!" Her face relaxed, and with a smile, she went back to playing.

A skinned knee represents a minor assault on the body compared to what one might suffer when facing a severe diagnosis. However, the same principle applies.

We magnify our fear and suffering by telling ourselves, "This is terrible. I can't handle this!" Our interpretations of pain amplify our fear, leading to greater emotional suffering. At first, after a scary diagnosis, we might say, "This can't be happening!" It is normal to struggle with disturbing news. We need time to take in the information and register how we feel.

The sooner we can accept our condition instead of resisting or fighting it, the sooner we lessen our suffering. Life requires a series of adaptations to events beyond our control. Sometimes those events include health crises. While talking about her recovery from cancer and colitis, Nicola Ranson says, "In recovering from both these conditions, practices which increased self-acceptance, which included my pain and physical distress, were enormously helpful. This, in turn, reduced the stress on my body as I became better at not fighting my own state."

Learning how to accept your whole self, including the parts that hurt, takes a bit of practice. Kimberly Joy, writer, physical therapist, and restorative yoga teacher has lived with Lupus, an autoimmune disease, for over twenty years. "By accepting my illness, I love myself as I am. This helps me reside in a soft, relaxed state, which supports healing," Joy says. She carries herself with the firm, upright posture of a yoga practitioner. In conversation, her intelligent eyes penetrate, framed by a long mane of blonde curls. I asked her how she manages her fear. She said:

The best way I've found to manage times of worry is by returning to the present moment. When my mind spins about the future or rehashes the past, I remember, much of what I worry about does not come to fruition and that challenging things pass. I lean into the knowing that I am resilient and able to handle difficult things.

This calms my mind and emotions, returning me to center and a sense of inner peace.

Like the *frazzle hacks* provided in this book, calming practices help soften our emotional and physiological responses to stress. That softening can help you accept, cope better, and suffer less from whatever pain you feel. Many of the *frazzle hacks* begin with deep breathing. Deep breathing sends a signal to your brain that everything is all right.

When we feel worried, we take quick, shallow breaths. This fast, shallow breathing sets off alarm signals in the brain. If we slow our breathing down and draw our breath in deeply, it calms the fear response. Kimberly Joy says, "When I feel my body becoming tense or my mind spinning with worrisome thoughts, I stop and breathe. I feel the cool air entering my nose. I sense the rise and fall of my chest and belly. I focus and breathe until relaxation starts to build and anxiety begins to fade."

It might feel like a struggle at first to just breathe when your mind floods with worries. That is perfectly normal. Just notice your mind wandering, then gently, without any judgment, draw your attention back to your breath. This exercise can help you cope with fear and back off from the urge to struggle.

When our body hurts, it can feel like an aggravation, an enemy that we must battle. We stiffen up against the pain, tightening muscles around the hurting parts, eventually hurting even more. "The journey to health involves differentiating between our well-programmed pull toward disaster avoidance: anxiety and endless attempts to figure it all out—and the call of the life force toward joy and expansion," Nicola Ranson says.

If you can train yourself to soften or relax into your pain, you might notice a softening of your suffering. Fear and anxiety tighten our muscles and turn us away from the "joy and expansion" we prefer. It helps to treat your body as a most treasured friend. Try the *frazzle hack* below to help you shift away from battling with your body to embracing it. The purpose of this exercise is to generate a relaxed, gentle, affectionate feeling toward the body—your whole body. Even the parts that hurt.

Frazzle Hack: My Body, My Friend

For this exercise, you will need paper and a pen or pencil. Begin with your eyes closed in a comfortable seated position. Take five deep breaths. Inhale through your nose. Exhale slowly through your mouth. With each breath, notice how the air feels entering your body and exiting your body. Observe whether the breath speeds up or slows down. After you feel a bit settled down, take a moment to imagine yourself watching your seated self. Imagine a deep affection for this person, this precious friend. Visualize a friendly face-to-face encounter and say to yourself, "I care about you. You are most precious to me; I want to take good care of you. I want you to be free from pain. I want you to be healthy and happy."

Imagine yourself holding this dear friend in your arms, providing comfort. Stay for a few moments with this gentle kindness and support. Take a few more deep breaths steeped in loving kindness. Next, open your eyes. Write a letter to yourself using your pen and paper. With that same spirit of gentleness, write how you will care for your precious friend, your body, your life. When you finish your letter, place it where you will see it every day. Let it act as a reminder to summon a kind and loving spirit toward your precious body.

Treatment for Gut Problems

The exercises in this book, along with medical treatments, can help restore your healthy gut functioning and improve your mood and health. These recommendations are not a substitute for medical advice. Be sure to get a proper diagnosis and treatment plan from a physician if you experience distressing physical symptoms. Many clients find relief from a comprehensive treatment plan that includes:

1. **Medication to help you manage symptoms and reduce the pain from conditions like IBS, IBD, GERD, etc.**
2. **Psychotherapy to lower anxiety, anger, and stress.** Cognitive Behavioral Therapy (CBT) and Somatic Experiencing (SE) therapies are two effective types of therapy.
3. **Support groups, both online and in real life, can provide helpful information and resources.** You might enjoy the good feelings that come from giving and receiving help within a community of support. (www.ibsgroup.org, www.crohnscolitiscommunity.org, etc.)

Managing problems of the gut requires multiple approaches for the best, most long-lasting positive effects. First, look for a doctor you trust and with whom you can be honest. Your primary care physician may order tests to determine a diagnosis and treatment plan for you. In addition to medical treatment, you may also find help from complementary practices that support stress and pain relief. Those include:

• **Naturopaths:** According to the American Association of Naturopathic Physicians, Naturopaths treat conditions of the body by encouraging the individual's self-healing capabilities through natural methods.

- **Osteopaths:** Osteopathic physicians, or DOs, cover the same curriculum as medical doctors and must pass a licensing exam. However, they receive additional training in the musculoskeletal system, sometimes specializing in the muscles, bones, and joints.
- **Functional medicine:** These practitioners often have medical training that specializes in identifying root causes for medical conditions. Often called "holistic health practitioners," these providers may examine nutrition, hormone imbalances, and other issues to help patients heal.
- **Acupuncturists:** These professionals use ancient Chinese medicine to insert tiny needles into points of the body to relieve pain, restore balance, and stimulate healing.
- **Reiki practitioners:** Using a Japanese form of stress reduction that involves laying hands on or over the body, these treatments promote relaxation, stress relief, and healing.
- **Massage Therapists:** These individuals employ stroking, kneading, tapping, and moving hands in a circular motion to produce a feeling of deep relaxation.

Perhaps scientists will one day analyze your gut bacteria to treat your anxiety or depression with psychobiotics. We know that striving for a healthy balance of bacteria in the gut will help your mood and overall health. What benefits the brain also benefits the gut, your second brain.

Frazzle Hack: Daily Stress Management Thirty-Day Challenge

Practice one of the following relaxation techniques every day for thirty days. You can alternate between the different activities or do one every day for thirty days. Notice any physical, mental, and emotional changes and record them in your frazzle hack journal:

- *20 – 30 minutes of meditation*
- *30 – 45 minutes of light to moderate aerobic exercise (walking, jogging, cycling, swimming)*
- *20 – 30 minutes of sitting in a massage chair*
- *20 – 30 minutes of light stretching or yoga*

Intentional behaviors that focus on managing anxiety, anger, and stress become habits. Those habits strengthen your resilience, your ability to bounce back from challenges and thrive. You dared to begin reading this book. If you dare to start, you can succeed. So, begin. I believe in you. You can do this.

Final Takeaway

When you care for your gut, your brain receives the fuel it needs to function effectively. You can help your digestion and gut functioning by eating mindfully, slowing down, eating a plant-based, low-sugar diet, and getting good sleep.

Listen to your body's music by paying attention to symptoms before they get too intense. Our gut acts as a second brain that communicates with the nervous system. You can minimize the symptoms in your gut and your brain when you regularly practice stress management. Healthy stress management includes:

- **Regular exercise**
- **Good sleep**
- **Light exposure**

In the next chapter, "Commune with Nature," we will explore what neuropsychology tells us about the effects of nature on the brain. You will learn about why it is essential to spend time in the natural world. Nature in all her forms provides healing effects that soothe and comfort.

FIVE

Commune
with Nature

Adopt the pace of nature. Her secret is patience.

RALPH WALDO EMERSON

One day I felt particularly frazzled with too many things to do while preparing for dinner guests. I planned to plant flowers in my front porch flowerpots. Lugging the bag of dark soil, I felt the strain on my back and worried about the lack of time to complete my to-do list. As I knelt and placed my hands in the rich, composted soil, I took in the fragrant aroma and started feeling better, calmer. I remember thinking, "It's okay if I don't accomplish everything. At least we will have nice flowers to greet our guests." After a few minutes of planting and watering, my mood improved. I felt a clear-headed sense of calm.

Modern life leaves many of us disconnected from nature.

Detachment from the natural world can alienate us from our natural senses. Higher rates of anxiety, irritability, and stress are associated with a lack of exposure to natural spaces. In this chapter, you will learn how connecting to the natural world can free you from *frazzlebrain*. You can walk in a park, get plants for your home, tend a community garden, visit a lake or ocean setting, and receive life-changing, stress-reducing benefits. Researchers found that spending just thirty minutes a week in an urban park could lower blood pressure and depression (Shanahan, et al. 2016). Planting some flowers in a pot of rich soil, as I did, can trigger the release of mood-boosting chemicals in your brain.

Scientists identified a bacterium in composted soil called Mycobacterium vaccae (m. vaccae). When people inhale particulates of m. vaccae, their serotonin levels increase. Serotonin is a neurotransmitter that relieves anxiety and depression. Psychopharmacology researchers found that chemicals isolated from m. vaccae:

- **Prevent inflammation of allergic asthma.**
- **Prevent stress-induced colitis.**
- **Improve learning** (Mathews and Jenks 2013).
- **Lower anxiety.**
- **Increase resilience to stress** (Smith, et al. 2019).

I felt the same reduction of anxiety as those mice when I planted flowers. When I took the time to get my hands dirty, it lowered my stress and helped me act smarter. Without the distraction of *frazzlebrain*, I managed to set more appropriate expectations, think more clearly, and relax. You can also relieve stress and achieve a sense of peace and calm by spending time near natural bodies of water.

Blue Spaces

When you wander near lakes, rivers, oceans, or streams, you receive great stress-relieving health benefits. Even brief walks near blue spaces improve mental health and well-being and lower stress (Vert, et al. 2020) (Volker and Kistemann 2011). Blue spaces invite us outdoors, encourage physical activity, and help the nervous system settle down and relax (White, Elliott, et al. 2020).

A visit to a city aquarium, with its wide variety of fish and plant life, can lower your heart rate, help you slow down and relax and feel happier (Clements, et al. 2019). You can even start your own home aquarium and notice the relaxing health benefits of bringing the sea indoors. You can lower anxiety, anger, and stress with time spent in both blue and green spaces.

Take a Forest Bath

The Japanese prescribe a leisurely visit to a forest called *shinrin-yoku*, or forest bathing, for relaxation and stress reduction. Scientists discovered that breathing in antimicrobial organic compounds called phytoncides (essential wood oils) reduces anxiety, anger, and depression. In another study, researchers looked at human immune system functioning after forest bathing. Surprisingly, they found a significant increase in Natural Killer cells, the tumor-killing cells of the immune system, after subjects spent time in the forest. They found that these positive effects on the immune system can last up to thirty days after a forest visit (Li 2010).

You do not have to be a hiker to enjoy the healing effects of the forest. Sitting in a car and looking out an open window at a forest can provide stress and anxiety-relieving benefits. The forest itself has healing properties even without exercise. In three reviews of multiple studies, researchers found that time in the woods (Farrow and Washburn 2019) (Kotera, Richardson, and Sheffield 2020) (Li 2019):

- **Lowers anxiety and depression.**
- **Improves cardiovascular health.**
- **Reduces anger and stress.**
- **Improves energy and vigor.**
- **Increases anti-cancer proteins and tumor-killing cells.**

Forest bathing provides an easy, relaxing, and refreshing way to turn off stress and turn on your healthy immune system.

Take a walk in the woods and listen to the sounds of life: the wind rustling through the sagebrush, woodpeckers rattling a rhythm on a nearby tree, the rush of a wild river, the various melodies of multiple species of birds, the sounds of your footsteps. The sounds, smells, and sites of nature can slow you down, clear your mind, and uplift your mood. Researchers found significant improvement in health and well-being when subjects spent 120 minutes per week in nature (White, Alcock, et al. 2019). Try the following *frazzle hack* to lower stress and improve your health.

Frazzle Hack: Natural High

Take a walk in a park or hike through your local mountains. Or walk by the ocean or a nearby body of water. If you are unable to walk, sit where you can view your environment. On this excursion, do not look at any electronic devices. Refrain from listening to music. Take out the earbuds. Focus your attention on absorbing yourself in the present moment. Allow yourself to notice the sounds, smells, sensations, and visual details of the natural environment. Observe closely any birds, flowers, insects, or other living creatures. Breathe deeply and smile. Notice any changes in mood, tension, or stress after spending some time in the natural world. Record your impressions in your frazzle hack *journal.*

Thriving in the Pavement Jungle

Sometimes we feel imprisoned in our work/life routines with no easy way to escape the stress. A *New Yorker* cartoon shows a prison with a sign out front that reads, "Stress Prison, the fictional jail you imagine being sent to so you can catch up on Netflix and reading." Some of my clients have told me that they wish they could go to the hospital to relax, read, and feel relieved of burdens. If you routinely unplug from work responsibilities to spend time in nature, you may never crave a stay in a hospital or Stress Prison.

But what if you do not live anywhere near a forest, lake, or park? What if you live and work in a pavement jungle where not a single living green thing can grow? Houseplants or office plants can reduce stress and improve your morale at work and home. Merely looking at a plant on your desk can lower your stress level (Toyoda, et al. 2020). Plants contribute to increased productivity and fewer absences from work due to illness (Fjeld, et al. 1998). Workplaces with more greenery produced happier, more patient, less frustrated workers (Kaplan and Kaplan 1989). Researchers found that merely looking at pictures of green spaces for five minutes helped lower stress by activating the body's self-calming mechanisms (Van den Berg, et al. 2015).

Spending time in a crowded city can trigger memory loss and irritability, as any city dweller can attest. Getting a little respite from the concrete and crowds, as you might find while having lunch in an urban park, can significantly improve your mental clarity and performance (Korpela, et al. 2010). The longer you linger in nature or park settings, the greater the level of stress reduction you will feel. Spending time in parks, especially biodiverse parks with a wide range of plant life, benefits your mood, reduces stress, and improves your concentration (E. Wood, et al. 2018).

Many communities, to foster a sense of connection and provide healthy food, have developed community gardens. Neighbors work the garden and enjoy social time together while they tend to the soil, plant, and harvest the food. Those living in poverty without access to fresh vegetables or good jobs can find a sense of empowerment in the community garden (Burls 2007). Gardening provides a respite from the stresses and worries of modern life. Green spaces encourage exercise, outdoor socializing, and play, all activities that benefit your mental health (Lee, Jordan, and Horsley 2015). Spending time in natural environments can even lessen attention deficit hyperactivity disorder (ADHD) symptoms, as it has a calming and centering effect on your nervous system (Kuo and Taylor 2004).

Aging Gracefully in the Garden

As you age, time in nature can lower anxiety, anger, and stress and improve your health and well-being. Studies of Alzheimer's patients found that time spent in gardens reduced their problem behaviors by as much as 19 percent (Mooney and Nicell 1992). Residents of long-term care facilities showed improved moods and reduced outbursts of anger after spending time in gardens

(Rappe and Kivela 2005). Dementia patients slept better, had better hormone balance, and decreased agitation after spending time outdoors in nature (Chalfont, et al. 2019). The research shows that natural environments help reduce stress and anger and improve your mood, energy, and physical health throughout your lifespan (Tu, et al. 2020).

Mud Matters

Parents need not recoil in horror when they find their three-year-old covered from head to toe in mud. Often the dark, sticky, muddy clay soil contains rich minerals that hold healing properties. Small amounts of ingested clay can help digestion and absorption of healthy minerals. The original formulation of the popular anti-diarrhea drug, Kaopectate, contained a clay mineral called kaolinite. Kaolinite's many medical benefits include an ability to absorb bacteria and viruses and treat intestinal ailments.

Africans on the Ivory Coast use clay to cure an infectious skin disease called Buruli ulcer disease. Some clays contain antibacterial qualities. The heat-generating properties of clay help those with rheumatism by increasing blood circulation, thus providing much-needed relief (Williams and Haydel 2010).

Spa treatments, some involving mud, provide relaxation and pampering that can refresh and recharge your whole body. If you can plan a one-hour spa treatment, massage, facial, or pedicure, it can add to your arsenal of stress busters. However, not everyone has access to the luxury of a spa treatment, and it is not necessary for a sense of well-being. You can get the same benefit from taking that gentle stroll near a park, forest, ocean, lake, or river.

The Sound of Things That Aren't Alive

At a film festival, my husband and I watched an inspiring documentary film, titled *All the Time in the World*, about a family who chose to live for nine months in the remote Yukon wild, without electricity or running water. Suzanne Crocker, filmmaker, and mother of three children ages ten, eight, and four, found the experience transformative for her and her whole family. After nine months of hauling water, gathering berries, cooking in a wood-burning stove, knitting, creating their own entertainment, stitching wounds, and running off a grizzly bear, the family loaded their gear into a boat and made their way back to civilization.

As they neared the town, the four-year-old daughter asked, "What's that noise?" Her brother replied, "That's the sound of things that aren't alive." That observation stunned me. I realized that most of the things we hear in the city, traffic, television, radio, digital music, disconnect us from life. We pay a cost for living wired to lifeless things. Nature connects you to your own imagination, heartbeat, vitality, life.

The Lifesaving Benefits of Pets

You can reap the relaxing benefits of nature by spending time with a pet. Pets can be therapeutic for people living with mental illness (Brooks, et al. 2018). Survivors of trauma and military veterans often report that a feeling of calm comes over them when they spend time with a dog. Pets help veterans relax and adapt better to civilian life. When you bond with a pet, you release the hormone oxytocin (Stern, et al. 2013). Oxytocin lowers blood pressure, reduces the stress chemical cortisol, and gives you a calm, comforting feeling (DeAngelis 2008). Pet ownership can even lower the stress of caring for an autistic child. Parents of autistic children show significantly less stress when they own a dog than those parents of autistic children without a dog (Hall, Wright and Mills 2016).

When you move at your dog's pace when you walk, you garner the relaxing benefits of both exercise and bonding with an animal. You obtain more relaxing benefits if you walk your dog without headphones or a radio. Electronic devices can distract you from the sounds of your footsteps and the outdoors.

Heart attack patients who owned pets were more likely to survive one year after surgery than those who did not own pets. The researchers found that the lifesaving benefit of pet ownership was not limited to dog owners, who typically get more exercise taking their pups on daily outings. Surprisingly, they found that owners of other pets like birds and cats also lived longer. Owning living creatures, and caring for them, seems to provide health benefits because we release lifesaving chemicals when we bond with pets, whether we get more exercise or not (Friedmann and Son 2008).

Just gazing into the eyes of your dog can increase levels of oxytocin in your body and boost your mood (Nagasawa, et al. 2015).

Perhaps you cannot have pets where you live, or you travel too much for work and cannot take on the responsibility of pet ownership. Maybe you suffer from allergies that make it an unhealthy option. You can still look for opportunities to enjoy the natural world and reap the benefits. Consider the following:

- **View exotic fish at a local aquarium or pet store.**
- **Swim in an ocean or a lake.**
- **Take a bird-watching hike.**
- **Cultivate houseplants or a garden.**

Many children and their parents live far from green or blue spaces. Bestselling author and journalist Richard Louv coined the term *nature-deficit disorder* to describe children raised with little or no connection to nature (Louv 2008). This worldwide trend of children spending less time in nature correlates with increased health problems, like obesity and diabetes, in children. Researchers found that lack of exposure to the sun contributes to high international rates of vitamin D deficiencies. Vitamin D deficiency is related to obesity, diabetes, low bone density, mental illnesses, and other health problems (Huh and Gordon 2008). You can improve the health of your whole family by spending time outside in nature.

A Nature Preserve in Your Own Backyard

Louv suggests that families develop a backyard nature preserve. He recommends that you plant more than five different species of plants for your nature preserve. Planting can provide bonding fun for the whole family. Research shows that restorative health benefits grow when we spend time in environments with a rich biodiversity (E. Wood, et al. 2018). Learn about the benefits of woody plants supporting caterpillars that attract birds. As you build your mini nature preserve, you can watch as creatures large and small come to play in your backyard. If you do not have a backyard, you can create a living wall garden inside your apartment. Grow herbs for cooking on your windowsills and enjoy house plants that provide natural air filtering for good health.

Frazzle Hack: Mini Herb Garden

Go to a local nursery and look for fresh herbs like rosemary, mint, thyme, or basil. Pick up small containers for a window garden and a small bag of soil. Return home and plant your favorite herbs in a few small pots. Place them on a windowsill or on a counter where they can receive adequate light. Take a small piece of each plant, rub it between your thumb and forefinger and inhale the aroma. Notice how it feels to pat down the soil, smell the rich earth, and the scent of fresh herbs. Allow the release of tension from nature's herbal hypnosis. Notice how adding live plants to your home can change how it feels. Record your impressions in your frazzle hack journal. Did it provide a bit of pleasure for you to dip into the earth in a small, tangible way?

Horticulture therapy, the use of farming to treat mental disorders, helps those suffering from anxiety, clinical depression, and other illnesses (Gonzalez, et al. 2011). Gardening lowers the stress hormone cortisol quickly after an acute stressor (van den Berg and Custers 2011). To learn more about how you might benefit from growing living things, read Ariel's story.

The Restorative Magic of Farming

A few years ago, I had the opportunity to live and work on a rural farm in South America called "Mama Roja" (Red Earth), where I learned about earthen building, organic farming, and natural medicine. I sought out this opportunity after three years of living in New York City. I felt fatigued and had become aware of my own limitations from participating in the competitive, fast-paced lifestyle that dominates and defines the educated class with which I identify. After a couple of weeks of being fully immersed in nature, using my physical strength to complete tasks throughout the day, and being held accountable by the other individuals living there, I noticed positive changes in my physical and mental health. My body felt stronger and my mind clearer. It satisfied me to sustain others and myself with the fruits of my labor. I was experiencing a deeper connection to myself: my feelings, my hopes and dreams, my body. Living in close community and being asked to participate in communal meetings accelerated my process of introspection and provided me opportunities to grow personally by working through personal and relational conflicts. These reflections led me to wonder about a broader healing power of connecting with nature (Schneider 2014). (Ariel Schneider is a clinical social worker and researcher of nature-based therapies in Los Angeles, California. She commutes by bicycle and keeps a small garden of succulents, herbs, and vegetables).

You do not have to get away and live on a farm to benefit from spending time with living things. Some people feel an aversion to the outdoors. Many of us grew up in families that discouraged outdoor activity. Some see it as dangerous, dirty, or just unpleasant. Even then, you can find a way to connect with living things, settle your nervous system, and *defrazzle*. Consider the case of my client Will, a teenaged boy with a strong aversion to getting dirty.

The Boy Who Was Afraid to Get Dirty

Years ago, I worked with a mother named Dawn. She made an appointment with me to help her socially anxious, overweight boy, Will. I asked the nervous mother what her son liked to do for fun.

"Video games," she replied.

"Does he like to go to the beach, play sports, go outside?" I asked.

"No, he hates the sand at the beach. He doesn't like to get dirty," she said.

I brought the boy into my office. He had a gaming device in his hands and appeared irritated when his mother told him to turn it off.

"When was the last time you had a lot of fun?" I asked.

"I don't know," he replied.

Dawn pulled a bottle of hand sanitizer out of her purse and rubbed a dab of it on her hands. Will reached for the bottle and did the same. I asked them about the hand sanitizer.

"Oh, it's important not to get germs that make you sick," the mom remarked.

"Tell me about your health," I inquired.

"We're all extremely healthy. We get regular check-ups every year. Other than all of us being a little overweight," she laughed, "we're in good health."

"Well, that's good to hear," I then asked, "when was the last time you did something fun outdoors?"

"Our neighbors had a backyard barbeque last weekend, and that was fun," she responded.

Dawn and Will lived a very hectic lifestyle, racing from job to school to computer camp to appointments. Their rushed lifestyle separated them from outdoor nature. I noticed that they had a hard time identifying their feelings and needs. Those who spend some time in parks, or other natural environments, enjoy the self-awareness and confidence that stems from quiet contemplation and physical movement.

Researchers working with teens in Norway found significant improvement in their mindfulness, well-being, and self-confidence after nine days of hiking in the mountains. Children who spend time in nature tend to take more physical risks.

Those children who engage in risky activities like climbing trees, wrestling in the grass, playing with puppies enjoy better physical and mental health. In our efforts to make things sanitary and safe for our children, perhaps we have gone too far by raising children who are squeaky clean but very frazzled (Brussoni, et al. 2015).

Dawn wanted Will to get more exercise, but he only wanted to play video games. So, she chose to "pick her battles" and focus on Will's homework and extracurricular computer classes.

"What would you like your life to be like when you grow up?" I asked Will.

"I want to have a dog and work at home on my computer and make a lot of money," he said with a rare smile.

"Have you ever had a dog?" I asked.

"No. My mom says it's too much work," he replied.

After talking with Dawn and her husband, I suggested getting a dog for Will, with the instruction that he had to do all the work to take care of the dog. That included training, feeding, walking, grooming, and cleaning up after the dog. We created a contract, and Will eagerly agreed to the arrangement.

A few weeks later, Dawn shared pictures of their dog, Sir Lancelot. In one photo, Will sported a huge smile as he hugged his new Labradoodle puppy.

"He's like a different kid," Dawn exclaimed. "He's with that puppy all of the time. He is even making friends at our neighborhood park. Everyone wants to play with Sir Lancelot."

At our last session, a few weeks later, Will seemed much happier. He spent many more hours outside, had made two new friends, and enjoyed sleeping every night with his beloved pup. His weight appeared normal; he had more color in his face and seemed more energetic and confident. I wish I could say my psychotherapy did the trick, but I think the real therapy magic arrived via Sir Lancelot and the great outdoors.

Studies show that families who frequent local parks and spend time engaging in outdoor activities experience greater happiness, need fewer trips to the doctor, and are more likely to volunteer to help their community. Social bonds get more robust, strengthening our resilience to stress. Crime and obesity rates go down in neighborhoods with community parks and recreation centers. When you live near an open space, you are more likely to walk, and that activity (otherwise known as exercise) helps you maintain a healthy weight. Exercise also boosts many neurotransmitters that ward off depression and anxiety, reduce anger and irritability, and allow for moments of happiness (White, M. et al. 2019).

Supermarket magazines and health blogs tout the value of exercise, yet many still find it challenging to accomplish regularly. Perhaps we find it difficult because we imagine it requires some painful, tedious, costly effort in a sweaty gym with hostile bodybuilders. Try to think of exercise as more like play, exploring, taking a break, and relaxing outside. A walk in the park exercises your body and your senses without the need for fancy exercise clothes or a gym membership. If you take that walk with a four-legged friend, you can compound the fun and the health benefits.

Final Takeaway

The pressures of modern life often force us to spend hours indoors or in vehicles that separate us from the natural world. When we get insufficient time in nature, we become alienated from our own nature. This alienation from nature can contribute to higher levels of anxiety, anger, and stress. Forest bathing can provide antidepressant effects that can calm your nervous system for up to thirty days after.

Spending time near oceans, lakes, or streams calms the body and eases stress. You can also achieve many stress-relieving benefits from gardening, planting a small herb garden, or caring for houseplants.

Keeping a live plant on your desk at work can help you focus better. Spending time outdoors in a garden or park or caring for a houseplant or a pet can help you stay healthier well into old age. Caring for a pet can lower your stress level and blood pressure and help you relax. You can achieve the same benefits even if you cannot own a pet by spending time in nature, caring for a neighbor's pet, or volunteering at an animal shelter.

In the next chapter, we will explore how performing acts of kindness benefit your brain. You will learn how cultivating a greater purpose that includes kindness toward others reduces anger, anxiety, and stress.

SIX

Cultivate Kindness

Constant kindness can accomplish much. As the sun makes ice melt, kindness causes misunderstanding, mistrust, and hostility to evaporate.

ALBERT SCHWEITZER

I
n Chapter Three, "The Power of Imagination," I shared how I decided to volunteer for a suicide crisis hotline when I was out of work and feeling quite blue. That wasn't the whole story. My closest friends had moved away. My other friends all performed in bands and worked from 9 p.m. to 1 a.m. Changing my career goals meant I would rarely see my music friends. I felt lonely and scared.

During that career crisis, I had to pull away from an entire community and lifestyle. Musicians often go to sleep at 4 a.m. and wake up at noon. Those night owl hours were incompatible with my demanding college schedule and the day jobs I soon worked. Yet, something about the idea of helping people in crisis sounded more meaningful to me than a career in music. Even though I felt desperately lonely and financially adrift, the decision to help others changed my life.

From that hotline work I gained a new group of dedicated and idealistic friends. A year later Crisis House offered me my first career track position. Everything I have today, including my husband and children, resulted from that moment when I said yes to an opportunity to help others.

Helpfulness and kindness possess healing properties. You, too, can obtain life-changing benefits from the intentional cultivation of kindness. In this chapter, you will learn how acts of kindness reduce *frazzlebrain* and increase health and happiness.

When we engage in selfless, kind, or compassionate behaviors, profound changes occur in the body and brain. Helping others lowers your blood pressure and heart rate. Acts of kindness trigger the production of mood elevators and bonding chemicals in the brain like oxytocin and endorphins. These physiological reactions accompany changes in the brain that strengthen our ability to recover from stress.

Acts of kindness can reduce *frazzlebrain* by making you less emotionally reactive to life's challenges. Those who contribute to the well-being of others report higher levels of happiness. This greater sense of happiness charms others, encouraging more social connections.

One blustery day in New York City, Brooklyn resident Delroy Simmonds waited at a subway platform on his way to a job interview. He noticed a woman with three children and a baby in a stroller waiting near him. Suddenly a strong gust of wind blew the stroller with the baby onto the tracks of the oncoming train.

Simmonds jumped onto the tracks in a burst of courage, rescued the baby, and barely escaped death as the train approached with horn blaring. When asked what would make him risk his own life, he said, "It was the fatherly instinct. I have two daughters of my own—eight and five. I was being a father. I would have done it for any baby," Simmonds said. Simmonds felt a common humanity with this desperate mother. We hear similar statements of shared humanity with a stranger in the stories of many heroes.

His act of compassion inspired another act of kindness. You see, Mr. Simmonds missed his job interview that day. When Guy Rodriquez, with ABM Janitorial Services, saw Mr. Simmonds's story in the paper, he offered him a maintenance position, like the one Simmonds missed when rescuing the baby. Acts of compassion can often inspire the generosity of others. Of course, Mr. Rodriquez had an excellent hunch he was hiring a person of character when he hired Delroy Simmonds (Lysiak and Hutchinson 2012).

Health psychologist Dr. Kelly McGonigal reports that the human brain is equipped with a social caregiving system. This system is regulated by the hormone oxytocin, produced mainly in the hypothalamus, and distributed into the bloodstream through the pituitary gland. When activated, this system creates a feeling of connection, trust, and bonding with others. Breastfeeding mothers produce oxytocin, contributing to the sense of love and connection between mother and child. Humans are social animals. When we feel close to others, we experience less activation of the amygdala, the brain's fear center. Bonded with others, we feel the courage to act. If we experience stressful events, oxytocin provides the chemical motivation to seek out support from others. It provides a cushion, protecting us from the paralyzing effects of overwhelming stress so that we cope better (McGonigal 2015).

If you feel stressed, as when a loved one faces surgery, the neurotransmitter dopamine strengthens motivation and the courage to do something helpful. When you offer that help, dopamine provides a boost even when it feels like the surgeon gave you an energy-ectomy. Sometimes *frazzlebrain* can cause you to freeze under pressure. If you ask yourself, "How can I be helpful, useful, or beneficial to others?" you activate the reward system of your brain. Doing something helpful, kind, or useful tells your brain, "You can make things better." And that feels empowering.

A study by UCLA neuroscientists demonstrated that helping others decreases your fear and increases courage and hope. In this study, scientists wanted to measure two different ways of coping with the distress of watching a loved one experience pain. Participants were given a sample electric shock to know what their loved ones were going to feel. They were told that they would be unable to prevent their loved ones from experiencing pain. Those who decided to continue with the study were given two ways to cope with the stress of watching their loved ones get shocked. For the first coping strategy, subjects could provide comfort by holding their loved one's hands. In the second coping strategy, they could distract themselves from the distress by squeezing a ball. Researchers then watched and recorded activity in the participant's brains.

The reward and caregiving systems of the brain showed more activation when participants held the hand of their loved ones. Providing comfort to another also lowered activity in the threat-sensing amygdala, decreasing the fear response. In stark contrast, those told to squeeze a ball (a distress avoidance activity) experienced a decrease in the reward and caregiving system of the brain. The stress avoidance activity provided no calming effect on the amygdala. When we merely avoid distress by doing some unrelated activity, it does not seem to help us feel better. In fact, it makes us feel more powerless (Inagaki and Eisenberger 2012). When we help others, we lower our own nervous system distress response and feel more empowered, with less fear and worry (Inagaki and Eisenberger 2016).

Time Stress

Comedian George Carlin observed, "When someone is impatient and says, 'I haven't got all day!' I always wonder how can that be? How can you not have all day?" The perception that you do not have enough time can set the stage for *frazzlebrain*. Deadlines—racing to get the kids to school, beat the rush hour traffic, write that paper—all these demands trigger anxiety, irritability, and distress. Researchers at the University of Pennsylvania Wharton School wanted to find a way to relieve time pressure at work. When we feel rushed and frazzled, we often make poor, unhealthy decisions.

Employers and employees alike could benefit if people felt less frazzled and more empowered. So, Wharton researchers placed people randomly into two groups. One group received an unexpected chunk of free time that they could use however they pleased. The other group was asked to spend their free time helping others. Afterward, the participants were asked to rate how much free time they had now and how little free time they felt they had in general.

Researchers found that the group that helped others during their free time perceived time as less scarce than those who were given more free time. Interestingly, those who helped others reported feeling more competent and capable than those who spent their free time on themselves. When we help others, we feel more self-confident. The demands we face feel less daunting. We see time as less scarce and ourselves as more able to cope with life pressures (Mogilner 2012).

When we cope with stress by tending and befriending others rather than isolating and escaping, we activate biological mechanisms that make us feel better, stronger, more competent, courageous, and less anxious. In addition, helping others encourages a positive feedback loop where others want to return the favor and help us when we need it (Klimecki, et al. 2014).

Goals for the Greater Good

Frazzlebrain can make you very self-focused and impatient, with a drive to find some relief. How can you help anyone else when you feel like you are the one who needs help? Perhaps you feel frazzled because you already help your aging parents, disabled spouse, and ungrateful children.

You can feel vampirized by other people's demands on your time. Sometimes you just need rest to replenish your energy. Give yourself permission to rest and recover. However, what you do and think about while resting matters. If your thoughts take you on a stress-cation instead of a vacation on that retreat, you might not get the real respite you need. Physical rest and mental rest are equally important.

One way to rest your mind is to savor pleasurable, positive, or comforting experiences. Savoring requires that you linger longer watching a beautiful sunset. Let delicious food melt in your mouth and draw your full attention to the pleasure you experience. Luxuriate in a warm bath. Savoring amplifies positive emotions allowing them to last longer. Take a photo so that you can remember positive experiences after you return to your usual routine. Savoring strengthens our resilience to stress and helps us recover and cope better (Irvin, et al. 2020) (Smith, et al. 2020). You can rejuvenate and recover from stress when you:

- **Do something pleasurable:** Enjoyable activities like playing a game, socializing with friends, or swimming in the ocean, pull your mind away from the worry treadmill.
- **Savor the experience:** Draw your full attention to pleasurable experiences. Activate all your senses. Linger longer with memories of enjoyable moments. Journal or photograph the experience to help you remember and savor later.
- **Think like a child:** For children, most experiences are wondrous and new. Free your mind of preconceptions and cultivate an openness to new experiences. You will notice more and find it easier to relax.

My husband and I love visiting New Mexico. We marveled at the painterly cloud formations while visiting Santa Fe in the spring. The artist Georgia O'Keeffe lived there and found inspiration for her paintings in the nearby landscape and sky. We bought a rock inscribed with a quote of hers, "Take time to look." When we returned to our home in California, we both started looking up at the sky more. It reminded us to look outside in the middle of a busy day. That trip away helped us marvel at our own San Diego sky.

When you return from resting, back to your work and responsibilities, it helps to adjust your perspective to avoid a recurrence of *frazzlebrain*. Take a pause and look at your life in its larger context.

When you think about the positive impact you would like to make on the people around you or society in general, it changes your brain chemistry. Studies show that focusing on a purpose larger than yourself helps you persist through frustration and setbacks. It also lowers two main stress hormones, cortisol, and adrenocorticotropic hormone (Abelson, et al. 2014). Focusing on the greater good beyond yourself increases your motivation and decreases burnout. It also helps you feel more enthusiastic, hopeful, curious, caring, grateful, and inspired. If you operate only from a sense of personal competition or self-focused goals, you tend to feel more frazzled, envious, and lonely. To illustrate, let me tell you the story of Desiree.

When You Have It All and Still Feel Frazzled

Desiree arrived for her first session, impeccably dressed as if for a magazine spread. Tall and blonde, with a fierce scowl of impatience, she rapidly regaled me with her success story. She had created a business that had made her a multimillionaire before the age of thirty-five. Her beach home had just been featured in a leading decorating magazine. She and her husband traveled and entertained extensively. They frequently appeared in the society pages of the local newspaper. Desiree had achieved everything she had hoped for, and yet she felt frazzled and unhappy.

"What is wrong with me? I have everything I ever wanted. I look at my best friend from college. She is so happy working for a non-profit agency. My other friend is a schoolteacher. They both seem so happy, and they make a fraction of what I make. I want to find something that makes me happy!" she said.

After ruling out health, relationship, and depression issues, I asked her, "What do you truly care about besides being happy and successful?" Desiree was stumped.

"How does your business, talent, and effort help other people?" I asked.

"I don't know. I am constantly on my employees, so not sure how that helps them. My husband likes me," she chuckled.

"So, your business provides jobs for people. Isn't that helping them?" I asked.

"Well, I guess the job helps them support themselves," she

agreed. "Isn't there something else I should be doing with my life that would make me happier?" she asked.

"It appears that achieving great success has not made you happy. Perhaps you will feel happier focusing on something else," I said.

I sent her home with an assignment. Instead of thinking about her own happiness, she was to examine precisely how her talents and efforts contributed to the greater good.

In the next session, Desiree shared her list of ways that her business and other activities helped others.

"I had to ask my husband for help on this assignment," she said. "I'm usually just focused on results."

I asked her what it felt like to think of herself as connected in an essential way to others in the community.

"It feels better," she said. "It makes me want to do more. I thought it might be fun to coordinate a charity fundraising gala this year." she said.

After a few more sessions, Desiree learned the secret to happiness and well-being. Kindness toward others provides far more happiness dividends than self-focused achievement. Simply thinking differently about our connection to the greater community can generate a sense of purpose and well-being.

Take a moment to think about how you currently influence others. How does your work intersect with the broader community around you? What kind of influence would you like to have on others? The following *frazzle hack* can help you explore your connection to the larger community around you. Take some time to think about your goals and record your answers in your *frazzle hack* journal:

Frazzle Hack: Greater Good Goals

1. How do your unique personality traits, talents, skills, background, or interests contribute to your family, friends, and the larger community? (Humor, technical skills, friendliness, communication skills, creativity, reliability, sensitivity, health, safety, technical knowledge, etc.)

2. How do you make a positive contribution to the lives of others? (Provide services, products, order, companionship, transportation, friendship, information, etc.)

3. Who benefits the most from your contributions? (Customers, family, city, country, etc.)

4. What kind of impact do you want to have on the people in your sphere of influence? (Better service, kindness, education, safety, entertainment, support, love, security, etc.)

5. What one change would you like to help create in the world? (Happier customers, healthy children, better service, more efficient products/services, safety, healthy environment, help the poor, humane treatment of animals, etc.)

6. Who could you join with to help you affect that change? (Church groups, friends, coworkers, environmental groups, philanthropic organizations, service clubs, community organizations, online communities, etc.)

7. In what way can you develop or grow to make more of a positive difference? (Education, communication, coaching, reading, better self-care, get more rest, join with others, volunteer, etc.)

Notice how you feel when you think about yourself in the larger context of your family and community. Greater Good Goals can provide that spark of motivation to help you persist when things seem overwhelming.

Coping with Resentment

Sometimes it feels too challenging to think about others when you feel resentful about your own unmet needs. You might harbor resentment toward those whose lives seem easier or happier. Maybe you have been unemployed too long and resent others who appear to have job security. Perhaps you feel burdened by family troubles or anger toward those who have harmed you. Sometimes you just need a break. It might feel burdensome to help others when you feel like no one is showing kindness toward you.

During these times, you can become stingy with your kindness, love, understanding, patience, and forgiveness. You might find yourself keeping score with the idea that you will start giving to others when others start giving to you. When you wait for others to do the giving, you give the keys to your happiness away. You will feel better faster when you take action to increase your well-being.

It helps to start with small acts of kindness and appreciation while expecting nothing in return. Begin with one of these three types of kindness:

1. **Daily:** Use common courtesy, social manners like saying "please" and "thank-you" to show kindness toward others at home, at work, and in public.
2. **Routine:** Remember birthdays, anniversaries, significant life events with a card, gift, or greeting. Respond to invitations, host a baby shower or retirement party for a friend or loved

one. Routinely volunteer at your children's school, a church, or a local community center.

3. **Random:** Praise someone on social media, open a door for a stranger, help a neighbor find a lost dog, donate to local causes, give a homeless person a meal.

Small acts of kindness increase your feeling of competency and improve your mood. You might notice others appreciating you more. That can help turn around that frazzled feeling and ease you back into life with renewed energy and optimism.

Forgiveness

Resentments and grudges aim the mind away from kindness. When we hold grudges, seek revenge, or dwell on past grievances, it raises our blood pressure, disrupts our immune system, and makes us more prone to illness and infection. Over time holding grudges can contribute to poor health and greater unhappiness (K. Weir 2017).

If you merely imagine forgiving the source of your injury, it can help your nervous system calm down. Forgiving does not mean that you just forget about the harm you sustained. It does not require that you condone the other person's behavior.

Forgiveness requires channeling your anger toward actions that help you heal. It does not mean that you forget.

Sometimes you might want to forgive someone too quickly so that you stop feeling the hurt and anger. Anger exists to protect us from harm. Make sure that the injury is indeed a past wound and not one continually reopened.

Karen and Jim planned a lovely summer poolside wedding on Karen's parents' property. Karen felt obligated to invite her brother Ron to the wedding but feared that he would make a scene due to his severe alcoholism and drug addiction. Ron had been in and out of alcohol and drug rehabilitation programs for many years. In the past, he had been arrested for punching a guest at a family birthday party. Ron had stolen money from the family to finance his addiction.

Karen and her parents decided to host an alcohol-free wedding reception and invite Ron. Two sober friends of Ron agreed to support him should he be tempted to misbehave at the wedding. Unfortunately, Ron arrived at Karen and Jim's wedding intoxicated and proceeded to shout obscenities in the middle of the ceremony. Ron's friends escorted him off the property and drove him home.

Karen felt devastated. "I want to forgive him because he's my brother," she said. Ron had no memory of what he had done to disrupt Karen's wedding. "I'm afraid of Ron. Every time there is a family event, he ruins it. I don't know how to forgive him." Karen continued to worry about what her brother might do next to hurt her and her family. I explained to Karen that she needed to establish safety boundaries to minimize harm.

Before trying to forgive, first, establish safety.

Karen and Jim attended a support group to help them define the limits of their relationship with Ron. With help, they agreed that Ron would not be allowed in their home unless he had established a year of sobriety. Until then, they would see him only in neutral settings where they could leave if his behavior became disruptive. Karen and Jim felt calmer after agreeing to specific limits on their relationship with Ron. They recognized that Ron had no control over his disease. However, Karen and Jim could limit the harm Ron's disease caused them. From that platform of safety, over time, Karen and Jim were able to forgive Ron.

Before focusing on forgiveness, ask yourself the following three questions:

1. **Is the person I feel anger toward continuing to injure me now?** If you answered yes to this question you need to focus on establishing emotional and physical safety first before attempting any forgiveness.

2. **Have I fully explored the effects of this injury and taken care of myself to repair the harm?** If you answered no to this question then it is best to inventory what harm you suffered and repair the damage through support, self-care, and perhaps counseling before trying to leap to forgiveness. Desmond Tutu writes, "We are not responsible for what breaks us, but we can be responsible for what puts us back together again." (Tutu and Tutu 2014).

3. **Do I feel psychologically and physically safe enough to forgive?** If the answer to this question is yes, then consider trying the following steps toward forgiveness. If the answer is no, focus on safety, recovery, and self-care to repair the parts that feel broken. The *frazzle hacks* in this book can help you lower your anxiety and stress to help you think with greater clarity about your next steps.

Melody Beattie, the author of eighteen books on codependency and addiction, writes, "Letting go helps us to live in a more peaceful state of mind and helps restore our balance." How do you let go of anger and move toward forgiveness? Forgiveness requires more than a passive letting go of angry thoughts. True forgiveness requires cultivating understanding, compassion, and empathy for the person who harmed you.

Forgiveness is an active decision to turn toward goodness in your thoughts and behavior.

Approach forgiveness with kindness and compassion toward yourself, rather than a harsh attitude. Researchers found that forgiveness protects your mental health and well-being no matter how much stress you have experienced in your life (Toussaint, et al. 2016).

Once you have established safety and feel ready to cultivate a forgiving attitude, try putting on some empathy glasses. Try to see from a different perspective the other person's humanity. The more time you spend trying to humanize the offending party, the less frazzled you will feel. Trying to forgive requires intentional action over time. Research shows that the more time you spend on forgiveness efforts, the greater the mental health benefits (Wade, et al. 2014). When you feel ready, use this guide to begin your process of forgiveness. Record your answers in your *frazzle hack* journal:

Forgiveness Guide

1. How do you feel now about the offense?
2. What actions have you taken to provide for your safety and recovery?
3. What makes you want to forgive now?
4. What needs, beliefs, or emotions may have induced that person to harm you?
5. What human failings, illnesses, or weaknesses may have influenced this person's behavior?
6. What cultural, financial, or social pressures may have motivated this person?
7. What part, if any, did you play in the situation?
8. What limitations, weaknesses, or behaviors of yours may have contributed to the injury?

You may not know the answers to all these questions. You can still benefit from attempting to answer them. Aiming your behavior toward empathy and forgiveness activates different regions of your brain. You still obtain stress-relieving benefits from the exercise even if you cannot answer every question with certainty.

If you did play a role in your injury, recognize, and take responsibility for it. Taking responsibility helps us to heal, grow and move on from suffering. Sometimes it is far more difficult to forgive ourselves. Shame and regret can fuel anger toward oneself. You can apply the above questions to yourself to foster self-forgiveness.

We can weather disappointment in ourselves better if we act kindly toward ourselves.

Self-Kindness

When we take time for ourselves, we sometimes feel guilty. We might steal away a little time to do something fun or relax. Yet, it does not feel quite right to neglect our priorities, such as work, spouse, children, or family demands.

I worked with a lovely thirty-five-year-old mother of two young children named Maria. Bright, accomplished, and very competent, she supported her hard-working husband in his business that consumed most of their waking hours. She sought counseling to manage the stress of her busy load made worse by the recent stress of caring for her sick and aging parents.

Maria's *frazzlebrain* had hit a critical point after she suffered a broken bone from a car accident. She admitted that she felt inattentive and preoccupied. That lack of attention contributed to her car accident. Now she required help from others to do basic things like dress herself.

Competent Maria began to feel anxious, resentful, and depressed. The stresses of her life weighed her down, and she felt unable to meet all the demands placed on her.

"I need someone in my life like me, who takes care of things and doesn't complain!" she exclaimed in frustration.

"Well, you do have you," I said. "What would you tell your dearest friend in a situation like this?"

Maria thought for a moment. "I would tell her that she's amazing, and she will recover, and everyone else can take care of themselves for a while, and that she should take care of herself."

"In what way can you show that kindness to yourself right now? The kindness that you would show your dearest friend," I asked.

With tears in her eyes, Maria began to see that she could give that kindness, understanding, and support to herself and not just to others. As Maria showed more kindness to herself, she began to feel happier by asking for help, performing physical therapy exercises, and getting massages. Over time her resentment toward others in her family lifted, and she felt a renewed sense of confidence in her ability to handle adversity.

Acts of kindness for yourself make room in your heart for more empathy and compassion for others. Relationships with others improve when we properly care for ourselves. Self-kindness reduces *frazzlebrain* as we replenish our well of comfort and support. We can then weather the tsunamis of life with greater courage, optimism, and determination.

Frazzle Hack: Intentional Kindness

1. Pick one way you can show kindness toward someone today. Choose a stranger, a friend, neighbor, or family member and do one unsolicited act of kindness for that person. Be sure to expect nothing in return. Not even a "thank you."

2. *Choose one person that you can help during your day. Even minor things like giving directions or holding a door open for someone counts.*

3. *Choose one way to show kindness to yourself today. Ask yourself, "What do I feel right now?" Then ask yourself, "What do I need right now?" Do one thing to address your current need.*

4. *Notice how just thinking about ways to be kind and helpful, even to yourself, can change the way you feel. Record your experiences and impressions in your* frazzle hack *journal.*

Final Takeaway

Engaging in selfless, kind, and compassionate behaviors provides many mental and physical health benefits. When you help others in your free time, it increases your feelings of competence and makes you feel as if you have more time.

Cultivating goals for the greater good of our family, community, and society helps us feel connected and significant. We feel happier, less frazzled, and more motivated when we see how our life influences others in positive ways.

Daily, routine, and random acts of kindness help us move past resentment and feel happier. Acts of kindness often create a positive feedback loop encouraging others to want to be kind to us.

Forgiveness offers many mental and physical health benefits. Forgiveness requires an active engagement in compassion, empathy, and understanding. You obtain more significant physical and psychological health benefits when you spend more time actively forgiving.

In the next chapter, you will learn how relationships can change your brain, why they matter, and how to create a supportive relationship network. We will discuss how you can cultivate close relationships that help you recover from *frazzlebrain*.

Healing

Experiences

In Part III, we will explore how healing experiences like good relationships change the brain and help repair damage from anxiety, anger, and stress. You will learn how to cultivate positive emotions and how mindfulness can expand your capacity for happiness and mental flexibility.

SEVEN

How Relationships Can Change Your Brain

There is a deep interconnectedness of all life on earth, from the tiniest organisms, to the largest ecosystems, and absolutely between each person.

BRYANT MCGILL

H uman relationships behave like a complex ecosystem. We produce, reproduce, and consume in an intricate exchange of energy. Pioneering psychiatrist Carl Gustav Jung said, "The meeting of two personalities is like the contact of two chemical substances: if there is any reaction, both are transformed." Interactive experiences with others change the structure and function of the living brain through our lifespan.

As we get older, relationships get complicated. We seek connection with others but retreat when we feel hurt or betrayed.

If our actions caused another pain, we feel anxiety, anger, stress, and guilt. Our actions affect the neurochemistry of others. And their behavior influences us.

In this chapter, you will learn the secret of healthy relationships. You will discover how relationships buffer the effects of *frazzlebrain*. Meaningful and uplifting experiences with others protect your physical and mental health. Included are tools to help you build your own healthy human ecosystem. It all begins during the first two years of life with the development of the social brain.

The Social Brain

From the time I took my first-born son into my arms and fed him, I felt enormous relief that I could nourish him. When he squeezed my finger and looked into my eyes, I felt a swelling of love. His sweet smell, soft skin, and baby giggles spirited a comforting awareness that my son would be all right.

Nursing mothers release the hormone oxytocin, fostering a warm, relaxed feeling of attachment to the child. The baby gains nourishment, satisfaction, and comfort, forming the early food-means-love connection.

Oxytocin can be delivered to other parts of the brain, such as the amygdala, where it eases our fear; the hypothalamus, where it lowers our stress response; and the hippocampus, where we store memories.

"When dogs and humans make eye contact, that actually releases what's known as the love hormone, oxytocin, in both the dog and the human," says evolutionary anthropologist Dr. Brian Hare.

Oxytocin is released during orgasm as well. Our neurochemistry stimulates a feeling of connection, warmth, and attachment. Bonding with others lowers our stress. We feel safer. Oxytocin even provides natural pain relief. (Ishak, Kahloon, and Fakhry 2011).

When my daughter was two, I developed lower back pain from two years of holding her, putting her in car seats, lifting her onto slides, and bending over to help her dress. On one errand, I put her down and said, "Mommy's back hurts, so I can't carry you now." She held my hand as we walked through the store, gathering items. As we parted the store, she said, "Mommy, does your back still hurt? Can you pick me up?" My heart warmed at her concern and empathy for my feelings. I shouldered the shopping bag, bent down, whisked her into my arms, and happily hoisted her up. She smiled, "I love you, Mommy! Don't hurt your back!" "I love you too, honey, and I won't hurt my back," I said.

Somehow my pain lessened at her tender expression of concern. Her caring inspired me to want to give back to her in a loving exchange of affection. My actions shaped her behavior, and her actions shaped mine.

Like the example I just shared, small interactions between parent and child build the social brain over time. Our relationships shape the growth of connections in the brain. Neurons (brain cells) and neurotransmitters (brain chemicals) activate, and change based on our experiences with other people (L. Cozolino 2014).

Fathers of newborn babies showed a bulking up of gray matter in regions of the brain linked to nurturing behavior. These brain changes occur within the first four months of parenthood (Kim, et al. 2014). New fathers and mothers show changes in neural networks that help them attune to the needs of their newborn (Abraham, et al. 2014).

When a parent comforts a crying child, the parent's soothing voice, smell, and touch stimulate the release of several other neurochemicals besides oxytocin. Brain chemicals such as prolactin, endorphins, and dopamine provide parents and children with warm and pleasurable feelings.

The transfer of comforting energy fosters a mutual feeling of security, love, and connection. This interpersonal neurobiology delivers the raw materials to form close bonds with others. These caring relationships help one better manage stress and cope with loss (L. Cozolino 2010).

Unfortunately, some children are born into war zones, deprivation, suffering, and despair. This early trauma influences how the brain develops. Fortunately, however, healthy relationships can help the brain recover from trauma.

Healing from Childhood Trauma

When children grow up with verbal, physical, sexual abuse, neglect, or witness violence, the stress from those experiences directly alters the development of the brain.

Early childhood maltreatment stunts the development of the hippocampus, the seat of long-term memory. The greater the number of harmful early childhood events, the more significant the decrease in the volume of the hippocampus (Carrion and Wong 2012).

Emotional abuse does something different to the brain. Those who suffered emotional abuse in childhood showed a thinning in two parts of the brain. One part processes self-awareness in the prefrontal cortex, and the other part helps us understand and cope with our own emotions in the medial temporal lobe. Thinning in these regions of the brain help explain the high rates of anxiety and depression in those who have experienced emotional abuse and neglect (Aghamohammadi-Sereshki, et al. 2021); (Teicher and Samson 2016).

Traumatic experiences are common. In fact, 80 percent of us will experience at least one traumatic event in our life. Most of us will endure multiple traumatic events (Lewis, Jones and Davis

2020). Fortunately, the mighty human brain is built to withstand many dangers. Your living brain learns from experience and adapts (Yusifov, et al. 2021).

Multigenerational Trauma

Many of us grow up with stories of family trauma that can go back for generations. Trauma and addiction expert Dr. Gabor Mate says, "Stress is not an individual problem. Stress is a social problem." For example, Daphne, a witty, fifty-five-year-old Black American school teacher, told me in conversation about how she came to California.

"When I was a little girl in Alabama, my mom came into my room in the middle of the night and said, 'get up, we gotta go!' My dad and mom threw stuff into suitcases and stuffed them into the car as fast as they could move. I was scared and didn't understand what was happening. My little brother was crying, and I just grabbed what my mom told me to take. Dad's business was doing well and cut into the business of a Klansman. The KKK (Ku Klux Klan) threatened to kill our family, so we left. We left our home, business, friends, everything," she said.

Daphne's parents had traumatic stories passed down to them from their parents who faced brutality, the legacy of slavery, and discrimination. They received no police protection from threats of violence because local police officers were also members of the KKK.

Stories of survival can both inspire and trigger a stress response when people of color recognize an unmet need to feel safe in the world.

Jewish families exploring their genealogy find significant gaps in their family tree. Many discover relatives killed in the Holocaust or pogroms. Stories of fleeing persecution, escape from war, or economic struggle amid prejudice cause multigenerational suffering. Many Jewish people do not know what happened to their relatives. Synagogues routinely receive bomb threats, shootings, vandalism, and desecration of graves.

Descendants of Holocaust survivors show changes in the HPA axis (hypothalamic-pituitary-adrenal) responsible for regulating our stress response. Descendants of combat veterans with post-traumatic stress disorder (PTSD) show similar changes in the HPA axis. These changes (lower cortisol levels and higher glucocorticoid sensitivity) are the same changes observed in people with PTSD. Descendants of survivors show these genetic changes even though they did not suffer trauma themselves (Yehuda, Bierer and Schneidler 2000) (Yahyavi, Zarghami, and Naghshvar 2015).

The human need to feel safe is fundamental to well-being, yet it remains unmet for many of us.

Multigenerational trauma is nearly universal. Here are a few more examples:

- *First Nations, Native Americans, and other indigenous people forced from their lands, culture, economic opportunity, and dignity continue to fight for recognition of multigenerational harm.*
- *Cambodians, Vietnamese, Armenians, Rwandans, Palestinians, and those from the former Yugoslavia have experienced displacement, genocide, war, violence, mass killings, rapes, starvation, and many other traumatic events as part of their family history.*
- *Immigrants from Mexico, Central America, South America, Asia, Europe, Africa, and the Middle East, who suffered poverty, violence, political unrest, forced sterilization, and*

*discrimination, feel the legacy of those traumatic
events today.*

- *Japanese Americans interned during World War II lost
property, businesses, relationships and were treated as
enemies by their own country, leaving unhealed wounds that
last for generations.*
- *Multigenerational substance abuse, addiction, family
violence, rape, and incest leave descendants feeling unsafe
even within their own families.*

Fortunately, the effects of multigenerational trauma are not permanent (Yehuda and Lehrner 2018). Your brilliant brain adapts to new environments and experiences. The trauma your family experienced may provide you with unique wisdom, strength, and survival skills. Those strengths include, but are not limited to:

- **A deeper appreciation of a safe, welcoming community.**
- **Ability to appreciate everything you have after experiencing significant losses.**
- **Specific survival skills that help you cope with economic downturns or physical dangers.**
- **Gratitude for the sweetness of life itself.**

Those who suffered economic deprivation or devastation learn to savor and enjoy every precious thing they acquire. For example, when I was a little girl, my mother's close friend Stella watched me occasionally. Before fleeing to America, Stella hid from the Nazis for years after Hitler invaded Holland. She could only venture out at night to scavenge for food, even boiling her own hair for nourishment.

One day I was helping her cut vegetables for a salad. I started to throw away the discarded ends of the celery when she exclaimed, "What are you doing? Don't waste that! I will make soup with that!" She saved vegetable ends, roots, and meat bones for savory soups. Her casseroles, created from leftovers, tasted tremendous and honored her fierce need to waste nothing.

Having lived close to starvation, she valued every morsel of nourishment. Stella tastefully furnished her home with used pieces, repaired, and refinished herself. Though she had the means for more extravagance, Stella lived frugally, with a rich appreciation of art and culture, well into her 90s.

Take a moment to acknowledge the trauma your ancestors experienced and consider how that suffering may impact you today. Multigenerational trauma may sensitize you to interpersonal conflict, political conflict, or other triggers because of the feeling of being unsafe.

You can benefit from recognizing the strength and wisdom you gained from the traumatic experiences your family endured. Trauma survivors often possess carefully honed survival skills, character, and adaptability that can improve every area of life.

If your family has suffered multigenerational trauma, you can find healing in collective experiences that aim to make the world better. When we direct our imagination and behavior toward the future we want to see, healthy hopefulness emerges. Begin with these three steps:

1. **Acknowledge the past:** How has multigenerational trauma affected you? What feelings arise when you think about family stories and facts you've learned about this trauma?
2. **Recognize present strengths:** What personal strengths have you developed due to this collective trauma? Awareness,

resilience, adaptability, interpersonal sensitivity, assertiveness, survival skills, resourcefulness, etc.

3. **Aim for future growth:** What positive change(s) would you like to see in yourself and your community? What people or organizations can you partner with to work toward that change?

Our ancestors paved the way for us. Our descendants will walk the paths we build. No matter what you have endured in life, new experiences reshape your brain. Healthy relationships can lower stress and help you cope better with trauma. Bonding with a social community can help you feel safe and secure. For example, researchers found that black women who suffer from anxiety benefit from "sister circles" or safe places for women of color to meet, feel connected, and receive emotional support (Neal-Barnett, et al. 2011).

A rich social ecosystem strengthens your overall health and well-being. From that rich soil of supportive relationships, you cultivate caring experiences that heal the frazzled brain.

Cultivate Caring Experiences

To enrich your social ecosystem, begin with acts of service, thoughtfulness, and caring. In the last chapter, we talked about the stress-relieving impact of kindness. Here we learn that shared experiences, infused with acts of caring, enrich our human ecosystem. Studies show that just thinking about doing something beneficial for another reduces your stress. It also increases happiness (Nelson, et al. 2016).

Years ago, a loved one's breast cancer returned after a period of remission. Soon after we received that bad news, our families vacationed together at a mountain cabin. We shared meals and day hikes in the Sierra Nevada mountains with our children. We all felt the fear, anxiety, stress, and anger at that monster cancer.

After our vacation, two of my friends and I decided to participate in the Susan G. Komen three-day breast cancer walk. It required a fundraising effort and walking sixty miles in three days.

We raised the required funds and joined thousands of women, men, breast cancer survivors, teens, and children for three days of walking. Along the route for the walk, we were cheered on by a father with his little girl. They called themselves "the Smile Guy and the Little Grin." Dressed in bright yellow smiley face pajamas, they offered us candy and smiley face buttons. The Little Grin's mommy was battling breast cancer. Every time we saw her, throughout the three days, it boosted our energy.

On the third day, we arrived at the stadium in downtown San Diego. A gauntlet of volunteers gave us high fives for finishing the strenuous walk. We all wore matching blue T-shirts. Cancer survivors wore pink shirts. At the closing ceremony, the survivors went to the center of the group. The rest of us surrounded the survivors in a spirit of healing and support. Tears streamed down my face as I looked at this sea of caring people, many of them also overcome with emotion. I felt a warm energy flood my body. It numbed the aching pain I felt from the long walk. We all loved someone struggling with cancer. We all cared.

Caring experiences can heal the frazzled brain. Don't wait for others to show caring. Take a moment to look at the following list. See which caring experiences you might try:

- **Host a birthday party or baby shower.**
- **Join a Habitat for Humanity build.**
- **Share lunch with an elderly neighbor or relative.**

- Join a charity run or walk.
- Help a friend with childcare.
- Organize a game night with friends.
- Take chicken soup to a sick friend.
- Coach a Little League or soccer team.
- Join a community mural project.
- Work in a community garden.
- Volunteer at a hospital.

Generosity toward others lowers our stress and boosts our happiness even more than spending money on ourselves. Connecting with kindness also provides many stress-relieving benefits for the body, including:

- Changes in oxytocin and progesterone.
- Alters nervous system arousal in the hypothalamus-pituitary-adrenal axis.
- Alters the sympathetic nervous system.
- Changes in leukocyte gene regulation associated with lower inflammation and higher well-being levels (Nelson-Coffey, et al. 2017).

Shared experiences that demonstrate caring and generosity change us at the cellular level. We can be a source of healing for others, and they can help us mend. These interactive experiences can sustain us through any trauma or adversity.

Growth from Trauma

Trauma survivors often flourish from what psychologists call "post-traumatic growth." (Schubert, Schmidt, and Rosner 2016). Character grows from adversity. Many survivors develop unique strengths and talents as a direct result of trauma. Growth from traumatic events includes:

- **Self-confidence:** "If I could survive this, I can handle anything."
- **Courage:** "I already know that scary things happen. Everyday risks are nothing in comparison."
- **Gratitude:** "I'm grateful that I survived. I appreciate all the little things life has to offer."
- **Empathy:** "I care about people who suffer trauma as I did. I feel fortunate that I can offer support and understanding."

Like mangrove trees adapt to brackish and salty water, survivors can adapt to harsh conditions and flourish. When you move from a poisonous ecosystem to a healthier one, your living brain grows as it acclimates to the new fuel. Consider the story of Titus.

Surviving and Thriving After Abuse

Titus, six-foot, three inches, and all smiles, sought career coaching with me. He wanted to learn better ways to impress on his superiors that he deserved a promotion. I asked Titus about his background. He was born in upstate New York. As an infant, his parents left him out in the cold so they would not be disturbed by his crying. He was rescued by a concerned neighbor and placed in a foster home, where he witnessed domestic violence between his foster parents. Authorities removed him from that home after his foster father beat him. Eventually, a loving family adopted Titus at age five.

I asked him about his rough beginning and how it contrasts with his current life. "I'm grateful for my adoptive parents," Titus said. "They loved me and gave me everything I needed. They love my wife and kids too. I think I appreciate them more than if they were my biological parents. They didn't have to take me in. They chose me. I want them to be proud of the man I've become."

Titus survived abuse, neglect, and violence. Loving relationships, including adoptive parents, friends, and church community, helped his brain grow, adapt, and heal from that early trauma. Titus felt proud of his family and grateful for their love. And to my eyes, he gave a lot of love back to them.

Titus developed several strengths that allowed him to flourish. Rather than dwelling on the suffering he endured as a child, he lived with gratitude for the loving-kindness he received. He had seen the worst of human behavior but chose to focus on the best. Through his work, family, and community relationships, he felt his life had meaning and significance. Titus's story reveals:

Three Secrets to Healthy Relationships

1. **Gratitude:** When you appreciate the kindness of others, you strengthen your attachments. When you share your appreciation, it inspires others to do the same.

2. **Amplify the good:** Our relationships flourish when we magnify the positive qualities we notice in others. We also feel happier when we recognize and amplify the good around us. Amplify the good by noticing it. Let your mind linger in the good longer. Then mention that good in all your relationships.

3. **Commitment and meaning:** Our work, family, social obligations, and responsibilities provide purpose beyond selfish desires. Maintaining our commitments makes our relationships stronger. Obligations and commitments offer us a sense of significance and meaning.

Some children spend their entire childhood in abusive homes, refugee camps, or suffer great neglect. No matter how rough your upbringing, warm relationships can strengthen your resilience to stress. To break free from stress and strengthen your resilience, try the following *frazzle hack*:

Frazzle Hack: Amplify the Good

—ⴰⴰⴰ—

Take a moment to allow your nervous system to settle down. Sit comfortably, where you feel supported and relaxed. Take five deep breaths, inhaling deeply through your nose and exhaling slowly through your mouth. Think about someone for whom you have caring feelings. Visualize that person as if they were standing before you. Notice all the good qualities you can find about that person. Is she intelligent, funny, kind, hard-working? Is he responsible, loving, talented, empathetic? Are they loyal, thoughtful, considerate? Do you admire this person for their accomplishments? Bravery? Integrity? Let your mind linger in appreciation of all the qualities you admire about this person. Now open your eyes and look around you. What can you see in your immediate environment that you appreciate? Let your eyes linger on the beautiful plant, colors, furnishings, anything in your surroundings that you find pleasing. Record your impressions and observations in your frazzle hack journal.

Embrace Your Inner Geek

Even fictional characters can inspire and help us cope and flourish. Characters in literature, television, and film often exemplify values we admire. Research shows those with social anxiety gain improved well-being by connecting with fictional characters (Jarzyna 2020). Many people bond over their passion for the *Harry Potter* books and films. Fans of the television show *Star Trek* call themselves Trekkies. Trekkies attend conventions, wear costumes from the show, and form long-term relationships around their shared fandom. Cosplay and role-playing games (in real life and online) offer a way to bond with others over a shared love of fantasy and creativity.

Studies show that favorite television shows can provide a sense of belonging and reduce feelings of loneliness (Derrick, Gabriel, and Hugenberg 2009). Digital media offers opportunities to find people with similar interests. Many develop close friendships and even find love in shared fandom communities.

Meaningful cognitive improvements can occur even when you connect through online social media (Mintzer, et al. 2019). No matter how you connect, close, meaningful relationships can help you live a longer, happier life.

Relationships Help Us Survive and Thrive

Our survival depends on the diversity of our relationship ecosystem. We depend on loved ones for companionship, emotional support, and a sense of significance. Employers, educators, and coworkers contribute to our economic survival. Grocers, healthcare professionals, security, and service personnel ensure our physical survival in modern society.

The human brain has special cells, called mirror neurons, that help us observe, understand, and learn from others. Researchers at the University of California, Los Angeles, were the first to observe mirror neurons. They found that these cells respond when you perform an activity and when you watch someone else act. When your piano teacher shows you the correct fingering of a piece of music, mirror neurons activate auditory and motor neurons in your brain to help you perform the music. These brain cells form the building blocks of empathy, the capacity to recognize and feel the emotions of another (Keysers and Gazzola 2010).

Children with high levels of empathy are rated as more popular by teachers and peers (Marcus 1980). The ability to resonate with the emotions of others strengthens all our relationships. When others show caring for our feelings, we are more likely to trust them.

Trusting and supportive relationships can influence your health in significant ways. If, for example, you have a good relationship with your doctor, you will more likely adhere to prescribed medical treatment (Fuertes, et al. 2007).

Married couples tend to take better care of themselves and encourage each other to engage in healthier behaviors (Umberson 1987).

When your friend orders a salad for lunch, you are more likely to pick a healthy option. Do you want to become more physically fit? Hang out with more physically active friends.

When you watch your partner, friends, or family members demonstrate healthy habits, it influences your brain to see those behaviors as standard and makes you more likely to choose healthy options as well (Reblin and Uchino 2008).

In a review study of more than 300,000 people under sixty-five years of age, those with strong social relationships had a 50 percent increase in odds of survival over 7.5 years than those with inadequate social relationships. Having a solid network of relationships provides as great a benefit to your health as quitting smoking. Good relationships produce a more substantial health effect than exercise or tackling obesity. Relationships can save your life (Holt-Lunstad, Smith, and Layton 2010).

Hostility Poisons the Ecosystem

While good relationships provide feelings of comfort and security, bad relationships can harm. Social stress, such as living with a violent or chronically angry spouse, can damage our immune system. Living with a chronically hostile person accelerates aging and shortens the lifespan (Razzoli, et al. 2018). Abusive relationships can make you more prone to anxiety, depression, and stress-related illnesses.

Fortunately, you can heal your human ecosystem in several ways:

- **Establish safety:** Find safe people and tell them the truth. Identify safe places for refuge. Call a crisis hotline, domestic violence shelter, or find temporary lodging.
- **Ask for help:** Psychotherapists, family, mentors, clergy, and close friends can provide support and a fresh perspective.
- **Lower the stresses you can control:** Prioritize commitments. Make time for relaxation and self-care. Ask for help when you need it. Practice some *frazzle hacks* to calm yourself.

When you take charge of what you can control, the health of your ecosystem improves, even if no one else changes. Why? Because you influence the ecosystem too.

Strengthen Your Social Ecosystem

You can develop and maintain a healthy social support community at any age. What is social support? Like a healthy ecosystem containing a wide diversity of life, a social support system includes a variety of meaningful connections. The National Cancer Institute defines social support as "a network of family, friends, neighbors, and community members that is available in times of need to give psychological, physical, and financial help."

Social relationships protect your brain, increase your resistance to viruses, and help you heal more quickly from illness and injury. If you feel you can depend on a few people for friendship, childcare, help with a move, or a financial gift when needed, you possess an adequate support system.

Most research demonstrates that the quality of our relationships better predicts good health than quantity. A handful of close friends provides more benefit than a hundred superficial acquaintances. We need both a close group of intimate relationships and a broader spectrum of people with whom to socialize (Ozbay, et al. 2007).

As we get older, friends and family members move away, drift away, or pass away. It helps to remain open to new friendships while strengthening the relationships you cherish throughout your lifespan.

New friendships require tending and feeding for them to flourish. Other relationships, like those with family, may have strong roots, like a sturdy oak tree. Long-term relationships still need nourishing. Take a moment to identify some relationships that you would like to strengthen. Then try the following *frazzle hack*. You might warm the heart of someone you love.

Frazzle Hack: Strengthening Relationships

Make a list of people who matter to you. Choose someone for whom you feel grateful. It could be a coworker who agreed to work a shift for you. Maybe a neighbor who let you borrow a tool. Perhaps a friendship that has provided you welcome companionship during a tough time. Now think about one kind thing you could do for that person to show them you care. Could you write a letter or thank-you note? Perhaps you could invite them out for a meal or coffee. Think about one unique way you could show that person what they mean to you. Say to yourself, with intention, "I wish to uplift this person. I expect nothing in return, not even a thank-you." Pick a day and a time to provide that care. Record your impressions in your frazzle hack *journal.*

Tending the Social Garden

While it feels life-sustaining to surround yourself with supportive people, you gain even more from tending to others. Studies show that seniors and retirees who feel needed live longer, healthier, more fulfilled lives. One study discovered that older adults who felt socially useful had lower levels of disability and mortality. Seniors who suffer financial strain can lower their stress by giving their time and service to a community or church group.

Tending actions, such as bringing a hot meal to a widow, lower blood pressure in the giver. Helping others reduces physiological stress. As your social garden blossoms, you enjoy a sense of safety and community. Those who give support to others also receive more support. When you give to others, you demonstrate to yourself that you can provide something of value. If you remain connected to a community of support, it can provide meaning, significance, and life-saving help (Reblin and Uchino 2008).

Sometimes, during periods of loss or loneliness, we tend to dwell on heartache. That can create a feeling of emptiness or disconnection from the community. When you act to help someone else, it stimulates a sense of empowerment. When we feel more empowered and less helpless, we cope better with stress.

Sometimes traumatic events are so massive in scope that they impact most people on the planet. World wars, natural disasters, and global pandemics tax our emotional, physical, and financial resources. During times of great stress, relationships help us survive and thrive.

Coping with Global Crises

During the COVID-19 pandemic, many suffered the loss of loved ones. To make matters worse, they could not comfort their dying relatives because of hospital safety rules.

Routines of daily life became stressful. "Where are the clean masks?" was a frequent issue in our home. The stress of adapting to mask-wearing, handwashing, and social distancing strained our patience. People lost jobs. Entire industries shut down. The comfort of going out to dinner or a movie with friends or safely going to worship services abruptly ended.

Healthcare workers and first responders had to cope with severe daily stresses through the pandemic. They suffered anxiety about personal exposure to COVID-19. They worried about the risk to family members. Many experienced extreme stress watching patients die at alarming rates.

Danielle Kaplan, a registered nurse in a COVID-19 unit in Rapid City, South Dakota, explained, "I remember holding my patient's phone up so that her family could talk to her (maybe even for the last time), and the daughter was in tears. After hearing their emotional exchange, I had to leave the room, stood in the hallway, and tried not to cry. It didn't work. I paced up and down the hallway for a few minutes, tears flying down my face. The doctor went in after me to tell my patient that there was nothing else we could do for her. When the doctor came back out, our eyes met, and we embraced one another with tears streaming down our faces. I felt so much sadness, but in the end, I was able to stay strong and supportive for the family members experiencing such a great loss."

I asked what helped her cope with that overwhelming stress. "The ability to have optimism amongst a time of stress and sadness truly gave me the strength I needed to cope with the stress of my work," she said. "I knew that I was making a difference, even if it was small."

"Witnessing the extensive losses of people all over the country and my own COVID-19 diagnosis gave me the courage to tell my best friend that I'm in love with him. He returned my feelings, and having him as my rock and support system made some of my hardest days lighter in a way. By allowing myself to be vulnerable and open, it helped me handle stress in a healthier way," she said.

Her parents live in a different state, but she credits her almost daily conversations with them as a vital source of support. I asked her what else she did to manage her stress. "Having my dog Bailee with me during the peak of the pandemic truly helped me cope. And my newfound love of plants gave me the perfect distraction I needed to disconnect from social media and gloomy news stories. I ended up with thirty-five plants in my apartment!"

Nurse Kaplan mustered optimism and courage even during times of great stress and sadness. She shows how finding meaning and purpose can get you through many bad days. The ability to experience positive emotions even during painful times helped her summon strength. It even gave her the courage to be vulnerable with her best friend, deepening that precious relationship.

Even her non-human ecosystem, with dog Bailee and her menagerie of plants, provided a sense of well-being and offered stress relief.

Finding support from puppy love also helped Lizzy Tsen, a critical-care nurse from Portland, Oregon. "Training two puppies in an apartment," she said, "has provided me with a great distraction and focus that has helped me in my healing this year."

Nurse Tsen asked me to refer to her as Lizzy. Her work as an ICU nurse during the pandemic hit her hard. "I've cried about work more times than I can count and have seen more death in the last three months than I have in my three years of nursing prior to COVID. It can feel so defeating to be working so hard for little reward. However, on the flip side, when we do have success stories, we celebrate and cherish them, and those lives we save make us work that much harder."

Lizzy lost both of her grandparents during the first year of the pandemic. She had to isolate from her family to protect them from exposure to the virus. This separation gave her tremendous empathy for families who could not be with their loved ones in the hospital.

"I have found meaning in my work by attempting to be a stand-in for them," Lizzy said. "Whether this means holding someone's hand as they pass away or brushing their hair every morning, I've tried to find ways to give patients some final moments of peace during an incredibly isolating time. This has also helped me in my own stress and grief because although I was not able to be there in those moments for my grandparents, at the very least, I can be there for someone else's."

Lizzy felt tremendous gratitude for her colleagues. "My coworkers have been the greatest support system during this pandemic. We formed a special bond going through this shared trauma together. After rough shifts, we find time to debrief and vent to each other. Receiving the vaccine has also done a lot to mitigate my stress." She also expressed gratitude for her partner, who "had to deal with the worst of my emotions this past year... He has been very encouraging, and I wouldn't have gotten through this year without him."

She also had to provide support to other nurses in her role as head nurse. She began to feel the secondary trauma of helping everyone else through their suffering. Lizzy realized she needed someone to talk to about her stress. "This made me start the process of getting into therapy and seeking out people I viewed as mentors," she noted. "Both things have helped my burnout and helped me be a better leader."

Seth Firstman, a nurse in Olympia, Washington, said "the girlfriend and pups" helped him cope with stress. "One of my favorite things about being a nurse is being able to comfort people when they are anxious and scared about going into surgery," he said. "I love the Maya Angelou quote that says, '...people will forget what you said, people will forget what you did, but people will never forget how you made them feel.' I think that's especially true in nursing."

Danielle, Lizzy, and Seth found many relationships helpful to them through this time of severe crises. Coworkers, partners, family, puppies, therapists, and mentors helped them function at an extremely high level despite the sadness, stress, anger, and pain. The meaningful relationships they developed with patients and their families gave them strength.

Uplifting Influences

Several years ago, our office experienced a baby boom. Over two years, seven babies were born to seven new moms. When a mom would return to visit the office with her new baby in her arms, the office's mood shifted. As we watched staff members coo, giggle, and interact with the new baby, we all felt uplifted.

When someone shares their happiness with you, it can give you a bit of a mood boost, too, if you allow it. Playing with a neighbor's new puppy can stimulate production of endorphins and oxytocin generating positive feelings. Those positive feelings might make us feel more warmly toward our neighbor the next time we meet. We move closer to those people we associate with positive emotions.

Sharing physical activities like sports, hiking, dancing, and swimming release the joy chemicals, endorphins. When we generate these natural chemicals, we feel less pain, anxiety, stress, and anger. We also develop positive feelings that build and strengthen friendships (Anderson and Shivakumar 2013).

We can choose uplifting influences to reduce feelings of fear and anxiety. When we uplift others, we boost our mood, generating feelings of calm, safe connection.

Hearts Beat as One

Sometimes we feel disconnected from the community. That might happen when friends and family move away, or if you take a job in a new town. Or disconnection can occur when you feel frazzled. Studies show that those who feel a sense of oneness and connection, regardless of religious beliefs, experience greater life satisfaction (Edinger-Schons 2020).

Oneness, or feeling part of something larger than oneself, stems from openness to the experience of transcendence (Van Lente and Hogan 2020). When you open yourself to experiences of oneness and connection, you obtain many benefits:

- **Reduced anxiety and depression** (Mills, et al. 2018).
- **Prolonged positive mood, attitude, and behavior** (Boyd-Wilson and Walkey 2015).
- **Mental flexibility** (Vago and Silbersweig 2012).

One way to feel more connected to others is to participate in synchronized group activities. Synchronous activities provide many physiological and psychological benefits.

Swedish researchers found that choir singers' heart rates synchronized when they sang in unison or a canon. Respiration and heart rate go up and down in unison, along with the music. We know that heart rate variability (HRV) and respiration rate influence one another. This relationship is called respiratory sinus arrhythmia (RSA). When we control our breathing and slow it down, as we might while singing or performing yoga breathing, we slow our heart rate as well (Vickhoff, et al. 2013).

Messages sent through the vagus nerve contribute to an increase of vagal tone, a measure of well-being. Similar effects occur in group yoga classes where breathing is synchronized, during church services while singing and praying in unison, and when meditators chant together. An experience of unity, connectedness, and harmony with others creates a sense of social safety. It also increases happiness.

Friendships often develop from shared experiences. If you regularly attend sports, choir, or other activities, you plant yourself in fertile soil for relationship growth. Familiarity with the group creates a sense of emotional safety. Try the following *frazzle hack* to see how connecting with others can enrich your social ecosystem.

Frazzle Hack: Connecting with Community

The purpose of this frazzle hack is to help you experience a sense of connection, oneness, and community with others. If you already engage in any of the following activities, commit to continue regularly. If you do not participate in any connection activities, pick one that you would like to try from the following list. Or select another action that sounds appealing to you. Just make sure the activity you choose has a synchronized, shared component. As you participate, allow yourself to feel a part of something larger than yourself. Respond to others with kindness. Show appreciation for the action itself. Record your impressions in your frazzle hack journal.

Connecting activities list:

- *Join a community or church choir.*
- *Participate in a sport or recreation community.*
- *Take classes in Yoga, Tai Chi, or Qi Gong.*
- *Join a dance group.*
- *Participate in a community theater or improvisation group.*
- *Join a book club or a writing read and critique group.*
- *Engage with a quilting, sewing, or scrapbooking community.*
- *Join a musical group.*
- *Help with a community planting, construction, or clean-up project.*

We feel safer and happier when we engage in activities that connect us with a community. Synchronous activities move our mental energy away from the self-centered focus of shame.

We also feel happier when we spend time with people we genuinely enjoy. Our stress lowers and makes space for happiness to bubble up inside. Sometimes those feelings develop into passionate love.

Love, Loss, and Shame

Neuroscientists investigated the blissed-out brains of couples in passionate love. Hot passionate love looks different in the brain than maternal love or friendship. Lovers feel euphoria, as if on opiates. The passion of love charges up our motivation. It activates higher-level thinking, memory, and self-awareness. We idealize our loved ones and feel an expanded sense of self. Passionate love can make us feel fearless.

Friendship love helps us feel calm, connected, and secure. It activates oxytocin and vasopressin, making us feel warm and content (Cacioppo, et al. 2012).

We experience something akin to opiate withdrawal when we lose a loved one. Stomach aches, fatigue, physical pain, and deep sadness accompany the loss of our significant relationships.

We feel physical pleasure with bonding and attachment, and physical pain with separation and loss. This emotional distress often appears as irritability, anger, anxiety, or *frazzlebrain* (Lieberman 2013).

Frazzlebrain temporarily interferes with our ability to experience love and connection. It narrows our perspective. We focus on threat and safety only. It prevents us from exploring broader options of behavior. We forget about fun, playfulness, creativity, joy, and delight.

When we lose connection with others, as in divorce, we feel shame. We feel shame when rejected or when excluded from a group. It can feel like banishment from our comfortable tribe, leaving us alone to wander in the wilderness.

When others become too close, demanding, or abusive, we can experience a sudden jolt of embarrassment or shame. We also feel shame if we experience a loss of status, influence, or power, as might happen with a demotion at work or a financial loss.

Most people describe shame as wanting to "fall into a hole" or "disappear." That desire to hide appears to stem from survival instincts built into the human brain (Lanius, Terpou, and McKinnon 2020). Embarrassment, humiliation, and shame make us feel like we are unacceptable to others. We feel like we do not belong.

Shame activates our pain receptors and makes us feel agitated, angry, and defensive. This results from activation of the midbrain and hypothalamus, triggering defensive reactions. Shame activates the amygdala, amplifying our sensitivity to threats (Pulcu, et al. 2014).

We all feel shame. Shame is one of the most painful of human emotions. If you feel shame, you are not alone. You are human. Mother Teresa said, "If we have no peace, it is because we have forgotten that we belong to each other." It is important to remember that you belong here too.

A Healthy Response to the Pain of Shame

During times of significant loss and shame, we retreat into our turtle shells to feel safe. I hear my clients say they stay away from others because they do not want to bring anyone down. It can be hard to face people when we feel bad. Threats to our standing in our social group or family can often feel like threats to our existence.

Shame, and its cousin guilt, are two self-conscious emotions (Michl, et al. 2012). When we feel shame, we become very self-focused. We lose bandwidth for empathy. We assume others will find us unacceptable. Sometimes we get mad and push others away.

To heal from shame, we need to experience ourselves as acceptable to the community. The experience of feeling useful, productive, playful, connected changes our perspective. If we feel rejected by one part of our community, it is healing to experience acceptance by another.

One healthy way to respond to shame is to focus on an activity that you care about that connects you with others. Ask yourself the following three questions:

1. **What activities do I enjoy that involve others?**
   (Sports, video games, music, book club, dance, volunteering, religious services, political campaigns, social clubs, art classes, educational programs.)
2. **Which do I feel is most important to me right now?**
3. **What action can I take today to join that activity?**

For example, one of my clients, Marta, is a forty-two-year-old bookkeeper. She and her husband recently divorced after a ten-year marriage. Her husband had engaged in an affair with a friend in their close group of coupled friends. After she found out about the affair, she was devastated to learn that several of her friends knew it had been going on for two years. Not one of her friends told her about the betrayal of trust.

"I feel like such a fool. Everyone knew about the affair but me. We went on vacations together! I can't look at any of them now. He can have those friends. None of them really cared about my feelings, or they would have told me. Now I feel like I have no one," she said.

Marta had behaved with integrity in her marriage and friendships, yet she blamed herself for trusting those who betrayed her. I explained that recovery from shame required new experiences of connection and belonging. I asked Marta what activities she could do with others that might inspire joy, interest, curiosity, or pleasure.

"I have always loved music. I love singing, but I'm scared to get in front of people. As a child, I loved the youth choir. Since then,

I haven't done anything. We always did the things my husband wanted to do," Marta said.

I recommended she investigate joining a choir. Even though she was scared, she was tired of feeling lonely. "I need to start doing things for myself now. My husband called all the shots. Now I must be brave enough to do what I want to do on my own," she said.

Marta auditioned for a local choir and was accepted. That action changed her life. A year later, Marta was singing lead parts in her choir performances. "I'm so excited that I was invited to sing on a professional recording for the choir!" she exclaimed. Marta had found a new tribe where she could freely express her love of music.

When you focus on creating new connecting experiences, you will respond in a healthier way to shame. Acting on something we value moves us in the direction we want to go.

Investing time in something we care about pulls us out of the painful alienation of shame. We can observe progress toward a goal. We feel less frazzled. You can also work through feelings of shame by seeking out therapeutic relationships.

Healing from Therapeutic Relationships

Therapeutic relationships buffer the harmful effects of *frazzlebrain*. They can help you move beyond the self-consciousness of shame and rejoin a community of support. Psychotherapy is one example of a therapeutic relationship.

Psychotherapy is a process that uses psychological tools, rather than medical ones, to help people with emotional, behavioral, or mental issues. A licensed psychotherapist provides a safe and supportive environment for self-awareness.

You can learn new skills to manage difficult emotions. Healing stems from psychotherapy experiences that include:

1. **A safe, supportive, and trusting relationship with the therapist.**
2. **Stress management strategies.**
3. **Exploration of emotions, thoughts, and actions.**
4. **Fostering a fresh outlook on problems.**

As you learn to cope with stress and manage difficult emotions, your brain chemistry changes over time.

For some people, severe symptoms require medical help. Medication can help them improve their functioning. Studies show that antidepressant medication can spur new growth in the hippocampus (Malberg, Hen, and Madsen 2021). This new growth helps promote positive behavioral changes, like exercise and socializing, that help people recover from anxiety and depression.

You can learn more about therapeutic relationships and how to find the right one for you in the appendix of this book.

No matter how rich or barren your current landscape of relationships appears, you can create meaningful experiences with others. Experiences with people can help your brain recover from trauma and heal. When you join with others, doing activities you care about, you will feel happier and healthier.

Final Takeaway

Relationships change the brain beginning at birth. Neurochemicals like oxytocin, prolactin, endorphins, and dopamine activate in response to our interactions with others. These chemicals provide us with warm and pleasurable feelings. Many people suffer from relationship traumas. You can heal from trauma by seeking out uplifting relationships and experiences.

You can enrich your human ecosystem with kindness, consideration, and acts of service. These positive interactions with others can heal the frazzled brain. Experiences like volunteering, hosting a baby shower, or sharing lunch with a neighbor can help you feel happier.

Three secrets to healthy relationships include gratitude, amplifying the positive, and engaging with commitment and meaning. When we commit to meaningful relationships and activities, we strengthen our mental and physical health.

Hostility poisons the ecosystem. If your relationship often erupts with hostility that leaves you shaken and hurt, first establish a safe place to go. Then ask others for help and lower the stresses you can control. We strengthen our connections when we tend to others. We can boost our happiness by uplifting others.

Even in times of crisis, relationships with coworkers, friends, family, and even pets can help us through. When we engage in synchronous activities with others like sports, choir, or yoga, we receive mental and physical health benefits.

Losses, like divorce or a job loss, can trigger feelings of shame. Shame makes us want to isolate ourselves from others. One healthy response to shame is to do something we value. Focusing on what we can do, rather than past injuries, helps us recover. We can also obtain help from therapeutic relationships.

In the next chapter, Cultivate Positive Emotions, you will learn how to perk up your joy with the power of play. I will show you how experiences of awe and wonder can heal. You will discover how to build resilience from *frazzlebrain*. It starts when you learn how to generate a wide variety of positive emotions within yourself.

EIGHT

Cultivate Positive Emotions

I'm especially excited these days about investigating how positive emotions change the very ways that our cells form and function to keep us healthy.

BARBARA FREDRICKSON

Sometime between childhood and adulthood, we often get caught in the cycle of striving. The pressure to work hard to get through school, get a good job, a car, a house can feel unrelenting. Always striving for more in the quest for future fulfillment can trigger anger, anxiety, and stress. Many of us wake up one day surprised to find that we have more stuff and less happiness. Long hours of striving without pausing to enjoy life can build up tension and increase anxiety and irritability.

It is comforting to know that positive emotions relieve

frazzlebrain. In this chapter, you will learn how to generate positive emotions at will. You will discover the mental health benefits of recreation and playfulness. When you expand your repertoire of positive emotions to include awe and wonder, you gain many stress-relieving, life-enhancing benefits. Positive emotions strengthen your resilience and mental flexibility (Wang, Chen, and Yue 2017). Feeling happier even helps the body heal faster after injury or illness (Pressman, Jenkins, and Moskowitz 2019).

What are Positive Emotions?

When someone asks, "How are you?" what do you typically reply? Most of us respond with a polite, pleasant word like "fine" or "good," or if we are feeling exuberant, we might reply, "great!" Focused on the tasks at hand, we might not give much attention to our positive feelings. Yet if we name and savor our positive emotions, we strengthen the ability to experience them.

Positive psychologists have identified several positive emotions worth exploring (Armenta, Fritz, and Lyubomirsky 2016):

- Amusement (enjoyment, fun)
- Amazement (awe, wonder)
- Gratitude (appreciation)
- Optimism (hopefulness)
- Inspired (motivated, energized)
- Admiration (delight)
- Elevation (feeling uplifted)
- Curiosity (interest)
- Joyfulness (happiness)
- Love (affection, fondness)
- Pride (self-respect, confidence)
- Serenity (peacefulness, calm)

Look at this list and make a note of any of those emotions you have felt recently. What were you doing when you experienced that emotion? Were you alone or with others? Working or were you engaged in a recreation activity? Take a moment to remember a positive recollection. Savor or linger longer with the feeling by conjuring up physical details in your imagination.

When we worry, the brain magnifies negative emotions. One of my clients could skillfully take any worry and morph it into her inevitable death. *If I eat this burrito, I'll become obese and die of a heart attack. If I get lost while on vacation, I will become stranded and starve to death in the middle of nowhere.* Worry can take us to dark places quite quickly.

Yet positive emotions come from the very same wellspring of neurochemical abundance.

If we move some of that worry energy just a little to the left in our brain, we can summon more of these expansive emotions. Our brain's left side tends to activate more when we feel good feelings (Alexander, et al. 2021).

How do we generate positive emotions at will? It starts with Part I of this book. Focused thoughts help you support and soothe yourself, tame your hostile and cynical thoughts, and generate hope that you can feel better. Use your imagination to delight and inspire yourself.

From the Intentional Behaviors section, Part II, you learned that when you balance your gut chemistry with good habits, you give your brain the fuel it needs to generate uplifting feelings. Time in nature and engaging in acts of kindness can help you feel happier too.

In Part III, Healing Experiences, you learn to choose positive and meaningful relationship influences. These thoughts, behaviors, and experiences form the foundation for a happier life.

You can generate positive emotions throughout your whole lifespan if you maintain one specific childhood habit—the habit of play.

Play Power

Mammals appear hard-wired for play. Watch puppies, kittens, bear cubs, and baby apes wrestle, pounce, roll, tickle, and play like human pups. Neuroscientists discovered that play stimulates neural growth in children. Dr. Terry Marks-Tarlow studies the neuroscience of play. She and other experts refer to play as the "work" of childhood. "When young children engage in free play, they learn all about culture at large, and adult society in particular," she says. "They practice the roles, rules, and types of relationships they will need later in life. Beyond this, when young children use their imaginations to play, they forge the seeds of their own identities."

In a paper she wrote for the *American Journal of Play*, called "The Fractal Self at Play," she states that we can all look back at our childhood imagination games to find the beginnings of our early sense of self. The way you played as a child reflects your interests and even your professional choices today (Marks-Tarlow 2010). The philosopher Plato wrote, "you can discover more about a person in an hour of play than in a year of conversation." Take a moment of self-discovery and engage with your playful self:

Frazzle Hack: Engaging Your Playful Self

Settle yourself into a comfortable chair. Take five deep breaths. Inhale through your nose and exhale slowly from your mouth.

Think back on your childhood. How did you play? What activities did you engage in just for fun? What made you feel the most joy, vitality, or pleasure? Did you play more with others or enjoy more solitary exploration? Did you prefer outdoor activities? Did you lead or organize others, or did you join in something already established? Does your current occupation share some of those elements of your early childhood play? Do you lead others or belong to an organization with its own structure? Do you engage more with people or things? How can you bring more of your favorite childhood play into your life now? Record your impressions in your frazzle hack journal.

Life satisfaction improves when you find ways to incorporate the elements of childhood play into your work. Children learn better when lessons incorporate fun, play, or physical activity. Play helps us learn to socialize, take turns, and stimulate our imagination. Without a rigid organized structure, children who play freely manage stress better and are more resilient (Ginsburg and Jablow 2020).

Adult play motivates us, stimulating goal-directed activity. For example, if you wish to exercise more, you will more likely persist if you combine it with fun. One way I stay on the exercise bike longer is when I mix it with a page-turning novel. I only read the book when I exercise. I am motivated to get back on that bike to see what happens next. The brain recovers from stress more quickly when it receives a burst of the neurotransmitter dopamine from a fun activity.

Fun helps us focus on the present moment, stay engaged, and feel more fully alive. When our positive feelings outnumber our negative emotions by a three to one ratio, we become more resilient in life and love (B. L. Fredrickson 2001). Our patience and tolerance for distress grow. Play expands one's capacity to enjoy life. A pleasant side effect of play is that it can combat the adverse effects of *frazzlebrain*.

Positive Emotions Expand Our Options

People who lead happy, contented lives do not have perfect lives. Most people, even happy people, experience at least one violent or life-threatening situation during their lifetime. (Ozer, et al. 2003). Happy people also suffer losses, pain, frustration, traffic jams, financial woes, illnesses, and all the problems their grumpy counterparts experience. Our life experience does not determine our happiness. Instead, our reaction to those life experiences determines whether we will become bitter and resentful or content and fulfilled (Masten 2001).

If happy people experience the same number of negative experiences as unhappy people, what makes the difference? Happy people seem to know something about how to generate positive emotions inside of themselves. They do not wait for good things to happen.

Positive emotions broaden and build our perspective. Our thoughts and actions expand in the moments when we feel joy. Even our visual scope of attention extends, allowing us to see more when we feel happier (Fredrickson and Losada 2005).

For example, I attended a meditation class for several weeks at the same location in San Diego. It was a medical rehabilitation facility. Every week I walked the walkway into the front of the building, stressed from work, my eyes on the front door aimed straight for the classroom. It was only during our Saturday meditation retreat when I felt relaxed, content, and peaceful, did

I notice the gorgeous garden next to the building entrance. I never saw it before, even though I had walked by it for several weeks.

We need positive emotions so that we will see the beauty all around us daily.

Interest and curiosity are two positive emotions that propel us to explore new things. Contentment fosters savoring of the present moment and calms the worried mind. Love motivates us to think and act in ways that help us maintain close relationships.

In contrast, negative emotions, like anger or fear, narrow our range of thoughts and behaviors. When angry, we feel motivated only to attack or distance ourselves from the object of our anger. Our range of thoughts and behaviors shrinks.

The word anger derives from the Latin word *angustus*, meaning narrow, and the Ancient Greek *anchein*, meaning to squeeze. When we feel anger, our arteries constrict, and our blood pressure rises. We feel pressed, trapped, cornered, and limited.

Positive emotions, in contrast, open us to new thoughts and actions that foster creative ideas, solutions to problems, and strengthen social bonds. The word inspired stems from the Latin meaning to inflame or breathe into. Imagine blowing air onto a flame, making it grow. Positive emotions give us that sense of expansiveness, fire, life, vitality.

Have you noticed that you are more likely to want to try something new, engage in a social activity, or explore a talent or skill you wish to improve when you feel good? When we know how to make ourselves happy, we broaden our behavioral options and build new relationship connections.

Even very mild pleasant emotions, such as the contentment you might feel watching a puppy play, can generate enough change in your brain chemistry to counteract the adverse effects of a recent stressful event. Gentle, positive emotions even help your cardiovascular system recover faster from stress. Mild positive emotions such as interest or curiosity increase resilience and might even help you live longer (B. L. Fredrickson 2001).

The Language of Happiness

Positive psychologist Tim Lomas, PhD, studies the linguistics of happiness around the world. He translates words for happy emotions into English. For example, the Finnish word *hyppytyynytyydytys* (hyp-ya-teyrna-teyrna-dish) means the relaxing, cushiony feeling you get when you settle into a comfortable chair. Or the Hebrew word, *nachat*, the joyful pride you feel when one of your students or children enjoys a success.

The Danish word *morgenfrisk* describes the morning fresh feeling you get after a good night's sleep. *Kaif* is a Russian word for euphoric pleasure mixed with a sense of calmness.

Lingering on words that describe positive emotions helps you remember those feelings better. People even make up words, or neologisms, for emotions.

You may have heard the term *hangry*, the cranky feeling of being hungry and angry at the same time. You can make up words for positive emotions too.

My husband, a playful jokester, made up the word *frappy*, a combination of fresh and happy. *Frappy* is when you feel fresh and clean, dressed up, and anticipate a happy outing. An old friend coined the word *chingles*, a portmanteau of chills and tingles. It is that goosebump feeling you get when touched softly.

In the animated movie classic *Bambi*, the rabbit Thumper felt *twitterpated* or captivated by a giddy spring fever love and infatuation. I stumbled upon the word *respair* online (systemagicmotives.com). It means the return of hope after a period of despair.

Positive emotions can be limitless. Use your imagination; think about how you might describe some of your positive feelings. Try to make up a new word that better describes how you feel. Share that new word with your friends and family. Record your new word ideas in your *frazzle hack* journal. Allow yourself to bask in positive feelings longer. You might surprise yourself.

Awe and Wonder

On most clear nights, I look up at the stars and feel a sense of awe and wonder. I contemplate the vast distance and mystery of outer space and my humble place in the universe. When I first studied astronomy in college, I felt astonished when considering distances, like a light year (the distance light travels in a year). To get your mind around a light year, first think about the distance between the earth and the sun, 93 million miles. That's a lot of miles to try to imagine. Astronomers call that distance 1 AU or astronomical unit. One AU consists of only eight seconds of a light-year. Freaky, right?

You might feel awe and wonder when you witness a great Olympic athlete complete a record-breaking swim, run, jump, or inspiring gymnastics routine. Years ago, my husband and I went hiking with our five-month-old son asleep in a backpack. As we came around a narrow part of the trail, we heard a waterfall rush and felt the quickening air and cooling temperature. Our son woke up and excitedly exclaimed, "ooh ooh!" his mouth and eyes wide open with wonder. The three of us shared a thrilling moment of awe, gazing at this powerful display of natural beauty.

Awe inspires feelings of social connection (Bai, et al. 2017). My husband and I experienced awe, wonder, and social connection at a concert by Sir Paul McCartney. At Dodger Stadium in Los Angeles, with the full moon rising behind the stage, the seventy-two-year-old McCartney hit all the high notes and rocked out like a twenty-five-year-old to a multi-generational audience of loving fans.

At the end of the concert, the couple next to us, strangers, but fellow fans, embraced us, and we wished one another well. We felt a collective joy, moved by the infectious energy of a shared musical experience. It made us feel close and connected.

Awe makes us kinder and less self-centered. Social psychology researchers found that those with a higher capacity for awe tend to behave more generously toward others. They discovered that many types of experiences of awe and wonder reduce self-centeredness and promote kindness and more pro-social behaviors. We transcend ourselves and view the world and the people around us with mysterious fascination when we experience awe and wonder (Piff, et al. 2015).

Awe helps us to see things from a new perspective. It motivates us to stop, think, pay attention to details, and remain open to new information (Shiota, et al. 2017). Albert Einstein said, "He who can no longer pause to wonder and stand rapt in awe is as good as dead; his eyes are closed." He referred to awe as "the source of all true art and science."

Awe increases our critical thinking abilities making us less likely to believe a weak argument (Griskevicius, Shiota, and Neufeld 2010). People who watched awe-inspiring videos were more likely to recall details of a story accurately. Awe provides mind-expanding benefits that allow us to see the world as it is instead of what our biases expect (Danvers and Shiota 2017).

The experience of awe makes us feel as if time has stopped. When we experience an expanded sense of time, we are more likely to volunteer and help others. Wonder makes us more likely to spend our money on meaningful experiences rather than binging on the shopping channel. We feel more satisfied and more fully alive (Rudd, Vohs, and Aaker 2012).

Several years ago, I saw a YouTube video (double rainbow guy) viewed now over 48 million times. A man hiking in Yosemite, California, sees a double rainbow. He gasps, shouts, and sobs in awe-struck wonder for several minutes. His over-the-top reaction inspires laughter. Yet the double rainbow guy gets the last laugh on us. He likely derived many positive physical and psychological benefits from that awe-struck double rainbow hiking adventure.

Awe and wonder appear to lower inflammation and promote better health and immune system functioning. Jennifer Stellar (appropriately named) from the University of Toronto found lower levels of cytokines, chemical markers of inflammation, in those subjects who reported more experiences of awe, wonder, and amazement (Stellar, et al. 2015).

Noticing nature in your neighborhood can improve your mood, lower inflammation in your body, and engender a feeling of warm connection with your environment. Everyday experiences open us to opportunities for awe and wonder. Whenever I fly on an airplane, I think about the years of dreaming, attempts, and failures, that went into this machine that takes us into the sky at high speeds. It's wondrous.

Frazzle Hack: Conscious Awe

Settle comfortably and take a few deep breaths. Think back on a time when you felt a positive feeling of awe, amazement, or wonder. What did you experience, see, smell, or hear?

What sensations did you feel in your body? Were you alone or with others? How did the experience affect you emotionally? What thoughts passed through your mind? How do you feel remembering it now? In your frazzle hack journal, make a list of at least five occasions when you experienced awe, wonder, or amazement. Record your thoughts, feelings, and impressions as you summon these memories.

If you find it challenging to feel awe and wonder, you can learn how to cultivate it. When I was a young girl, we had an expression, "too cool for school," for those peers who seemed above all human emotions. They acted aloof, distant, unflappable. Coolness is one step away from coldness. Remaining detached from those awe-struck moments might rob you of life-enhancing joy.

Here are five ways that you can open yourself to awe and wonder in your everyday life:

1. **Sensing walk:** Take a slow walk in a park, canyon, or near a lake, ocean, or another place of natural diversity. Put away your phone and pay attention to what your body senses. Notice the sound of crunching leaves under your feet—bird song, the wind through the trees, the lapping of water. Notice the temperature and how light plays on the landscape. Slowly examine the trees, shrubs, flowers, insects, and any other life you see. Notice the texture and colors of a rock, the sand, clay soil, or the feel of a leaf or pinecone. Smell the bark of a tree, a leaf, a flower, the air. Let yourself notice each sensation as if for the first time.

2. **Visit a local art museum, aquarium, planetarium, or zoo.** Let your eyes linger on anything you find interesting, beautiful, inspiring, or unique. Observe how you feel inside as you look at something new and different. Let yourself experience your emotions without judging them.

3. **Listen to music that pleases, amazes, or inspires you.** Let yourself fully attend to the music without any other distraction. Open yourself to whatever the music feels like in your body. Write about how the music moves you.

4. **Drive to the desert or an area with little light pollution and gaze up at the night sky.** Watch a lunar eclipse or meteor shower. Gaze at planets through a telescope. Try to imagine the expanding vastness of the universe you inhabit.

5. **Go to a local lake, creek, or estuary and observe the tiny creatures that live there.** Observe spiders spinning webs, fireflies, pollywogs, and insects as they occupy and play their unique part in the natural order.

Record your experiences, impressions, and emotions in your *frazzle hack* journal. When you notice, name, and amplify your positive emotions, you strengthen your ability to access them.

Building Resilience

Sometimes life can present us with overwhelming pain and challenges that seem beyond our capacity for coping. When hit by hard times, we can cultivate our resilience, the ability to bounce back or bounce forward from adversity.

Consider the inspiring story of Gary Doan, from Eagan, Minnesota. He became sick in 1993 while on a cruise. At that time, doctors did not know about hepatitis C, so he was diagnosed with "non-A and non-B" hepatitis. Doctors determined that he contracted the disease from a blood transfusion obtained after a motorcycle accident. He actively followed his doctor's advice (practicing self-care), stopped drinking alcohol, had regular blood tests, and slowed down. Feeling chronically tired, he was eventually put on a liver transplant waiting list. His doctors said it might take three years.

Doan quit working, moved close to his children, and began to face the real possibility of imminent death. The disease weakened him so much that he could only focus mentally for three hours a day. Doan spent that precious time dreaming about something that delighted him. He dreamed up a business.

His short-term memory was like that of an Alzheimer's patient, yet he kept jotting down business ideas. Instead of angry fantasies of getting back at those who had prematurely shortened his life, he dreamed of an automated data storage business that could help small companies protect and store their data.

He slept through the call for his first opportunity for a liver transplant. Learning from that mistake, he put all his friends and family "on the hospital's speed dial" so he would not miss the next opportunity for a liver. In 2001 Doan received his transplant and survived. The company he created, Intradyn, when he had little energy and no short-term memory, became a significant competitor in the data management industry. Doan chose to focus on something that delighted his imagination rather than the painful likelihood of his imminent death (Flynn 2004).

Resilient people do not have easy, problem-free lives. Instead, when problems appear, they take care of themselves. They seek out healthy, happy individuals for friendship, advice, support, and companionship.

Resilient people continue functioning healthily, even when they grieve the loss of a loved one or suffer from a violent or life-threatening situation. (Bonanno 2004). They strive to generate humor, social connections, and positive emotions even in the face of adversity.

You can increase your resilience too by generating positive emotions, often alongside painful emotions. I have been to many memorial services filled with laughter, tears, shared memories of joy, and loving social connection. You can feel grief and positive emotions at the same time. The simple pleasure you might experience from a good meal or laugh can help you through hard times.

Positive emotions motivate us to take better care of ourselves. Gratitude is one such motivating emotion.

Gratitude

Gratitude is a recognition that something good has occurred and that someone or something else is responsible for that good. Most world religions recognize gratitude as a virtue. We teach our children to say thank you as a regular expression of everyday gratitude. Social manners require expressions of gratitude like thank-you notes after receiving gifts. These displays of gratitude help strengthen our social connections by fostering goodwill.

Gratitude motivates us to want to improve ourselves. When we receive kindness from someone, it sets a standard for good behavior. It makes us want to give back to the person who demonstrated that kindness. Feeling gratitude expands our emotional repertoire to include:

- **A feeling of connectedness**
- **An elevated, uplifted feeling**
- **Humility**
- **Indebtedness** (Armenta, Fritz, and Lyubomirsky 2016).

Now you may wonder, what is so great about feeling indebted? When we feel indebted, it makes us feel obligated to reciprocate after someone provides a favor. We might feel a little guilty that we have not done more for our benefactor. It can feel a bit uncomfortable. We want to do something nice in return. It motivates us to improve our social behavior.

For example, when our daughter was born, we came home exhausted from the hospital with nothing in the refrigerator to make a meal. Famished and depleted, we were trying to figure out what to eat for dinner when my dear friend, Kelly, appeared at our door with a delicious hot meal and freshly baked cookies. We felt overwhelming gratitude for her act of kindness. It inspired us to want to give back to her. It strengthened our friendship.

I felt a little guilty that I had not done more for her. The indebtedness made me feel connected to her with a more profound sense of obligation and appreciation. Indebtedness and appreciation motivated us to provide support when she needed it. She inspired our lifelong gratitude for her thoughtful generosity.

We felt humbled by her expression of caring. She called family members to find out when we would arrive home so she could provide a perfectly cooked, warm meal. I marveled at her effort. It made me want to work harder for all my friends. She set an excellent example of thoughtfulness that I wanted to try to emulate.

Gratitude also inspires a kind of "pay it forward" desire to treat others better. I enjoyed making lasagna casseroles for other new moms in my neighborhood, inspired by my friend Kelly's kindness.

Grateful people obtain many physical health benefits:

- **Better overall health** (Krause and Hayward 2014).
- **More engagement in healthier behavior** (Hill, Allemand, and Roberts 2013).

- **Better and longer sleep** (Ng and Wong 2013).
- **More likely to seek help for health issues** (Hill, Allemand, and Roberts 2013).

People with a grateful attitude receive mental health benefits as well. Those with higher levels of gratitude have lower levels of stress, depression, and anxiety (Wood, et al. 2008) (Froh, et al. 2011) (Petrocchi and Couyoumdjian 2016) (Disabato, et al. 2017).

People in a substance abuse recovery program who displayed a grateful disposition demonstrated better coping strategies. They dealt with stress more effectively and were less likely to use drugs (Leung and Tong 2017). Twelve-step programs promote gratitude as an essential part of recovery. Because gratitude strengthens relationships, those in recovery programs would likely benefit from its goodwill effects.

Cynical appraisals of behavior can get in the way of our ability to experience gratitude. For example, one of my clients felt suspicious of any expression of kindness from others. "They just want something from me. I'm not interested in feeling obligated to reciprocate," he would say. His cynical attitude robbed him of the ability to feel uplifted and grateful. It requires a bit of humility to appreciate the goodwill of others.

When we resist cynicism (the assumption that others have sinister motives), we can bask in gratitude's benefits. Cynicism can block your ability to recognize kindness even when it is right in front of you. If you notice a tendency toward cynical interpretations, review Chapter Two, From Hostility to Hope. You might also benefit from the following *frazzle hack*:

Frazzle Hack: Finding Gratitude

Settle yourself down into a comfortable chair. Take five deep breaths, inhaling through your nose, exhaling from your mouth. Notice any sensations in your body as you breathe deeply. Now think about an accomplishment or something you have achieved that makes you feel proud, content, or satisfied. Perhaps you graduated from college, created a business, purchased a home, or started a family. Maybe you feel pleased with organizing your home or completing a challenging project at work. Now take a moment to think about all the people and things that helped you achieve. College professors, textbook authors, friends, family, books, accountants, coaches, trainers, doctors, and others all may have played a role in helping you achieve. Next, hold your hand over your heart and, with closed eyes, imagine feeling deep gratitude toward all the people who helped you accomplish your goal. Think about how each of them paved the way for your success. Make a note of specific things that helped you. Then, with your silent voice inside, say these words:

I am forever grateful for all the ways you helped me and all that you taught me. Thank you.

Record your thoughts, feelings, and impressions in your frazzle hack journal.

Positive emotions like love, inspiration, and curiosity, motivate us to expand our social relationships, behaviors, and knowledge. Curiosity, or the drive for information, is linked to the reward system of the brain. We get mood-boosting benefits from dopamine when we satisfy our need to know something (Kidd and Hayden 2015).

Curiosity

In Chapter Two you learned how flexible curiosity can help you shift your cynical thoughts toward an openness to new information. Curiosity offers many other benefits as well. The more curious you are about a subject in school, the more likely you will perform better in that subject. Curiosity motivates you to dig deeper and try harder. While you may have heard the disparaging expression "curiosity killed the cat," it is more likely the cat found some better food source, or place to sleep, during its exploration.

When my husband and I watch movies, we often pull out our smartphones and look up the actors, screenwriters, and directors to learn more about them. Since we both play musical instruments, we also love learning about the musical artists featured in the films we watch. It expands our appreciation of the artists and movies.

Curiosity diminishes when we feel depressed and frazzled. We stop caring about exploring interests and become hyper-focused on stress instead. The word curious derives from the Latin root *cura* meaning "to care." When we care about something, we put effort into it. We feel motivated.

You can strengthen your mental health and well-being when exploring your interests (Gallagher and Lopez 2007). Even a tiny little flicker of curiosity can grow if you act on it. When a question pops into your head, like *When did the Challenger space shuttle explode?* You can look up the answer, January 28, 1986. If you do not scratch that itch to know, you dim the flame of curiosity. You can cultivate curiosity, like any other positive emotion.

Trying new activities to satisfy your curiosity offers several benefits:

- **Strengthens learning, even about things about which you have no interest.**
- **Improves memory.**
- **Aids in decision making.**
- **Activates reward centers of the brain, increasing motivation** (Kidd and Hayden 2015).
- **Helps maintain cognitive functioning, mental and physical health as we age** (Sakaki, Yagi, and Murayama 2018).

Curiosity helps distract the mind, in a pleasurable way, from the static of *frazzlebrain*. When you feel motivated to learn, try new things, and research something new, you bolster your ability to combat anxiety, anger, and stress. You can strengthen curiosity by trying the following frazzle hack:

Frazzle Hack: Strengthening Curiosity

Take a few moments to settle yourself into a comfortable position. In your frazzle hack journal, write about any fields of study, people, or things in which you have shown a mild to moderate interest. For example, television, films, video games, books, cars, gardening, business, children, finance, science, engineering, art, nature, politics, philosophy, family ancestry, famous people, etc. Then pick one subject, person, or thing about which you would like to know more. Begin a research

> *project on that subject, starting with a simple computer search. See what you can learn in twenty minutes of searching. Record your impressions in your* frazzle hack journal.

Positive emotions combat the foggy-headed gloom of *frazzlebrain*. You can generate positive emotions on purpose without waiting for anything special to happen. Permit yourself to bask in gratitude, explore with curiosity, and love with abandon. You will be glad you did.

Final Takeaway

Positive emotions offer life-sustaining physical and mental health benefits. Positive emotions counteract the adverse effects of stress and *frazzlebrain*. You can generate positive emotions throughout your lifespan by engaging in the habit of play. Playful activities encourage physical and mental flexibility.

You expand your visual field and see more when you feel good. This expanded view allows you to enjoy the beauty that surrounds you.

Awe and wonder encourage social connection and a sense of humility. They make us kinder and more generous toward others.

Gratitude strengthens our connection to others. It uplifts our spirits. It also motivates us to want to do more for other people.

Curiosity improves memory, increases learning and motivation. It helps our brain maintain cognitive functioning well into old age.

The next chapter, How Mindfulness Heals, will show you how mindfulness lowers angry reactivity and improves relationships. We explore easy-to-use techniques to ease stress and increase your ability to experience positive emotions.

NINE

How Mindfulness Heals

**Meditation is not evasion;
it is a serene encounter with reality.**

THÍCH NHẤT HANH

After returning home from work one evening, I noticed I had no conscious memory of driving home. Preoccupied with client stories and mental lists, I went almost all the way home, completely unaware. Once home, I noticed pain in my neck and shoulders. The awareness of pain forced me to attend to my discomfort.

Pain often functions as a wake-up call to pay attention to the present moment.

How often do we go through the motions of daily life, unaware of ourselves and others? Distracted by our phones, preoccupied with worry and nervous irritability, we live in a kind of foggy partial awareness. This distracted state can leave us feeling disconnected from ourselves, our environment, and others.

As I parked the car in my garage at home, I noticed my hands gripping the steering wheel. I had been overusing the muscles in my hands and arms without conscious awareness. This mindless, automatic state is a symptom of *frazzlebrain*. One remedy for this mindlessness is mindfulness.

Mindfulness lowers anxiety, anger, and stress, freeing energy to pursue what you most love. In this chapter, you will learn how mindfulness can reduce your reactive irritation and improve your relationships. You will gain simple exercises you can perform anywhere. Let's begin with a basic understanding of mindfulness.

Jon Kabat-Zinn, PhD professor of medicine emeritus at the University of Massachusetts Medical School, defines mindfulness as "paying attention on purpose, in the present moment, and nonjudgmentally, to the unfolding of experience moment to moment." Dr. Kabat-Zinn founded the Center for Mindfulness in Medicine, Health Care, and Society and created the Mindfulness-Based Stress Reduction (MBSR) program for seriously ill patients to reduce their anxiety and pain. MBSR classes are now offered all over the world.

Most of the world's major religions practice some form of meditation. From Christianity's "contemplative prayer" to Buddhism's "vipassana," learning to sit quietly and reflect is a near-universal value. The word meditation stems from the Latin *meditatum*, meaning "to ponder." Mindfulness meditation stems from Buddhist philosophy brought to Westerners as a tool for self-awareness and relaxation.

Mindfulness meditation requires intentional awareness without the usual critical commentary in your head. Judgments like *this is a waste of time* or *I hate heavy traffic* can muddle mental clarity and fuel *frazzlebrain.*

We experience frazzled distress when the mind worries about what might happen. *What if this medical treatment fails?* or *If I'm late to work, my boss will reprimand me again*, or *I'm not saving enough money, I'm going to end up on the streets.* This kind of thinking takes us out of the present moment of life. It removes us from reality and transports us into worry land.

When we pay attention to the present moment, on purpose, moment by moment, without judgment, we notice more. As a side effect of that noticing, we feel calmer. The future we imagine is only a potential that may or may not occur. The past is an idea, a set of memories that we have molded into a story. These memories represent a distorted, tiny fraction of what has happened. Memory imperfectly captures reality because memories fade, change, and only record fragments of our experience. The reality we can grasp resides in the present moment.

Mindfulness helps us fully appreciate life as we live it.

Meditation and Your Brain

When we meditate, distinctive brain patterns emerge. These brain patterns differ from any other mental state, including relaxation (Kaur and Singh 2015). Whether asleep, watching television, or at rest, our brain is in a constant state of electrical activity that scientists measure in waves.

The electroencephalograph (EEG) measures brain wave changes in real-time. During meditation, Theta waves appear more prevalent in the frontal and middle parts of the brain. Also, during meditation, Alpha waves appear more pronounced in the posterior part of the brain. This combination of Theta and Alpha waves creates a state of both relaxation and wakeful alertness (Ahani, et al. 2014).

Experienced meditators can get into this state very quickly. They also show more robust brain activity than beginning meditators. Researchers, using magnetic resonance imaging, compared the brains of long-term meditators with non-meditators. They found significantly higher gray matter density in the lower brain stem regions of meditators. As a result, meditators enjoy better cardiorespiratory control, immune system health, and emotion control (Vestergaard-Poulsen, et al. 2009). In other words, long-term meditators enjoy the antidote to frazzlebrain.

When frazzled, your brain behaves differently. Often the right prefrontal cortex of the brain is overactive and out of balance. Excessive neuroelectrical activity can result in a cascade of chemical messengers that can change our mood, metabolism, and hormone levels.

The amygdala, the threat-sensing part of the brain, responds to stimuli several times faster than the reasoning prefrontal cortex part of the brain. The amygdala serves a protective function so that you can quickly duck if something is flying at your head. Afterward, you might then ask, *what was that thing flying at my head?* The amygdala exists to make sure you do not waste time analyzing the situation; you duck or block the flying object and ask questions later.

The trouble comes when the amygdala triggers a threat response in reaction to your teenager using disrespectful language or your boss failing to give you credit for your work. You might find yourself feeling bad about losing control of your emotions. When the amygdala overreacts to something, like an insult, it triggers a stress response that activates the hypothalamus, pituitary, and adrenal systems (HPA).

HPA axis hyperactivity appears in many psychiatric disorders, including major depression, obsessive-compulsive disorder, panic disorder, and alcoholism. Our mental health improves when we can calm this hyperactivity of the HPA axis.

You can learn to calm your response to stress with meditation practice. Meditation trains your brain to work in a more balanced way. You lower your baseline level of nervous system arousal so that you react to life events with more resilience. From a calmer state, it takes a lot more distress to arouse your ire. When you learn to lower the frazzle response in your body, you feel happier, with greater self-control. (Smith and Vale 2006).

Carry Water Chop Wood

Years ago, a scrappy and resourceful twelve-year-old boy named Cody snapped me out of *frazzlebrain* in a single moment. At that time, I was a recreation coordinator for a city youth recreation center. Cody attended our after-school and summer recreation programs. I grew enormously fond of him and his little brother, raised by a disabled single mom and without a dad. Rushed and stressed, as I gathered supplies for our summer beach trip, Cody approached my desk. He pointed the index finger of his right hand up and looked down at his watch on his left wrist, "fifty-seven, fifty-eight, fifty-nine…" he then looked up at me and exclaimed with a grin, "It's a brand-new minute!" I laughed and replied, "You're right, Cody. It is a brand-new minute. Let's make the most of it."

Cody reminded me to seize the moment with relaxed wonder and fun. The shift instantly happened when he alerted me to that simple truth. It is a brand-new minute. Right now.

Think about this moment. It is a precious gift infused with possibilities. As you read these words right now, allow your mind to consider that this moment holds wonder for you to discover.

A Chinese Zen master wrote a poem a millennium ago:

Magical power,
Marvelous action!
Chopping wood,
Carrying water.

This poem reminds us that we can marvel at any moment if we fully summon our attention, without criticism or judgment, to that moment. The most ordinary actions can enliven and enrich us when practiced mindfully.

Most of us experience mundane chores in life as dull, tedious, and overwhelming. We need not feel oppressed by housework if we stop characterizing it as a crushing burden. Even though life can overwhelm us with responsibilities, some too challenging to bear, daily tasks do not need to make us crazy. When you remove the editorial commentary in your head, chores can feel calming, even blissful.

I have learned to enjoy washing dishes. The comforting waterfall sound, the warm water, the fresh smell of soap, and the simple motion, feel almost like a relaxing meditation when I take the judgment out of it. If you look at daily tasks as an opportunity to practice mindfulness, you can lower your bodies' stress response and feel better. Try the following *frazzle hack* and see if you notice a difference in how you experience daily tasks.

Frazzle Hack: Mindfulness and Chores

Pick a task that you find annoying. Perhaps it is cleaning the bathroom, folding laundry, washing dishes, running errands, car maintenance, or driving your children to activities. Before you begin the chore, notice your judgments about the task. It's too much work, boring, a waste of time, exhausting, unimportant, unfair; I never get any help; it's not fun. After identifying your judgments about that chore, ask yourself to imagine clearing your mind of all expectations of how you should feel or think about it. Imagine how you would feel if you were a child, eager to try something new, exploring a large laundry basket of unwashed clothes, splashing in dishwater. With that playful child's mind, begin the chore slowly.

Notice your body sensations and the rhythm of your physical movements. Breathe deeply. Take note of the smells, sounds, and sights of this simple chore. When your mind wanders away from your actions, gently draw your attention back to the task. As judgments reappear in your mind, identify them as unworthy of your attention. Aim your mind at the job and the simple ballet of movements required. Think of nothing else. There is nothing else. Just that present moment, without judgment. Record your impressions in your frazzle hack *journal.*

Mindfulness and the Vagabond Nerve

Meditation improves the tone of the vagus nerve. The vagus nerve regulates autonomic nervous system processes like heart rate and respiration. Vagus means "wanderer" in Latin, an appropriate name as the vagus nerve stems from two thick branches in the cerebellum, located at the back of the head. These branches wander to every major organ in the body, including the heart, and have roots in the abdomen. A good vagal tone occurs when your heart responds to stimuli within a healthy range. Those with poor vagal tone are less resilient to stress and can suffer from mood issues, gastrointestinal issues, inflammation, and heart problems (Gerritsen and Band 2018).

Athletes and meditators often have an excellent vagal tone as measured by a slow resting heart rate and quick cardio recovery times. Most stress management programs call for deep breathing exercises because you can achieve an almost immediate positive impact on your vagal tone by performing them. Meditation improves vagal tone by lowering your nervous system's reactivity to stress. Meditation makes you able to cope better with life's difficulties while achieving a calmer state of mind.

As a teenager, I was curious about meditation. My favorite band, the Beatles, studied meditation, as did a few of my friends. With a bit of skepticism, I signed up for a class in Transcendental Meditation (TM). This technique uses a mantra or sound that you think to yourself as a focus for your meditation. The mantra was a Sanskrit word provided by my teacher, who explained the meditation process.

From the first time I meditated, I noticed an extraordinary change in consciousness. The relaxation effects felt like I had received an hour-long massage or acupuncture treatment. Surprisingly, I felt these effects within ten minutes of meditating. My skepticism vanished, and I meditated twice daily for more than ten years.

After obtaining a doctorate in psychology, I attended a Mindfulness-Based Stress Reduction (MBSR) training, adding mindfulness as a tool in my practice. Later I completed a nine-week course called Compassion Cultivation Training (CCT) and an eight-week class called Mindful Self-Compassion (MSC) developed at Stanford Medical School's Center for Compassion and Altruism Research and Education (CCARE). These classes, based on mindfulness meditation techniques, specifically cultivate a compassionate mind.

Scientists have studied TM and mindfulness meditation for decades. Over forty years of scientific research demonstrate significant health and wellness benefits of meditation. Research findings show that meditation:

- **Improves immune system functioning** (Black and Slavich 2016).
- **Decreases pain and inflammation within the cells of your body** (Zeidan and Vago 2016) (Rosenkranz, et al. 2013).
- **Decreases anxiety, depression, and stress** (Song and Lindquist 2015).
- **Increases social connection and reduces loneliness** (Hutcherson, Seppala, and Gross 2008) (Creswell, et al. 2012).
- **Boosts self-control and emotion control** (Friese, Messner and Schaffner 2012), (Elkins-Brown, Teper, and Inzlicht 2017).
- **Increases brain tissue volume in the hippocampus, responsible for emotion control** (Holzel, et al. 2011).
- **Increases cortical thickness in areas related to attention** (Grant, et al. 2013).
- **Improves memory and creativity** (van Vugt and Jha 2011) (Capurso, Fabbro, and Crescentini 2014).

If meditation provides so many health and happiness benefits, why isn't everyone doing it? Perhaps it seems too complicated, takes time, classes cost money, you're too frazzled to sit still, or you don't believe it will help you. It requires change, and humans find that difficult. Resistance to change is natural and worth some attention here. We fear change because:

- *We don't want to feel incompetent. Trying something new when we don't have the skills makes us feel stupid. We don't like feeling stupid.*
- *We don't trust that the change will make anything better.*
- *It takes energy to change, and we already feel too tired and frazzled.*
- *It's hard to decide how to change. Too many choices make it hard to determine the best course of action.*

To overcome your resistance to change, ask yourself what concerns you about making this change. Are you worried about how other people in your family might react? Do you feel concerned about adding another thing to your already busy schedule? After you determine your main reasons for not trying meditation, develop a plan to address your concerns.

For example, if you do not believe that meditation will do anything for you, perhaps you could address that concern by telling yourself to try it out for a short period, maybe two weeks, and see if you notice any changes. If you're not sure you can sit for very long, just start with a one-minute meditation. Address each of your concerns so that you feel able to try something. Think of it as an experiment on yourself. You get to decide if the investigation is a success.

If you feel skeptical but want a low-risk way to meditate, I will give you a simple introduction. I still recommend that you get some formal meditation training. With a teacher, you can ask questions, correct errors in your meditation technique, and learn how to cope with anything that makes you uncomfortable. You can benefit from meeting other meditators. Group meditation provides an experience of calm relaxation in the presence of strangers. That experience alone often helps those with social anxiety learn to feel more relaxed in a crowd. It can help you form a support system to talk about the process, benefits, and difficulties of maintaining a daily meditation practice.

Frazzle Hack: Mindful Moment Meditation

Until you can find the time to take a class in meditation, here is an easy way to start right now:

Sit comfortably with your feet on the floor. I recommend that you start with fifteen minutes as a target time, gradually increasing it to twenty or thirty minutes as you can tolerate it. It's okay to recline, but you might fall asleep, and that's okay too because if you fall asleep while meditating, you probably need sleep. But if you want to take a few minutes to refresh yourself and meditate, it's best to sit.

Next, begin to settle your mind a little by inhaling through your nose for six counts, holding your breath for six counts, and then releasing your air out of your mouth for six counts. You can do this cycle (inhale, hold, exhale) six times to slow your breathing down a bit and settle yourself. Counting your breath can help you quiet your mind and give you something to focus on, like a mantra.

After the breathing exercise, gently draw your attention to your normal breathing. Notice the sensations in your nose, through your airway, and into your abdomen. When your mind drifts, gently draw it back to your breathing. When you notice that your attention is not on your breathing, do not judge yourself or criticize yourself for doing it wrong; see where your mind is focusing and gently draw your attention back to your breathing. Continue until your designated time is up. Then let yourself sit quietly for a minute or two to adjust before you get up and start moving about your day. It's that easy! Record your impressions in your frazzle hack journal.

If you cannot sit still for fifteen minutes, just do it for five minutes or one minute. Set aside time every day to meditate. A client of mine likes to meditate in his parked car before he drives home from work. Meditation helps him relax and prevents his work stress from infecting his home life. Others like to start their morning with meditation to obtain some mental clarity and calm. Another client prefers to meditate in the mid-afternoon for an energy boost.

I prefer to meditate for twenty minutes two times a day, before breakfast and before dinner. Meditating before you eat helps you digest your food better because your nervous system is calmer.

Often, I will take a brief one-minute meditation break between sessions with clients. A one-minute meditation allows me to clear my mind and feel refreshed for my next client. Decide on a schedule and do it for a few weeks. Take note of any changes you observe. You may find that your friends, family, or coworkers notice a calmer you.

Meditation Improves Physical Health—Jay's Story

Several years ago, I was diagnosed with Type 1 insulin-dependent diabetes. The disease requires a lot of attention to diet, insulin, equipment and sometimes can lead to stressful and potentially life-threatening mistakes if I don't pay attention to what I'm doing. I use an insulin pump and continuous glucose monitor that helps me stay healthy. However, the pump is a computer that needs attention and maintenance. A mistake in managing my equipment could be fatal. I'm required to get regular check-ups, including the A1C test that measures what percentage of hemoglobin—a protein in red blood cells that carries oxygen—is coated with sugar (glycated). The higher the A1C level, the poorer my blood sugar control and the higher my risk of diabetes complications. After nine weeks of training in mindfulness meditation, my A1C tested at the lowest level ever. While I can't say for sure that meditation was the only reason for improvement, I believe it helped me slow down, pay better attention to my diabetes management, and take better care of my health.

Mindfulness meditation alone does not make one more happy, generous, or kind. If your mindset is competitive, self-centered, materialistic, and independent, you might become more selfish with a mindfulness practice. If you see yourself as more interdependent, part of a network of others, mindfulness fosters more generosity and kindness (Poulin, et al. 2021).

Self-centeredness leads to ups and downs, between happiness and disappointment. If you get that promotion, you feel great. When you lose your job, you feel bad. Selflessness, in contrast, is when we feel connected to others. We can transcend ourselves in peaceful acknowledgment that there is more to life than just getting what we want. Selflessness provides a more durable, authentic happiness. When we feel part of a family, a community, a purpose beyond mere personal fulfillment, we can better weather life's disappointments (Dambrun 2017).

The *frazzle hacks* and earlier chapters' recommendations can help you strengthen your interconnectedness with the environment and other people. When you pay attention to your thoughts, turning them away from hostility and worry toward hopefulness, you broaden and build your potential. Intentional behaviors like addressing your gut health, spending time with nature, and cultivating kindness, provide you the building blocks of a happy and healthy life—healing experiences including healthy relationships, positive emotions, and meditation tame amygdala reactivity. Taming the amygdala helps you keep your cool under stress.

Regular meditation helps foster resilience to stress. When you learn meditation, it gives you the skills and confidence to calm down. If you value joy, compassion, empathy, and kindness, meditation can help you tap into the abundance within you.

Final Takeaway

Mindfulness benefits mind and body health. Mindfulness requires that we attend to the present moment, on purpose, without judging that moment. We can perform any action mindfully. As a side effect of mindfulness, we feel calmer.

Mindfulness meditation practice can help us become more resilient to stress. It helps our immune system, improves heart health, and aids in healing from surgery or illness. If we develop a sense of interdependence with others, mindfulness can increase our generosity and strengthen our relationships.

In this final chapter, "CalmBrain for Life," I will share tools that will help you track your transformation from frazzlebrain to CalmBrain. You will learn strategies to help you maintain your progress, stay connected to your goals, and strengthen your resilience.

TEN

CalmBrain for Life

To change your behavior for good, you need to start believing new things about yourself.

JAMES CLEAR, *ATOMIC HABITS*

Dear reader, you have come to the last chapter. Here you will get a chance to put together what you have learned. I invite you to use this chapter as your personal *frazzlebrain* coach. The worksheets, charts, and exercises offer you a way to set goals and organize your progress. These tools will help you access your *CalmBrain* for life.

Healing from *frazzlebrain* requires creating the conditions for your mind to heal. A physician setting a broken leg makes it possible for the bones to heal or grow back together by positioning the broken parts with a cast. The body does the healing all by itself. In the same way, our brain can heal from anxiety, anger, and stress, when we create the conditions for calm to occur.

Remember, *CalmBrain* is that state of awareness when your breathing is deep and slow. Your muscles feel loose and relaxed. Your mind is agile and absorbed in the present moment. You feel wrapped in a comfortable blanket of serenity.

Focused thoughts, intentional behaviors, and healing experiences rewire your *frazzled* brain, opening new pathways to serenity. The *frazzle hacks* and exercises teach you how to create the conditions for *CalmBrain* to occur naturally. When you regularly strengthen your brain's calming neuropathways, you experience less stress even when faced with challenging situations (Goldfarb, et al. 2020).

Neuroscientists discovered that it takes the same amount of mental energy to focus on a change goal as it does to follow a habit or even rest. Yes, that's right, your brain can do some fancy thinking using the same amount of energy as it does at rest. The reason we quit trying to change is not that the brain gets tired. If that were true, all we would need to restore brainpower would be a short break and a good night's sleep (Berkman 2018).

We fail to change because we get distressed and feel depleted. Our emotional reactions drain our energy, not brain strain. That drained feeling happens when we see our change goals as something we *must* do rather than something we *want* to do.

You generate more energy and motivation when you link the change to something you want (Berkman 2018). If your goals are all obligation-based or focused on preventing something bad from happening, it can suck the joy out of life. If it depletes your joy, it drains energy. In contrast, when you focus on things you want, your motivation and energy increase (Inzlicht, Schmeichel, and Macrae 2014).

Motivation also expands when you link that change to your identity, core values, and beliefs (Berkman 2018). It's hard to sustain effort toward a goal when you believe it's just not you.

For example, I worked with a woman named Sasha who struggled with obesity her entire life.

"I'm just not an athletic person," she said. She couldn't imagine herself exercising.

I asked Sasha how she liked to play as a child. "My friends and I loved to listen to music and dance, talk and laugh," she said.

"So, you liked to dance?" I asked.

"Oh yes, we had fun trying all the new dance moves," she said.

I asked Sasha if she could believe that she was someone who liked to dance.

"Absolutely! That's easy," she said.

Sasha could see herself as a dancer but not as an athlete. She discovered dance-based exercise videos that she could do at home alone or with family and friends. Her vision of herself as a child, dancing with friends, made her so happy she felt motivated to try it again as an adult.

Sustainable change requires three things.

1. **You want the change.**
2. **You can imagine yourself as that changed person.**
3. **The change connects to something you believe in and value.**

Start by identifying what you genuinely esteem. The following is a list of values to help you better determine what matters to you. Which ones do you demonstrate in your personal or professional life? Which values, if you adhere to them, would make you the proudest? Think of the people you most admire and love. Which values do they emulate? Check the five that are most important to you:

Serenity	Fairness	Independence	Generosity
Community	Humor	Compassion	Adventure
Beauty	Courage	Creativity	Curiosity
Loyalty	Forgiveness	Gratitude	Integrity
Respect	Humility	Excellence	Kindness
Leadership	Love	Knowledge	Tenacity
Social justice	Personal growth	Self-control	Social connection
Spirituality	Playfulness	Teamwork	Enthusiasm

After picking your top five values, write down which ones connect with the change you want. Here are five examples of how this works:

Want to feel relaxed giving training presentations?
Imagine: Mentally practice presenting with poise and humor.
Value: You care about increasing *knowledge* in a *playful*, fun way.

Want to be patient with your children when they misbehave?
Imagine: Visualize yourself calmly teaching them, implementing discipline with love in your heart.
Value: You *love* your children and want to create a happy family.

Want to feel more confident on dates?
Imagine: Mentally rehearse standing tall, feeling comfortable, with an openness to learning about another person.
Value: You admire socially *courageous* people and would like to act that way.

Want to get along better with your in-laws?

Imagine: Visualize yourself negotiating calmly and respectfully, considering their needs as well as the needs of your immediate family.

Value: You value *kindness* and *forgiveness* and want to model those behaviors for your children.

Want your manager to see you as a leader?

Imagine: Picture yourself leading, using good judgment, managing difficult people with calm confidence.

Value: You care about good *leadership* and want to treat others *fairly* and *justly*.

You will feel happier and less frazzled if you live according to your top values. When we act against what we believe, it causes internal conflict, stress, and *frazzlebrain*.

For example, as a teen, I became a vegetarian and had a keen interest in nutrition. I took a job at a fast-food hamburger restaurant to pay the bills. Every day I served very unhealthy-looking people food that I wouldn't eat. I felt guilty. My job conflicted with my strong desire to live and promote a healthy lifestyle. I quit that job and found one more in alignment with my beliefs. With that internal conflict resolved, I felt happier.

Take a moment to think about the most significant change you would like to make to help you break free from anxiety, anger, and stress. What do you want the most? How does that change connect with your top values? Be specific. The more clearly you state your goal, the more likely you will achieve it.

For example, *I want to be calmer* is a goal that's difficult to measure. Instead, saying *I want to respond more calmly when my spouse criticizes me* gives you a more precise, measurable, and achievable way to make progress.

Make your goal something you can accomplish without requiring another person to change. You will be more successful if you take control of your own behavior.

Complete the following:

1. **The specific change I want most is:**
2. **I imagine myself behaving calmly in this specific situation_____when I do the following:**
3. **This change aligns me with the following value(s):**

Changes that harmonize with your beliefs give you an evergreen reason to maintain the new behavior. The behavior becomes a part of your identity and sense of self. That kind of change sticks.

For example, Lydia wanted to reduce her angry outbursts at her children. When she entered therapy with me, she had three children under four years of age. Exhausted, depleted, discouraged, and resentful, Lydia needed help.

"My husband goes off to work in the morning, and he thinks I don't do anything all day because I don't have a job. He has no idea how hard it is to manage three crying, hungry, needy kids all day," she said.

I asked Lydia when she felt the most frazzled.

"I do pretty well until it's time to start dinner, right before my husband comes home. The kids are hungry, demanding. I can't get anything done. I feel like I'm losing my mind sometimes," she said.

I asked her to visualize how she would like to feel during those periods.

"I want to feel calm, in control, and in a good mood. Instead, I'm just hating being a mom," she replied.

Lydia identified the specific behavior she wished to change. She wanted to stop yelling at her children at the end of the day. This goal did not require anyone else to change. She could manage her reactions without needing her children to behave or anyone else to help her.

Next, Lydia needed to determine her core values. She looked at the values list and chose these five:

1. *Love*
2. *Playfulness*
3. *Creativity*
4. *Beauty*
5. *Loyalty*

"So how does calmly making dinner without yelling at your children align with these values?" I asked.

"I want to have a loving relationship with my kids and my husband. If I'm always mad at the end of the day, that's all my husband sees. I don't want to make them unhappy just because I'm frustrated," she replied.

Next, I asked her to imagine feeling calm and content while managing dinner and her children. Lydia visualized her more relaxed self:

I greet my husband with a smile. I've created welcoming aromas from food cooking in the kitchen. I laugh with my kids, watching them play with pots and plastic containers on the kitchen floor while I finish making dinner. I look good in my cute yoga pants, light makeup, brushed hair, and matching jewelry.

"That's great, Lydia! You visualized demonstrating your core values of love, beauty, playfulness, and maybe a little creativity too," I said.

"It's all wonderful to imagine, but how do I handle it when I feel exhausted, hungry, and angry? How do I keep from losing it? How do I calm down?" she asked.

Lydia needed a strategy or a plan of attack to help her change. *Frazzlebrain* made it hard for her to cope with her children's demands. She was too tired and hungry at the end of the day to summon much patience.

"If you're too tired and hungry to make dinner patiently, what do you need?" I asked.

"I need a break. Rest. A snack maybe," Lydia said.

I suggested she create a quiet time for the children. They could watch a children's program with her in bed, and she could listen to a guided meditation recording with earbuds to block out other sounds. I recommended she try twenty to thirty minutes of meditation time before preparing dinner. Lydia liked this idea because one of her favorite parenting rituals was "snuggle time" with her children right before bed.

On a follow-up appointment, I asked Lydia how the new routine worked.

"My kids and I love the cuddle time. I noticed that we all needed an afternoon snack. So, I changed the routine. We have snack time at 3 pm. Then at 4:30 pm, we have cuddle time. I listen to my meditation, and they watch a show. Sometimes they want to goof off, but they settle down a bit after a few minutes. It's so relaxing. Then I start dinner around 5 pm. My husband said he wants to meditate now," she said with a laugh.

Reward Effort

Progress happens one step at a time. You will see faster progress if you start with a modest, achievable goal and give yourself rewards for small steps toward that goal. Lydia's overall aim, to patiently make dinner and care for her children, gave her a focus for change. To incentivize her to try something new, she needed to imagine something pleasurable and rewarding for her effort.

It is essential to reward yourself for effort, not success. Success serves as its own reward. We need an incentive to work at something. Typically, our first efforts at change are inconsistent and imperfect. It's easy to get discouraged. If we don't get rewarded for our efforts, we tend to quit trying.

I asked Lydia to list things that she found rewarding. She needed something to look forward to, something positive to uplift her mood. Here is her list of rewarding things:

- *Time with girlfriends*
- *Decorating magazines*
- *Date night with husband*
- *Manicure/pedicure*
- *Massage*
- *Swimming*
- *Shopping for clothes*

From the list, I asked Lydia what she wanted the most right this moment.

"I miss seeing my friends," she said. So, Lydia chose girlfriend time as her reward. She looked forward to hikes, happy hours, and coffee breaks with her friends. After every five days of meditation, she rewarded herself with friend time.

Lydia was not rewarding herself for calmly making dinner; she rewarded herself for the effort she made to remain calm. For Lydia, that effort was daily meditation practice combined with a quiet time with her children.

Putting it all together, change that lasts requires the following:

1. **Choose something you want.**
2. **Imagine the ideal behavior.**
3. **Align behavior with your values.**
4. **Start with small steps.**
5. **Reward your incremental efforts.**

Be sure to give yourself the promised reward after completing the small step. When you deprive yourself of an earned reward, you can quickly become resentful and discouraged. So don't let yourself down!

When Lydia first started trying to meditate, she became frustrated and yelled at her children. I urged her to continue to reward herself for meditating, even if her children would not cooperate with the new schedule. She felt guilty for rewarding herself with girlfriend time after yelling at her kids.

I explained that if she meditated, even if fitfully, she demonstrated progress. After a few days, Lydia and her children looked forward to their quiet time together. The tension eased as they adapted to the new routine. She enjoyed more time with her friends, which made her feel happier. The meditation practice helped her regularly access her *CalmBrain*.

To help you make progress use the following Goal Setting Guide. You can make copies of the form and use it for every specific behavior you wish to change. Track your progress each day by checking the box indicating your small-step effort.

Record with a check mark each day that you do the unwanted behavior, imagine the ideal behavior, exercise your values, perform your small step, and reward your effort. Make a check under progress for each day that you work your plan.

Goal Setting Guide

		SUN	MON	TUE	WED	THU	FRI	SAT
UNWANTED BEHAVIOR	*Yelling at kids*							
IMAGINED IDEAL BEHAVIOR	*Calmly making dinner*							
VALUES	*Love, playfulness*							
SMALL STEP	*Meditation with rest time*							
REWARD FOR EFFORT	*Time with friends*							
PROGRESS								

Letting go of *frazzlebrain* requires regular attention to your nervous system. Many people don't notice how stressed they feel until the tension gets so great that they have symptoms. Symptoms like irritability, anxiety, panic attacks, gastro-intestinal issues, hives, inflammation, pain in the neck, shoulders, and back make you pay attention. Those symptoms show that your nervous system is ramped up and needs to calm down.

When you regularly practice caring for your nervous system, you are less likely to experience anxious distress. You likely engage in daily grooming habits without realizing that your nervous system needs regular maintenance too.

You probably know how to work hard and accomplish things. Maybe you follow through with medical and dental checkups, but relaxation doesn't make the priority list. Many people list the following as their top relaxing activities:

1. *Watching television/playing video games*
2. *Drinking alcohol or consuming marijuana*
3. *Going on vacation*

Did you know that you can still agitate your nervous system even if you're lying on your couch watching television? Television and video games are entertainment, not relaxation. Entertainment is fun. We all need it and enjoy it. However, your brain experiences a mini version of everything you watch. Most television shows and video games, even children's cartoons, depict conflicts, violence, people in distress, pain, and suffering. Even if you're watching the baking channel or nature documentaries, the entertainment provides escape and enjoyment, but not deep nervous system relaxation (Takeuchi, et al. 2016).

Alcohol as a primary relaxation tool quickly leads to problem drinking. According to research from the US Department of Health and Human Services, drinking more alcohol is linked to an increased risk of death from all causes (accident, cancer, heart disease, etc.) (DietaryGuidelines.gov). You can include multiple relaxation methods into your daily life without risking the early death, addiction, and relationship issues linked to problem drinking.

Marijuana users often say they use the drug for its relaxation effects. In a recent study, 58.1 percent of medical marijuana users reported using it for anxiety (Stoner 2017) (yes, that is the researcher's real name). THC, the compound in marijuana that causes intoxication, is known to cause anxiety. Anxiety also returns when the effects of the drug wear off. CBD, another chemical compound from marijuana, has some anxiety-relieving effects

(Todd, et al. 2017). Yet tolerance for both THC and CBD develops very quickly. Tolerance means that you must consume more and more of the drug to get the same benefit.

The use of THC and CBD for anxiety creates a dependency on the drug. It tickles the reward system of your brain. You feel anxiety, do the drug, get rebound anxiety, and then consume even more to obtain the calming effects (Stoner 2017). Dependency on a drug to calm down leads to worse problems later.

If a vacation is your primary relaxation method, you may only relax once or twice a year or on the weekends. That is not enough to keep your nervous system calm all year round.

Optimal mental and physical health requires daily stress management. It is best to weave a wide variety of calming thoughts, behaviors, and experiences into your everyday life. Using a wider variety of soothing strategies strengthens your coping skills. When you have many self-calming tools available, you can use them in all types of situations. That makes you more adaptable and resilient.

Look at the list of calming tools below. Pick one from each category that you can implement today.

Calming Tools

FOCUSED THOUGHTS (Chapters One–Three)	INTENTIONAL BEHAVIORS (Chapters Four–Six)	HEALING EXPERIENCES (Chapters Seven–Nine)
Name your feelings	Eat real food/ drink water	Nurture relationships
Five senses soothing	Eat mindfully	Volunteer
Flexible curiosity	Exercise	Amplify the good

FOCUSED THOUGHTS (Chapters One–Three)	INTENTIONAL BEHAVIORS (Chapters Four–Six)	HEALING EXPERIENCES (Chapters Seven–Nine)
Compassionate affirmations	Sunshine and light	Choose uplifting influences
Hopefulness	Regular sleep	Play
Compelling fantasy	Commune with nature	Awe, wonder, gratitude, curiosity
Optimistic life story	Acts of kindness	Meditation

You will obtain the maximum benefit if you select from all three categories. When you make small changes in your thoughts, behaviors, and experiences, you notice significant improvements in your well-being over time. Please answer the following questions and record them in your *frazzle hack* journal.

Calming Plan

1. The *focused thought* I plan to use today is:
2. The *intentional behavior* I plan to begin today is:
3. The *healing experience* I plan today is:

I worked with a married father of three young children named Haruki. He felt well suited to his career as a mechanical engineer; however, he displayed frequent outbursts of anger that he and his family found disturbing.

Haruki learned that he suffered from social anxiety or a fear of being around new people. Whenever he had to attend a social work function or give presentations in public, he felt overwhelmed with stress. His anxiety leaked out as irritability and anger. Haruki felt embarrassed, out of control, and weak.

I worked with Haruki on soothing and self-calming methods. In the beginning, it was exceedingly difficult for him to identify how he felt. "My parents never talked about emotions. They worked hard and made sure that we had everything we needed," Haruki said.

I suggested that his stress and anxiety served an important function. "This suffering you are experiencing is a gift. Without it, you might have ignored your emotions your whole life," I said. Haruki was surprised to learn that stress could provide any benefit at all. Stress encourages us to:

- **Pay attention.**
- **Feel motivated to change.**
- **Use the energy it provides.**
- **Seek help from others.**
- **Become sensitive to other's feelings.**
- **Learn from experience and grow** (McGonigal 2015).

Anxiety, anger, and stress motivate us to change and grow. Many people, like Haruki, were taught to ignore negative emotions and instead focus on responsibilities. However, emotional pain, like physical pain, serves an important protective function. Emotional distress makes us notice what we need.

Haruki's anxiety, anger, and stress taught him that he was disconnected from himself. He had never learned the importance of attending to his own emotions. As a result, he overlooked the feelings of his wife and children. He felt socially anxious because he did not know how to cope with emotions in himself and others.

Over time he learned to name his feelings and introduce calming thoughts, behaviors, and experiences. Haruki's calming plan looked like this:

1. **The *focused thought* I plan to use today is:**
   "I plan to name my feelings when I notice myself becoming irritable or distressed and write about those feelings to understand better what I need."

2. **The *intentional behavior* I plan to begin today is:**
   "I will get daily exercise every morning either on the treadmill or a run outside if it's not raining."

3. **The *healing experience* I plan today is:**
   "I plan to be more playful with my wife and children to nurture those relationships. We all like board games, so I will suggest a weekly game night for the family."

As Haruki became more comfortable noticing his feelings, he grew more aware of his family member's feelings as well. He eventually added meditation to his daily stress-management regimen.

"I feel so much better," Haruki said. "Now I know how to calm myself down. It's even helping me with my son. I think he has some anxiety too. He and I listen to guided meditations together when I put him to bed. My wife said she feels calmer too because I feel better."

Let *frazzlebrain* become your teacher. If you stop fighting, escaping, or ignoring it, you just might find a way to learn and grow from that uncomfortable feeling.

As I worked on this book, our family experienced many dramatic events: four significant deaths, four new babies (including two grandsons), moved two aging parents, converted to telehealth and online training practice, canceled our daughter's big out-of-state wedding due to the COVID-19 pandemic, then safely shared her backyard wedding with friends and family on Facebook

Live, attended virtual funerals and college graduations, and I was airlifted off a mountain after breaking my foot in a hiking accident.

As I reflect on this time of great tumult, I remember a verse by the Chinese philosopher, Lao Tzu from the *Tao Te Ching*:

Follow your path to the end.
Accept difficulty as an opportunity.
This is the sure way to end up with no difficulties at all
(Verse 63, Tao Te Ching).

Adversity and emotional pain present us with a choice. We can view our problems as terrible deviations from the norm or see them as opportunities for growth. Each moment holds within it the seeds for wonder, joy, curiosity, and hope. I invite you to join our community of fellow *frazzlebrain* students finding new pathways to the *CalmBrain* within.

There is honor, grace, and beauty in the effort to cultivate calm. You can make it happen.

ACKNOWLEDGMENTS

To **Cathy Scott,** I owe a forever debt of gratitude for her brilliant and generous mentorship, friendship, tutoring, editing, and for connecting me with the fabulous **Valerie Killeen** at Central Recovery Press. Thank you, **Valerie**, **Patrick Hughes**, and **Kirby Gann,** the talented team at **Central Recovery Press**, for your kind professionalism. It's been pure joy to work with you. **Marni Freedman** arrived like a miracle to coach this book into existence. She is a gifted writer, master coach, therapist, and builder of dreams. Warm thanks to the talented therapist **Judy Ervice** for recommending Marni. Appreciation for **Tracy Jean Jones** for your early research, encouragement, and pitch coaching.

A hearty shout out to **Marni Freedman's** talented **Feisty Writers** group for midwifery and support: **Donna Agins**, your gifts as an author/educator added so much to the organization and clarity in the book. Thank you, **Kimberly Joy**, for your sage advice on structure and tone. **Jen Laffler,** your enthusiasm, poetry, and quick wit helped keep the inner child laughing. To **Phyllis Olins**, praise for the gift of my title. Your generous encouragement kept me going. **Tania Pryputniewicz**, your poetic heart and compassionate wisdom made me go deeper.

Nicola Ranson, your inspirational writing and intelligent counsel polished the prose. Thank you, Lindsay Salatka, for your thoughtful critique and comic relief. Suzanne Spector, thank you for your wise advice. I hope my third act is as exciting as yours! Barb Thompson, thank you for your insightful analysis and keen therapist eye. Nancy Villalobos, thanks for your encouragement and helpful suggestions. Thank you, Anastasia Zadeik, for diagnosing my comma problem and for geeking out on the neuroscience with me.

Thank you, Curtis and Mary Anne Firstman, for the encouragement, laughs, and nurse referrals. Anthony Gibson, your *astute* editorial skills helped to polish and refine. Thank you, Victoria Pynchon, for your support, mentorship, and inspiration. Gratitude goes to dear friends Joe and Melody Stewart, who read through an early draft and provided critique and encouragement.

Thank you, "Turbo Man," Ryan Boule, for letting me share a bit of your inspiring story. Warm thanks to Hayley and Emily Rathburn for helpful commentary and Kelly and Gary Rathburn for inspiration and motivation. Thank you, sweet Ariel Schneider, for your therapeutic horticulture story.

Respect and gratitude to Seth Firstman, Danielle Kaplan, and Lizzy Tsen, extraordinary nurses.

Thank you, Loriann Oberlin, for teaching me how to write and for your kind foreword. I'm grateful for your generous mentorship and friendship.

To my lion-hearted husband, Jay, thank you for reminding me to rhumba. Your enthusiasm, humor, support, and wise editing advice elevated my spirits and the work. Heartfelt thanks go to our extraordinary children: Brandon for technical support and your intelligent, insightful suggestions; Daniel for your bright editorial ideas and encouragement; and Chloe for your empathy, optimism, and hopefulness.

Finally, I give a warm shout-out to the **San Diego Writer's Festival, San Diego Memoir Writers Association**, and **San Diego Writers Ink** for bringing writers together in community.

Finding Support for Change

Do You Need Professional Help?

Psychotherapists create a safe, confidential space to express your feelings and concerns. Licensed professionals learn techniques to help you reduce anxiety, stress, anger, and many other issues. Psychotherapy techniques can help you enhance your happiness, relationships, and overall mental health and effectiveness. Psychotherapists can save you time and heartache by guiding you toward thoughts and behaviors that can help you get through hard times without harming yourself or your relationships. Check any of the following statements that apply to you:

- You feel sad, helpless, worried, anxious, or nervous on most days of the week.
- You find it difficult to concentrate on essential things in your daily life.
- You have not made any progress trying to improve on your own.

- You've been skipping work or finding it hard to engage in the normal functions of everyday life, like bathing, meal preparation, hobbies, school, or social engagements.
- You have been drinking too much or using drugs or engaging in self-destructive behaviors that are hurting you or your loved ones.
- You sometimes feel that life is not worth living or that others might be better off without you.

If you checked any of the above statements, you should consider seeking the help of a professional. Your therapist can guide you to support groups or other helpful services as needed.

Which Type of Therapy Works Best?

When you begin to look for a therapist, you may have no idea what to look for or how to start. Reading online profiles of therapists can confuse you. Should you go to a practitioner of Dialectical Behavioral Therapy, Acceptance and Commitment Therapy, Bowen Family Systems, or Psychoanalytic psychotherapy? It can all look like a bunch of words meaning nothing. It helps to look at research on the therapeutic effectiveness of different approaches.

In a review of many studies, results showed that Cognitive Behavioral Therapy (CBT) effectively helps with anxiety, depression, stress, and other issues (Hofmann, et al. 2012). A therapist trained in CBT examines your thoughts or cognitions about events. When you interpret events primarily in a negative manner, your feelings follow that unhelpful pattern.

A CBT psychotherapist will also ask about your behavior. Specific behavioral choices can lead to healthier outcomes, and your therapist points out those things that can help your symptoms improve.

CBT therapists often use checklists, worksheets, homework, and charting of thoughts and behaviors so that you can monitor your progress. These exercises can help you quantify your growth, providing concrete tools to help you feel better and function better. At first, it may seem challenging as you learn to examine the workings of your automatic thoughts and beliefs. However, with practice, you can quickly change the negative thoughts and behaviors, leading to unhappiness, anger, anxiety, and stress. Like a muscle, your capacity to alter destructive thoughts and beliefs grows stronger with exercise and practice.

Many therapists receive training in multiple treatment methods. They can draw on tools from other approaches as well. I recommend that you choose a therapist with training in CBT, and if they have training in another method, you can ask your therapist about what treatment approach(es) or techniques they recommend for your specific needs.

What Type of Therapist Should I Choose?

It helps to know about the different types of professionals available to make an informed decision. In the United States, governing bodies regulate professions and set standards for education, experience, and issue licenses. Regulation of the practice of psychotherapy varies from state to state. I will list here a few of the terms typically used to describe psychotherapists and counselors and give you a bit of information about the training and background required:

- **Psychologists:** Clinical psychologists typically go to college from eight to twelve years, earn a PhD degree, and call themselves doctors. They are not medical doctors, so they usually cannot prescribe medication unless they practice in one of the few states that allow specially trained psychologists to prescribe medicines (New Mexico, Illinois, Louisiana, and Iowa). Psychologists must obtain 3000 hours of supervised experience in addition to coursework before they can take a licensing examination. They must complete continuing education units during each licensing period. Licensed psychologists can work in hospitals, universities and have a private practice.

- **Licensed marriage and family therapists (LMFT), Licensed clinical professional counselors (LCPC), Licensed professional counselors (LPC), Licensed mental health counselors (LMHC):** Licensed counselor requirements vary from state to state. Typically, these psychotherapists must have a master's degree in psychology, counseling, or marriage, and family therapy. They must also complete 3000 supervised hours and a written test before practicing outside of a supervised setting. They often have extensive training in individual, marital, and family counseling. Licensed counselors must complete continuing education credits, such as Law and Ethics, each licensing period to renew the license. They often do not have a doctoral or PhD degree. Therefore, they are not called doctors.

- **Licensed clinical social workers (LCSW):** These psychotherapists often have specialized training in social systems, such as elder care services, hospital grief counseling programs, or care programs for abused children or the disabled. In most states, they too are required to complete 3000 hours of supervised training before licensure, and continuing education credits, such as mandatory classes on chemical dependency and child abuse, before renewing the license. Most LCSW's have earned a master's degree, so they are not titled doctors. Those who have completed a doctoral degree in social work will have a DSW designation by their name.

- **Psychiatrists:** These professionals complete medical school and then a one-year residency in psychiatry before joining the profession. They can provide psychotherapy as well as prescribe medication, such as anti-anxiety or antidepressant medications. Psychiatrists are required to complete continuing education coursework to maintain the licensure. Medical school usually does not provide the direct supervised counseling experience that a psychologist or LPC, or LMFT receives in graduate school. Most psychiatrists get that experience in their year of psychiatric residency and continuing education outside of the university.

Your relationship with your therapist is the best predictor of your success in therapy. Do you feel this person understands you and communicates well with you? Does this person seem to care about helping you? Do you feel comfortable in their company? A therapist should not have any other relationship with you other than therapy. So don't pick someone from your friendship network or someone you're likely to see in another setting. The boundaries of psychotherapy protect you and the therapist. Therapists are people with complicated personalities that don't mix well with everyone. So, trust your gut (once you do your homework about their qualifications) and work with the therapist with whom you feel comfortable.

How to Find a Qualified Psychotherapist

You can find a qualified therapist in several ways. Ask your physician or friends for a referral to someone they may know personally. Look for referrals from your insurance provider. Get names of preferred providers and google their biographical information. *Psychology Today* has an easy-to-use therapist finder. You can plug in your location, and they can direct you to providers who specialize in anger, anxiety, stress, or other concerns. You can see a picture of the provider, read their statement, and follow links to their website. Most therapists do not require any time commitment. You have no obligation to remain with that person if you don't like them or their approach. You can also get referrals to qualified therapists from the major professional association websites:

- **American Psychological Association, www.apa.org**
- **American Association for Marriage and Family Therapy, www.aamft.org**
- **National Association of Social Workers, www.socialworkers.org**
- **American Psychiatric Association, www.psychiatry.org**

Many people can find comfort and support, direction, and encouragement from other, non-licensed counselors, such as clergy, life coaches, and unlicensed interns. I suggest that you consider the following criterion before choosing one of these professionals.

- **Unlicensed interns:** Sometimes, you can find help from someone early in their career, who has a master's degree or a PhD doctoral degree, but they are in the process of completing their supervised hours for licensure. They often charge less money, and they work under the supervision of a licensed professional. Many unlicensed interns can provide quality counseling for a reasonable price. If you feel that your issue is not too complicated, does not require medication, and may merely require a good listener who can provide sound advice at an affordable price, consider looking for an intern. The licensing board requires interns to let you know that they have not yet completed licensing requirements. When in doubt, ask if the individual has a license to practice and what type of license they practice under.

- **Clergy:** I recommend seeking spiritual counseling for spiritual or moral dilemmas. Pastoral counselors, rabbis, and other spiritual counselors are usually not trained in marital counseling or mental health counseling. They possess knowledge about spiritual matters and moral issues and guide you toward decisions that align with your spiritual values.

- **Life coaches:** Life coaches come from varied educational and experience backgrounds. To date, there are not consistent licensing standards for coaches. Coaches can help you work on a specific area of growth. Many people hire coaches to help them master, public speaking, business strategies, organizational skills, business management, time management, etc. Health coaches help people manage health issues like diabetes. If you've been diagnosed with attention deficit hyperactivity disorder, a specially trained coach can help you handle big projects effectively. I would not recommend a life coach for marriage counseling or mental health counseling as most are not qualified to perform that work. Coaches should not promise to help you with any mental health issues.

Should You Consider Medication?

Sometimes, before you begin therapy, you might fear that the therapist will push medication or some other treatment that seems frightening or worrisome to you. Some people believe that a pill will fix all their problems. Typically, people get better faster when they work with trustworthy psychotherapists who listen to their concerns and provide good reasons for the recommended approach. Psychotherapists can better help you the more you participate in the therapy process. If you don't feel comfortable with medication, ask your therapist to recommend non-medical approaches. If you think you need medicine, ask your therapist about that. You do not need to do everything your therapist suggests if it doesn't feel right to you.

Most therapists, including myself, will recommend a medication evaluation from a qualified psychiatrist (a medical doctor with specific mental health training) if patients demonstrate any of the following:

- *Suicidal thoughts and feelings.*
- *Self-destructive behavior such as cutting, recklessness, and excessive drug or alcohol use.*
- *Chronic insomnia.*
- *Difficulty functioning at work or school.*
- *Trouble completing normal daily life activities such as bathing, shopping, eating, taking care of children.*
- *Tried non-medical treatment for some time without getting better.*

It's usually best to see your primary care physician for a complete physical exam because some physical conditions may cause mental health symptoms. Most psychotherapists will ask in their intake interview about health problems and if you have recently obtained a complete physical exam. If you have not had a complete physical in the last year, your therapist will recommend that you get one soon so they can rule out any physical cause for your current symptoms.

It takes courage to begin a psychotherapy process. Just remember, you are allowed to change your mind, challenge what your therapist says, and find a new therapist if you feel your current one is not helping you. Your psychotherapist can be a supportive and helpful partner in your healing journey.

BIBLIOGRAPHY

Abelson, J. L., T. M. Erikson, S. Mayer, J. Crocker, H. Briggs,
N. L. Lopez-Duran, and I. Liberzon. 2014. "Brief Cognitive
Intervention can Modulate Neuroendocrine Stress Responses
to the Trier Social Stress Test: Buffering Effects of a
Compassionate Goal." *Psychoneuroendocrinology* 44, 60–70.
doi.org/10.1016/j.psyneuen.2014.02.016.

Abraham, Eyal, Talma Hendler, Irit Shapira-Lichter, Yaniv
Kanat-Maymon, Orna Zagoory-Sharon, and Ruth Feldman.
2014. "Father's Brain is Sensitive to Childcare Experiences."
Proceedings of the National Academy of Sciences, 9792–9797.

Abramson, L. Y., Seligman, M.E.P, Teasdale, J. D. 1978. "Learned
Helplessness in Humans: Critique and Reformulation." *Journal
of Abnormal Psychology*, 49–74.

Aghamohammadi-Sereshki, Arash, Nicholas J. Coupland, Peter
H. Silverstone, Yushan Huang, Kathleen M. Hegadoren,
Rawle Carter, Peter Seres, and Nikolai V. Malykhin. 2021.
"Effects of Childhood Adversity on the Volumes of the

Amygdala Subuclei and Hippocampal Subfields in Individuals with Major Depressive Disorder." *Journal of Psychiatry & Neuroscience* 46(1), 186–195. doi:10.1503/jpn.200034.

Ahani, A., H. Wahbeh, M. Nezamfar, D. Miller, Erdogmus Oken, and B., Oken. 2014. "Quantitative Change of EEG and Respiration Signals During Mindfulness Meditation." *Journal of NeuroEngineering and Rehabilitation* 11(1), 87. doi: 10.1186/1743-0003-11-87.

Alexander, Rebecca, Oriana R. Aragon, Jamila Bookwala, Nicolas Cherbuin, Justine M. Gatt, Ian J. Kahrilas, Niklas Kastner, et al. 2021. "The Neuroscience of Positive Emotions and Affect: Implications for Cultivating Happiness and Wellbeing." *Neuroscience and Biobehavioral Reviews* 121, 220–249. doi.org/10.1016/j.neubiorev.2020.12.002.

Anderson, Elizabeth, and Geetha Shivakumar. 2013. "Effects of exercise and Physical Activity on Anxiety." *Frontiers in Psychiatry* 4(27), 1–4. doi:10.3389/fpsyt.2013.00027.

Appleton, Jeremy. 2018. "The Gut-Brain Axis: Influence of Microbiota on Mood and Mental Health." *Integrative Medicine* 17(4), 28–32.

Armenta, Christina N., Megan M. Fritz, and Sonja Lyubomirsky. 2016. "Functions of Positive Emotions: Gratitude as a Motivator of Self-Improvement and Positive Change." *Emotion Review*, 1–8. doi:10.1177/1754073916669596.

Backhed, F., J. Roswall, and Y.: et al. Peng. 2015. "Dynamics and Stabilization of the Human Gut Microbiome During the First Year of Life." *Cell Host Microbe* 17(5), 690–703.

Bai, Y., L. A. Maruskin, S. Chen, A. M. Gordon, J. E. Stellar, G. D. McNeil, K. Peng, and D. Keltner. 2017. "Awe, the Diminished Self, and Collective Engagement: Universals and Cultural Variations in the Small Self." *Journal of Personality and Social Psychology* 113(2), 185–209. doi.org/10.1037/pspa0000087.

Balleine, B.W., and O. Hikosaka. 2007. "The Role of the Dorsal Striatum in Reward and Decision-Making." *Journal of Neuroscience*, 8161–8165.

Begley, Sharon. 2008. *Train Your Mind: Change Your Brain: How a New Science Reveals Our Extraordinary Potential to Transform Ourselves*. New York: Balantine Books.

Berkman, Elliot T. 2018. "The Neuroscience of Goals and Behavior Change." *Consulting Psychology Journal* 70(1), 28–44. doi:10.1037/cpb0000094.

Black, David S., and George M. Slavich. 2016. "Mindfulness Meditation and the Immune System: A systematic Review of Randomized Controlled Trials." *Annals of the New York Academy of Sciences* 1373(1), 13–24. doi:10.1111/nyas.12998.

Blackwell, S. E., M. Browning, A Mathews, A. Pictet, J. Welch, J.: Watson, P. Davies, J.R. Geddes, and E. A. Holmes. 2015. "Positive Imager-based Cognitive Bias Modification as a Web-Based Treatment Tool for Depressed Adults: A Randomized Controlled Trial." *Clinical Psychological Science* 3, 91–111. doi:10.1177/216770614560746.

Bonanno, George A. 2004. "Loss, Trauma, and Human Resilience: Have We Underestimated the Human Capacity to Thrive After Extremely Aversive Events?" *American Psychologist* 59(1), 20–28. doi:10.1037/0003-066X.59.1.20.

Bonaz, B., T. Bazin, and S. Pellissier. 2018. "The Vagus Nerve at the Interface of the Microbiota-Gut-Brain Axis." *Frontiers in Neuroscience* 12(49). doi:10.3389/fnins.2018.00049.

Boyd-Wilson, B. M., and F. H. Walkey. 2015. "The Enlightenment Scale: A Measure of Being at Peace and Open-Hearted." *Pastoral Psychology* 64, 311–325. doi:10.10071/s11089-013-0586-9.

Breit, S., A. Kupferberg, C. Rogler, and G. Hasler. 2018. "Vagus Nerve as Modulator of the Brain-Gut Axis in Psychiatric and Inflammatory Disorders." *Frontiers in Psychiatry* 9, 44. doi:10.33389/fpsyt.2018.00044.

Brooks, Helen Louise, Kelly Rushton, Karina Lovell, Penny Bee, Lauren Walker, Laura Grant, and Anne Rogers. 2018. "The Power of Support from Companion Animals for People Living with Mental Health Problems: A Systematic Review and Narrative Synthesis of the Evidence." *BMC Psychiatry* 18(1), 31. doi:10.1186/s12888-018-1613-2.

Brussoni, M., R. Gibbons, C. Gray, T. Ishikawa, E. B. Sandseter, A. Bienenstock, G. Shabot, et al. 2015. "What is the Relationship Between Risky Outdoor Play and Health in Children? A Systemic Review." *International Journal of Environmental Research and Public Health*, 6423–6454. doi:10.3390/ijerph120606423.

Brydon, L., J. Lin, L. Butcher, M. Hamer, J.D. Erusalimsky, E. H. Blackburn, and A. Steptoe. 2012. "Hostility and Cellular Aging in Men from the Whitehall II Cohort." *Biological Psychiatry* 71, 767–773.

Burls, A. 2007. "People and Green Spaces: Promoting Public Health and Mental Well-being through Ecotherapy." *Journal of Public Mental Health* 6: 3. 24–39.

Bushman, Brad J. 2002. "Does Venting Anger Feed or Extinguish the Flame? Catharsis, Rumination, Distraction, Anger, and Aggressive Responding." *Personality and Social Psychology Bulletin* 28(6): 724–731 doi.org/10.1177/0146167202289002.

Cacioppo, Stephanie, Bianchi-Demicheli, Elain Hatfield, and Richard L. Rapson. 2012. "Social Neuroscience of Love." *Clinical Neuropsychology* 9(1) 3–13.

Cani, P.D., and C. Knauf. 2016. "How Gut Microbes Talk to Organs: The Role of Endocrine and Nervous Routes." *Molecular Metabolism* 5(9): 743–752. doi:10.1016/j.molmet.2016.05.011.

Capurso, Viviana, Franco Fabbro, and Cristiano Crescentini. 2014. "Mindful Creativity: The Influence of Mindfulness Meditation on Creative Thinking." *Frontiers in Psychology* 4(1020). 1–2. doi:10.3389/fpsyg.2013.01020.

Carlsmith, Kevin M., T. D. Wilson, and D.T. Gilbert. 2008. "The Paradoxical Consequences of Revenge." *Journal of Personality and Social Psychology* 95: 1316–1324 doi:10.1037/A0012165.

Carpenter, Siri. 2012. "That Gut Feeling." *Monitor on Psychology* 43:50.

Carrillo, A., M. Rubio-Aparicio, G. Molinari, A. Enrique, J. Sanchez-Meca, and R. M. Banos. 2019. "Effects of the Best Possible Self Intervention: A Systematic Review and Meta-Analysis." *PLoS ONE* 14(9). doi:10.1371/journal.pone.0222386.

Carrion, Victor G., and Shane S. Wong. 2012. "Can Traumatic Stress Slter the Brain? Understanding the Implications of Early Trauma on Brain Development and Learning." *Journal of Adolescent Health*, S23–S28. doi.org/10.1016/j.jadohealth.2012.04.010.

Cates, David S., B. Kent Houston, Christine R. Vivak, Michael H. Crawford, and Meredith Uttley. 1993. "Heritability of Hostility Related Emotions, Attitudes, and Behaviors." *Journal of Behavioral Medicine* 16, 237–256.

Chalfont, G., J. Simpson, S. Davies, D. Morris, R. Wilde, L. Willoughby, and C. Milligan. 2019. "Personalized Medicine for Dementia: Collaborative Research of Multimodal Nonpharmacological Treatment with the UK National Health Service (NHS)." *OBM Geriatrics* 3(3), 26. doi:10.21926/obm.geriatr.1903066.

Clapp, M., N. Aurora, L. Herrera, M. Bhatia, E. Wilen, and S. Wakefield. 2017. "Gut Microbiota's Effect on Mental Health: The Gut-Brain Axis." *Clinics and Practice* 7, 987. doi:10.4081/cp.2017.987 .

Clements, Heather, S. Valentin, Nicholas Jenkins, Jean Rankin, Julien Baker, Nancy Gee, Donna Snellgrove, and Katherine Sloman. 2019. "The Effects of Interacting with Fish in Aquariums on Human Health and Well-Being: A Systematic Review." *PLOS ONE* 14. doi:10.1371/journal.pone.022054.

Colbert, Steven. 2006. *Commencement Address*. Galesburg: Knox College.

Conversano, C., A. Rotondo, E. Lensi, O. Della Vista, F. Arpone, and M. A. Reda. 2010. "Optimism and its Impact on Mental and Physical Well-Being." *Clinical Practice and Epidemiology in Mental Health* (6), 25–29. doi.org/10.2174/1745017901006010025.

Cozolino, L. 2010. *The Neuroscience of Psychotherapy.* New York: W.W. Norton & Company, Inc.

Cozolino, Louis. 2014. *The Neuroscience of Human Relationships.* New York: W. W. Norton & Company.

Creswell, David J., Michael R. Irwin, Lisa J. Burklund, Matthew D. Lieberman, Jesusa M. G. Arevalo, Jeffrey Ma, Elizabeth Crabb Breen, and Steven W. Cole. 2012. "MIndfulness-Based Stress Reduction Training Reduces Loneliness and Pro-Inflammatory Gene Expression in Older Adults: A Small Randomized Controlled Trial." *Brain, Behavior, and Immunity* 26(7), 1095–1101. doi:10.1016/j.bbi.2012.07.006.

Crum, Alia J., and Ellen J. Langer. 2007. "Mind-set Matters: Exercise and the Placebo Effect." *Psychological Science* 18(2), 165–171. dy.doi.org/10.1111/j.1467-9280.2007.01867.

Dambrun, Michael. 2017. "Self-Centeredness and Selflessness: Happiness Correlates and Mediating Psychological Processes." *Peer J,* 1–27. doi:10.7717/peerj.3306.

Danvers, Alexander F., and Michelle N. Shiota. 2017. "Going off Script: Effects of Awe on Memory for Script-typical and Irrelevant Narrative Detail." *Emotion* 17(6), 938–952. doi:10.1037/emo0000277.

Davidson, R. J., and S. Begley. 2012. *The Emotional Life of Your Brain: How Its Unique Patterns Affect the Way You Think, Feel, and Live-and How You Can Change Them.* New York: Penguin Group.

DeAngelis, Tori. 2008. "The Two Faces of Oxytocin: Why Does the 'Tend and Befriend' Hormone Come into Play at the Best and Worst of Times?" *Monitor on Psychology* 39(2), 30.

Derrick, L. L., S. Gabriel, and K. Hugenberg. 2009. "2010." *Journal of Experimental Social Psychology* 45(2), 352–362. doi.org/10.1016/j.jesp.2008.12.003.

Dinan, T.G., and J.F. Cryan. 2017. "Gut Instincts: Microbiota as a Key Regulator of Brain Development, Ageing and Neurodegeneration." *The Journal of Physiology* 565(2), 489–503. doi:10.1113/JP273106.

Disabato, D. J., T. B. Kashdan, J. L. Short, and A. Jarden. 2017. "What Predicts Positive Life Events that Influence the Course of Depression? A Longitudinal Examination of Gratitude and Meaning in Life." *Cognitive Therapy and Research* 41(3), 444–458. doi.org/10.1007/s10608-016-9785-x.

Doidge, Norman. 2007. *The Brain That Changes Itself: Stories of Personal Triumph From the Frontiers of Brain Science*. New York: Penguin Books.

—. 2015. *The Brain's Way of Healing: Remarkable Discoveries and Recoveries from the Frontiers of Neuroplasticity*. New York: Viking Penguin.

Eckburg, P.B. 2005. "Diversity of the Human Intestinal Microbial Flora." *Science* 308, 1635–1638.

Edinger-Schons, L. M. 2020. "Oneness Beliefs and Their Effect on Life Satisfaction." *Psychology of Religion and Spirituality* 12(4), 428–439. doi.org/10.1037/rel0000259.

Elkins-Brown, Nathaniel, Rimma Teper, and Michael Inzlicht. 2017. "How Mindfulness Enhances Self-Control." In *Mindfulness in Social Psychology*, by Johan C. Karremans and Esther K. Papies, 14. London: Routledge.

Farrow, Marc R., and Kyle Washburn. 2019. "A Review of Field Experiments on the Effect of Forest Bathing on Anxiety and Heart Rate Variability." *Global Advances in Health and Medicine* 8, 1–7. doi:10.1177/2164956119848654.

Fjeld, Tove, Kaj Veiersted, Leiv Sandvik, Geir Riise, and Finn Levy. 1998. "The Effect of Indoor Foliage Plants on Health and Discomfort Symptoms Among Office Workers." *Indoor and Built Environment* 7, 204–209. doi:10.1159/000024583.

Flynn, Laurie J. 2004. "Technology; A Start-Up, and a Fresh Start on Life." *New York Times*, March 29: Section C. Page 4.

Fredrickson, Barbara L. 2001. "The Role of Positive Emotions in Positive Psychology: The Broaden-and-Build Theory of Positive Emotions." *American Psychologist* 56(3), 218–226. doi:10.1037/0003-066X56.3.218.

Fredrickson, Barbara L., and Marcial F. Losada. 2005. "Positive Affect and the Complex Dynamics of Human Flourishing." *American Psychologist* 60(7), 678–686. doi.org/10.1037/0003-066X.60.7.678.

Friedmann, E., and H. Son. 2008. "The Human-Companion Animal Bond: How Humans Benefit 39(2)." *Veterinary Clinics of North America: Small Animal Practice*, 293–326. doi:10.1016/j.cvsm.2008.10.015. PMID:19185195.

Friese, Malte, Claude Messner, and Yves Schaffner. 2012. "Mindfulness Meditation Counteracts Self-Control Depletion." *Consciousness and Cognition* 21, 1016–1022. doi:10.1016/j.congog.2012.01.008.

Froh, J. J., R. A. Emmons, N. A. Card, G. Bono, and J. A. Wilson. 2011. "Gratitude and the Reduced Costs of Materialism in Adolescents." *Journal of Happiness Studies* 12(2), 289–302. doi.org/10.1007/s10902-010-9195-9.

Fuertes, J. N., A. Mislowack, J. Bennett, L. Paul, T. C. Gilbert, G. Fontan, and L. S. Boylan. 2007. "The Physician-Patient Working Alliance." *Patient Education and Counseling* 66(1), 29–36. doi:10.1016/j.pec.2006.09.013.

Gallagher, M.W., and S.J. Lopez. 2018. "Introduction to the Science of Hope." In *The Oxford Handbook of Hope*, by M.W. Ed. Gallagher, 3–7. Oxford: Oxford University Press.

Gallagher, Matthew W., and Shane J. Lopez. 2007. "Curiosity and Well-Being." *The Journal of Positive Psychology* 2(4), 236–248. doi.org/10.1080/17439760701552345.

Gerritsen, Roderick J. S., and Guido P. H. Band. 2018. "Breath of Life: The Respiratory Vagal Stimulation Model of Contemplative Activity." *Frontiers in Human Neuroscience* 12(397), 1–25. doi:10.3389/fnhum.2018.00397.

Ginsburg, Kenneth R., and Martha M. Jablow. 2020. *Building Resilience in Children and Teens: Giving Kids Roots and Wings*. Itasca: American Academy of Pediatrics.

Goldfarb, Elizabeth V., Monica D. Rosenberg, Dongju Seo, and Todd Constable. 2020. "Hippocampal Seed Connectome-Based Modeling Predicts the Feeling of Stress."

Nature Communications 11(2650), 1–10.
doi.org/10.1038/s41467-020-16492-2.

Gonzalez, Marianne T., Terry Hartig, Grete Grindal Patil, Egil
Wilhelm, Martinsen Kirkevold, and Marit. Kirkevold. 2011.
"A Prospective Study of Existential Issues in Therapeutic
Horticulture for Clinical Depression." *Issues in Mental Health
Nursing* 32:1, 73–81. doi:10.3109/01612840.2010.528168.

Grant, Joshua A., Emma G. Duerden, Jerome Courtemanche,
Mariya Cherkasova, and Gary H. Rainville, Pierre Duncan.
2013. "Cortical Thickness, Mental Absorption and Meditative
Practice: Possible Implications for Disorders of Attention."
Biological Psychology 92, 275–281.
doi.org/10.1016/j.biopsycho.2012.09.007.

Griskevicius, V., M. N. Shiota, and S. L. Neufeld. 2010.
"Influence of Positive Emotions on Persuasion Processing: A
Functional Evolutionary Approach." *Emotion* 10, 190–206.
doi.org/10.1037/a0018421.

Gritz, E.C., and V. Bhandari. 2015. "The Human Neonatal Gut
Microbiome: A Brief Review." *Frontiers in Pediatrics* 3.

Hall, S.S., H.F. Wright, and D.S. Mills. 2016. "What Factors
are Associated with Positive Effects of Dog Ownership in
Families with Children with Autism Spectrum Disorder? The
Development of the Lincoln Autism Pet Dog Impact Scale."
PLoS ONE 11(2). doi.org/10.1371/journal.pone.0149736.

Hanson, Rick. 2011. *Just One Thing*. Oakland: New Harbinger
Publications, Inc.

Hill, P. D., M. Allemand, and B. W. Roberts. 2013. "Examining
the Pathways Between Gratitude and Self-Rated Physical

Health Across Adulthood." *Personality and Individual Differences* 54(1), 92–96. doi.org/10.1016/j.paid.2012.08.011.

Hofmann, Stefan G., Ann Asnaani, Imke J. J. Vonk, Alice T. Sawyer, and Angela Fang. 2012. "The Efficacy of Cognitive Behavioral Therapy: A Review of Meta-analyses." *Cognitive Therapy Research* 36(5), 427–440.

Holt-Lunstad, Julianne, Timothy B. Smith, and J. Bradley Layton. 2010. "Social Relationships and Mortality Risk: A Meta-analytic Review." *PLoS Medicine* 7(7), 1–20. doi:10.1371/journal.pmed.1000316.

Holzel, Britta K., James Carmody, Mark Vangel, Christina Congleton, Sita M. Yerramsetti, Tim Gard, and Sara W. Lazar. 2011. "Mindfulness Practice Leads to Increases in Regional Brain Gray Matter Density." *Psychiatry Research* 191(1), 36–43. doi:10.1016/j.pscychresns.2010.08.006.

Huh, Susanna, and Catherine M. Gordon. 2008. "Vitamin D Deficiency in Children and Adolescents: Epidemiology, Impact and Treatment." *Reviews in Endocrine and Metabolic Disorders* 9, 161–170. doi:10.1007/s11154-007-9072-y.

Hutcherson, Cendri A., Emma M. Seppala, and James J. Gross. 2008. "Loving-Kindness Meditation Increases Social Connectedness." *Emotion* 8(5), 720–724. doi:10.1037/a0013237.

Inagaki, Tristen K., and Naomi I. Eisenberger. 2012. "Neural Correlates of Giving Support to a Loved One." *Psychosomatic Medicine* 74(1), 3–7. doi:10.1097/PSY.0b013e3182359335.

Inagaki, Tristen K., and Naomi, I. Eisenberger. 2016. "Giving Support to Others Reduces Sympathetic Nervous System-

Related Responses to Stress." *Psychophysiology*, 427–435. doi.org/10.1111/psyp.12578.

Inzlicht, M., B. J. Schmeichel, and C. N. Macrae. 2014. "Why Self-Control Seems (But May Not Be) Limited." *Trends in Cognitive Sciences* 18(3), 127–133.

Irvin, K. M., D. J. Bell, D. Steinley, and B. D. Bartholow. 2020. "The Thrill of Victory: Savoring Positive Affect, Psychophysiological Reward Processing, and Symptoms of Depression." *Emotion*. doi:10.1037/emo0000914.

Ishak, W. W., M. Kahloon, and H. Fakhry. 2011. "Oxytocin role in enhancing well-being: a literature review." *Journal of Affective Disorders*, 1–9.

Jarzyna, Carol Laurent. 2020. "Parasocial Interaction, the COVID-19 Quarantinve, and Digital Age Media." *Human Arenas*. doi.org/10.1007/s42087-020-00156.

Kaplan, R., and S. Kaplan. 1989. *The Experience of Nature: A Psychological Perspective*. New York: Cambridge University Press.

Kaptchuk, T.J., E. Friedlander, J.M. Kelley, M.N. Sanchez, E. Kokkotou, and et al. 2010. "Placebos without Deception: A Randomized Controlled Trial in Irritable Bowel Syndrome." *PLoS ONE* 5(12), e15591. doi:10.137/journal.pone.0015591.

Kaptchuk, T.J., J. M. Kelley, L.A. Conboy, R.B. Kerr, C.E. Davis, and et al. 2008. "Components of the Placebo Effect: A Randomized Controlled Trial in Irritable Bowel Syndrome." *British Journal of Medicine* 336, 999–1003.

Kaur, Chamandeep, and Preeti Singh. 2015. "EEG Derived Neuronal Dynamics During Meditation: Progress and Challenges." *Advances in Preventive Medicine*, 1–10. doi.org/10.1155/2015/614723.

Keysers, C., and V. Gazzola. 2010. "Social Neuroscience: Mirror Neurons Recorded in Humans." *Current Biology*, R353–R354.

Kidd, Celeste, and Benjamin Y. Hayden. 2015. "The Psychology and Neuroscience of Curiosity." *Neuron*, 449–460. doi.org/10.1016/j.jeuron.2015.09.010.

Kim, C. H. 2018. "Immune Regulation by Microbiome Metabolites." *Immunology* Mar. 22. doi:10.1111/imm.12930.

Kim, Pilyoung, Paola Rigo, Linda C. Mayes, Ruth Feldman, James F. Leckman, and James E. Swain. 2014. "Neural Plasticity in Fathers of Human Infants." *Social Neuroscience* 9(5), 522–535. doi:10.1080/17470919.2014.933713.

King, Katherine. 2012. "Aggravating Conditions: Cynical Hostility and Neighborhood Ambient Stressors." *Social Science Medicine* 75(12), 2258–2266. doi:10.1016/j.socscimed.2012.08.027.

Klimecki, Olga M., Susanne Leiberg, Matthieu Ricard, and Tania Singer. 2014. "Differential Pattern of Functional Brain Plasticity after Compassion and Empathy Training." *Social Cognitive Affective Neuroscience* 9(6), 873–879. doi:10.1093/scan/nst060.

Kong, J., R. L. Gollub, G. Polich, I. Kirsch, P. LaViolette, M. Vangel, B. Rosen, and T. J. Kaptchuk. 2008. "A Functional Magnetic Resonance Imaging Study on the Neural

Mechanisms of Hyperalgesic Nocebo Effect." *Journal of Neuroscience* 28(49), 13354–13362.

Kong, J., R.L. Gollub, I. S. Rosman, J. M. Webb, M. G. Vangel, I. Kirsch, and T. J. Kaptchuk. 2006a. "Brain Activity Associated with Expectancy-Enhanced Placebo Analgesia as Measured by Functional Magnetic Resonance Imaging." *Journal of Neuroscience* 26, 381–388.

Konturek, P.C. 2011. "Stress and the Gut: Pathophysiology, Clinical Consequences." *Journal of Physiology and Pharmacology*, 591–599.

Korpela, Kalevi, Matti Ylen, Liisa Tyrvainen, and Harri Silvennoinen. 2010. "Favorite Green, Waterside and Urban Environments, Restorative Experiences and Perceived Health in Finland." *Health Promotion International* 25, 200–209. doi:10.1093/heapro/daq007.

Kotera, Yasuhiro, Miles Richardson, and David Sheffield. 2020. "Effects of Shinrin-Yoku (Forest Bathing) and Nature Therapy on Mental Health: A Systematic Review and Meta-Analysis." *International Journal of Mental Health and Addiction*, 1–25. doi:10.13140/RG.2.2.12423.21920.

Krause, N., and R. D. Hayward. 2014. "Hostility, Religious Involvement, Gratitude, and Self-Rated Health in Late Life." *Research on Aging* 36(6), 731–752. doi.org/10.1177/016402751359113.

Kress, Laura, Mirko Bristle, and Tatjana Aue. 2018. "Seeing Through Rose-Colored Glasses: How Optimistic Expectancies Guide Visual Attention." *PLoS ONE* 13(2), e0193311. doi.org/10.137/journal.pone.0193311.

Kress, Laura, Mirko Bristle, and Tatjana Aue. 2018. "Seeing Through Rose-Colored Glasses: How Optimistic Expectancies Guide Visual Attention." *PLoS ONE*, 1–27. doi.org/10.1371/journal.pone.0193311.

Kubany, Edward S., Antonio Gino, Nathan R. Denny, and Rodney, Y. Torigoe. 1994. "Relationship of Cynical Hostility and PTSD among Vietnam Veterans." *Journal of Traumatic Stress*, 21–31. doi.org/10.1007/BF02111909.

Kuo, Frances E., and Andrea Faber Taylor. 2004. "A Potential Natural Treatment for Attention-Deficit/Hyperactivity Disorder: Evidence From a National Study." *Research and Practice* 94(9), 1580–1586.

Landau, M.J., B.P. Meier, and L. A. Keefer. 2010. "A Metaphor-Enriched Social Cognition." *Psychological Bulletin* 136(6), 1045–1067. doi.org/10.1037/a0020970.

Langer, Ellen J. 2009. *Counter Clockwise: Mindful Health and the Power of Possibility*. New York: Ballantine Books.

—. 2010. *Counterclockwise: A Proven Way to Think Yourself Younger and Healthier*. London: Hodder Paperback.

Lanius, Ruth A., Braeden A. Terpou, and Margaret C. McKinnon. 2020. "The Sense of Self in the Aftermath of Trauma: Lessons from the Default Mode Network in Posttraumatic Stress Disorder." *European Journal of Psychotraumatology* 11(1), 1–11. doi.org/10.1080/20008198.2020.1807703.

Lee, Andre Chee Keng, Hannah C. Jordan, and Jason Horsley. 2015. "Value of Urban Green Spaces in Promoting Healthy Living and Wellbeing: Prospects for Planning." *Risk Management and Healthcare Policy* 8, 131–137.

Leung, C. C., and E. M. W. Tong. 2017. "Gratitude and Drug Misuse: Role of Coping as Mediator." *Substance Use and Misuse* 52(14), 1832–1839. doi.org/10.1080/10826084.2017.1312449.

Lewis, Michael W., Russell T. Jones, and Margaret T. Davis. 2020. "Exploring the Impact of Trauma Type and Extent of Exposure on Posttraumatic Alterations in 5-HT1A Expression." *Translational Psychiatry* 10, 237. doi.org/10.1038/s41398-020-00915-1.

Li, Qing. 2019. "Effect of forest bathing (shinrin-yoku) on Human Health: A Review of the Literature." *Sante Publique*, 135–143. doi:10.3917/spub.190.0135.

Li, Qing. 2010. "Effect of Forest Bathing Trips on Human Immune Function." *Environmental Health and Preventative Medicine* 15, 9–17. doi:10.1007/s12199-008-0068-3.

Lieberman, Matthew D. 2013. *Social: Why Our Brains Are Wired to Connect*. New York: Random House LLC.

Louv, Richard. 2008. *The Last Child in the Woods: Saving Our Children from Nature Deficit Disorder*. Chapel Hill: Algonquin Books.

Luerssen, Anna, Anett Gyurak, Ozlem Ayduk, Carter Wendelken, and Silvia A. Bunge. 2015. "Delay of Gratification in Childhood Linked to Cortical Interactions with the Nucleus Accumbens." *Social Cognitive and Affective Neuroscience*, 1769–1776.

Lysiak, Matthew, and Bill Hutchinson. 2012. "Hero Who Saved Baby from Subway Tracks Gets New Gig After a Year Without a Job." *New York Daily News*. New York City: Tribune Publishing, June 27.

Malberg, Jessica E., Rene Hen, and Torsten M. Madsen. 2021. "Adult Neurogenesis and Antidepressant Treatment: The Surprise Finding by Ron Duman and the Field 20 Years Later." *Biological Psychiatry* 90(2), 96–101. doi.org/10.1016/j.biopsych.2021.01.010.

Marcus, Robert F. 1980. "Empathy and Popularity of Preschool Children." *Child Study Journal* 10(3), 133–145.

Marks-Tarlow, Terry. 2010. "The Fractal Self at Play." *American Journal of Play* 3(1), 1-32.

Masten, A. S. 2001. "Ordinary Magic: Resilience Processes in Development." *American Psychologist* 56, 227–238. doi.org/10.1037/0003-066X.56.3.227.

Mathews, Dorothy, and Susan Jenks. 2013. "Subcutaneous Mycobacterium Vaccae Promotes Resilience in a Mouse Model of Chronic Psychosocial Stress When Administered Prior to or During Psychosocial Stress." *Behavioral Processes* 96. doi:10.1016/j.beproc.2013.02.007.

Mayer, Emeran A. 2018. *The Mind-Gut Connection: How the Hidden Conversation with Our Bodies Impacts Our Moods, Our Choices, and Our Overall Health*. New York: Harper Wave.

McGonigal, Kelly. 2015. *The Upside of Stress: Why Stress is Good for You (and How to Get Good at it)*. London: Vermillion.

McKee, Ian R., and N. T. Feather. 2008. "Revenge, Retribution, and Values: Social Attitudes and Punitive Sentencing." *Social Justice Research* 21, 138. doi:org/10.1007/s11211-008-0066-z.

Messaoudi, Michaël, Robert Lalonde, Nicolas Violle, Hervé Javelot. 2011. "Assessment of psychotropic-like properties of a probiotic formulation (Lactobacillus helveticus R0052 and Bifidobacterium longum R0175) in rats and human subjects." *British Journal of Nutrition*, 755–764.

Michl, P., T. Meindl, F. Meister, C. Born, R. R. Engel, and M. et al. Reiser. 2012. "Neurobiological Underpinnings of Shame and Guilt: a Pilot fMRI study." *Social Cognitive and Affective Neuroscience* 9(2), 150–157.

Miller, T. Q., T.W. Smith, C.W. Turner, M.L. Guijarro, and A.J. Hallet. 1996. "A Metaanalytic Review of Research on Hostility and Physical Health." *Psychological Bulletin* 119, 322–348.

Mills, P.J., C. T. Peterson, M. A. Pung, S. Patel, L. Weiss, and K. L. et al. Wilson. 2018. "Change in Sense of Nondual Awareness and Spiritual Awakening in Response to a Multidimensional Well-Being Program." *Journal of Alternative and Complementary Medicine* 24, 343–351. doi:10.1089/acm.2017.0160.

Mintzer, Jacobo, Keaveny Anne Donovan, Arianne Zokas Kindy, Sarah Lenz Lock, Lindsay R. Chura, and Nicholas Barracca. 2019. "Lifestyle Choices and Brain Health." *Frontiers in Medicine* 6(204), 1–11. doi:10.3389/fmed.2019.00204.

Mischel, Walter. 1961. "Father Absence and Delay of Gratification." *Journal of Abnormal and Social Psychology*, 116–124. doi:10.1037/h0046877.

—. 2014. *The Marshmallow Test: Why Self-Control is the Engine of Success*. New York: Little, Brown and Company.

Mischel, Walter, and Ebbe B. Ebbesen. 1970. "Attention in Delay of Gratification." *Journal of Personality and Social Psychology* 329–337.

Mogilner, C. 2012. "Giving Time Gives You Time." *Psychological Science*, 1233–1238. doi.org/10.1177/0956797612442551.

Mohajeri, M. Hasan, Giorgio La Fata, Robert E. Steinert, and P. Weber. 2018. "Relationship Between the Gut Microbiome and Brain Function." *Nutrition Reviews* 76(7), 481–496. doi.org/10.1093/nutrit/nuy009.

Mooney, P., and P. L. Nicell. 1992. "The Importance of Exterior Environment for Alzheimer Residents: Effective Care and Risk Management." *Healthcare Management Forum* 5, 23–29.

Murphy, Tim, and Loriann H. Oberlin. 2016. *Overcoming Passive-Aggression, Revised Edition: How to Stop Hidden Anger from Spoiling your Relationships, Career, and Happiness*. Boston: Da Capo Lifelong Books.

Nagasawa, Miho, Shouhei Mitsui, Shiori En, Nobuyo Ohtani, Mitsuaki Ohta, Yasuo Sakuma, Tatsushi Onaka, Kazutaka Mogi, and Takefumi. Kikusui. 2015. "Oxytocin-Gaze Positive Loop and the Coevolution of Human-Dog Bonds 348." *Science*, 333–336.

Neal-Barnett, A., R. Stadulis, M. Murray, M.R. Payne, A. Thomas, and B. B Salley. 2011. "Sister Circles as a Culturally Relevant Intervention for Anxious Black Women." *Clinical Psychology: Science and Practice* 18(3), 266–273. doi.org/10.1111/j.1468-2850.2011.01258.x.

Neff, Kristin. 2011. *Self-Compassion: Stop Beating Yourself Up and Leave Insecurity Behind*. New York: William Morrow.

Nelson, S. Katherine, Kristin Layous, Steven W. Cole, and Sonja Lyubomirsky. 2016. "Do Unto Others or Treat Yourself?

The Effects of Prosocial and Self-Focused Behavior on Psychological Flourishing." *Emotions* 16(6), 850–861.

Nelson-Coffey, S. Katherine, Megan M. Fritz, Sonja Lyubomirsky, and Steve W. Cole. 2017. "Kindness in the Blood: A Randomized Controlled Trial of the Gene Regulatory Impact of Prosocial Behavior." *Psychoneuroendocrinology*, 8–13. doi.org/10.1016/j.psyneuen.2017.03.025.

Ng, M. Y., and W. S. Wong. 2013. "The Differential Effects of Gratitude and Sleep on Psychological Distress in Patients with Chronic Pain." *Journal of Health Psychology* 18(2), 263–271. doi.org/10.1177/1359105312439733.

Ozbay, Faith, Douglas C. Johnson, Eleni Dimoulas, C.A. Morgan, Dennis Charney, and Steven Southwick. 2007. "Social Support and Resilience to Stress." *Psychiatry*, 35–40.

Ozer, E. J., S. R. Best, T. L. Libsey, and D. D. Weiss. 2003. "Predictors of Posttraumatic Stress Disorder and Symptoms in Adults: A Meta-analysis." *Psychological Bulletin* 129(1), 52–73. doi:10.1037/0033-2909.129.1.52.

Pascual-Leone, A., D. Nguyet, L. G. Cohen, J. P. Brasil-Neto, A. Cammarota, and M. Hallett. 1995. "Modulation of Muscle Responses Evoked by Transcranial Magnetic Stimulation During the Acquisition of New Fine Motor Skills." *Journal of Neurophysiology* 74(3), 1037–1045. doi:10.1152/jn.1995.74.3.1037.

Petrocchi, N., and A. Couyoumdjian. 2016. "The Impact of Gratitude on Depression and Anxiety: The Mediating Role of Criticizing, Attacking, and Reassuring the Self." *Self and Identity* 15(2), 191–205. dio.org/10.1080/15298868.2015.1095794.

Piff, Paul K., Pia Dietze, Matthew Feinberg, Daniel M. Stancato, and Dacher Keltner. 2015. "Awe, the Small Self, and Prosocial Behavior." *Journal of Personality and Social Psychology* 108(6), 883–899. doi:10.1037/pspi0000018.

Poulin, Michael, Lauren Ministero, Shira Gabriel, Carrie Morrison, and Esha Maidu. 2021. "Minding Your Own Business? Mindfulness Decreases Prosocial Behavior for Those with Independent Self-construals." *PsyArXiv* April 9. doi:10.31234/osf.io/xhyua.

Pratto, F., J. Sidanius, L.M. Stallworth, and B.F. Malle. 1994. "Social Dominance Orientation: A Personality Variable Predicting Social and Political Attitudes." *Journal of Personality and Social Psychology* 67, 741–763.

Pressman, S. D., B. N. Jenkins, and J. T. Moskowitz. 2019. "Positive Affect and Health: What Do We Know and Where Next Should We Go?" *Annual Review of Psychology* 70, 627–650. doi.org/10.1146/annurev-psych-010418-102955.

Puig-Perez, Sara, Carolina Villada, Matias, M. Pulopulos, Mercedes Almela, Vanesa Hidalgo, and Alicia Salvador. 2015. "Optimism and Pessimism are Related to Different Components of the Stress Response in Healthy Older People." *International Journal of Psychophysiology* 98, 213–221.

Pulcu, Erdem, Karen Lythe, Rebecca Elliott, Sophie Green, Jorge Moll, John F. W. Deakin, and Roland Zahn. 2014. "Increased Amygdala Response to Shame in Remitted Major Depressive Disorder." *PLoS One* 9(1), 1–9. doi:10.1371/journal.pone.0086900.

Rabot, Sylvie, Mathilde Jaglin, Valerie Dauge, and Laurent Naudon. 2016. "Impact of the Gut Microbiota on the Neuroendocrine and Behavioural Responses to Stress in Rodents." *OCL* 23(1), D116. doi:10.1051/ocl/2015036.

Radavelli-Bagatini, S., L.C. Blekkenhorst, M. Sim, R. L. Prince, N. P. Bondonno, C. P. Bondonno, R. Woodman, et al. 2021. "Fruit and Vegetable Intake is Inversely Associated with Perceived Stress Across the Adult Lifespan." *Clinical Nutrition* 40(5), 2860–2867. doi.org/10.1016/j.clnu.2021.03.043.

Radzvilavicius, Arunas L., Alexander J. Stewart, and Joshua B. Plotkin. 2019. "Evolution of Empathetic Moral Evaluation." *eLife* 8, 1–17. doi.org/10.7554/eLife.44269.

Rappe, Erja, and S. Kivela. 2005. "Effects of Garden Visits on Long-Term Care Residents as Related to Depression." *Horttechnology* 15, 298–303.

Razzoli, Maria, Kewir Nyuyki-Dufe, Allison Gurney, Connor Erickson, Jacob McCallum, Nicholas Spielman, Marta Marzullo, et al. 2018. "Social Stress Shortens Lifespan in Mice." *Aging Cell*, 1–14. doi.org/10.1111/acel.12778.

Reblin, Maija, and Bert N. Uchino. 2008. "Social and Emotional Support and its Implication for Health." *Current Opinions in Psychiatry* 21(2), 201–205. doi:10.1097/YCO.0b013e3282f3ad89.

Rhee, S.H., C. Pothoulakis, and E.A. Mayer. 2009. "Principle and Clinical Implications of the Brain-Gut-Enteric Microbiota Axis." *Nature Reviews Gastroenterology & Hepatology* 6, 306–314.

Rogers, G.B., D.J. Keating, R.L. Young, M. L. Wong, J. Licinio, and S. Wesselingh. 2016. "From Gut Dysbiosis to Altered

Brain Function and Mental Illness: Mechanisms and Pathways." *Molecular Psychiatry* 21(6), 738–748.

Romain, Ligneul, Romuald Girard, and Jean-Claude Dreher. 2017. "Social Brains and Divides: The Interplay Between Social Dominance Orientation and the Neural Sensitivity to Hierarchical Ranks." *Scientific Reports* 7, 45920. doi:10.1038/srep45920.

Rosenkranz, Melissa A., Richard J. Davidson, Donal G. MacCoon, John F Sheridan, Ned H. Kalin, and Antoine Lutz. 2013. "A Comparison of Mindfulness-Based Stress Reduction and an Active Control in Modulation of Neurogenic Inflammation." *Brain, Behavior, and Immunity* 27C, 174–184. doi:10.1016/j.bbi.2012.10.013.

Rudd, M., K. D. Vohs, and J. Aaker. 2012. "Awe Expands People's Perception of Time, Alters Decision Making, and Enhances Well-Being." *Psychological Science* 23(10), 1130–1136. doi:10.1177/0956797612438731.

Sakaki, Michiko, Ayano Yagi, and Kou Murayama. 2018. "Curiosity in Old Age: A Possible Key to Achieving Adaptive Aging." *Neuroscience & Biobehavioral Reviews* 88, 106–116. doi:10.1016/j.neubiorev.2018.03.007.

Scarlet, Janina, Nathanael Altmeyer, Susan Knier, and R. Edward Harpin. 2017. "The Effects of Compassion Cultivation Training (CCT) on Health-Care Workers." *Clinical Psychologist* 21, 116–124.

Schneider, Ariel. 2014. *Finding Personal Meaning: Vocational Horticulture Therapy for Individuals with Severe and Persistent Mental Illness*. Master's Thesis, Northhampton: Smith College School for Social Work.

Schubert, C.F., U. Schmidt, and R. Rosner. 2016. "Posttraumatic Growth in Populations with Posttraumatic Stress Disorder-A Systematic Review on Growth-Related Psychological Constructs and Biological Variables." *Clinical Psychology & Psychotherapy* 23(6), 469–486. doi:10.1002/cpp.1985.

Seligman, Martin E. P. 2006. *Learned Optimism*. New York: Vintage Books.

Shanahan, Danielle F., Robert Bush, Kevin J. Gaston, Brenda B. Lin, Julie Dean, Elizabeth Barber, and Richard A. Fuller. 2016. "Health Benefits from Nature Experiences Depend on Dose." *Scientific Reports* 6, 28551. doi:10.1038/srep28551.

Sharma, R., D. Gupta, R. Mehrotra, and P. Mago. 2021. "Psychobiotics: The Next-Generation Probiotics for the Brain." *Current Microbiology* Jan. 4. doi:10.1007/s00284-020-02289-5.

Shiota, Michelle, Todd Thrash, Alexander Danvers, and John Dombrowski. 2017. "Transcending the Self: Awe, Elevation, and Inspiration." In *The Handbook of Positive Emotions*, by M. M. Tugade, M. N. Shiota and L. D. Kirby. doi:10.31234/osf.io/hkswj. New York: Guilford Press.

Singer, Tania, B. Seymour, J.P. ODoherty, K.E. Stephan, R.J. Dolan, and C.D. Frith. 2006. "Empathic Neural Responses are Modulated by the Perceeived Fairness of Others." *Nature*, 466–469.

Smith, David G., Roberta Martinelli, Gurdyal S. Besra, Petr A. Illarionov, Istva Szatmari, P. Brazda, Mary A. Allen, et al. May 2019. "Identification and Characterization of a Novel Anti-Inflammatory Lipid Isolated from Mycobacterium Vaccae, a

Soil-Derived Bacterium with Immunoregulatory and Stress Resilience Properties." *Psychopharmacology (Berl)* 236(5), 1653–1670. doi:10.1007/s00213-019-05253-9.

Smith, J. L., J. G. Bihary, D. O'Connor, A. Basic, and C. J. O'Brien. 2020. "Impact of Savoring Ability on the Relationship Between Older Adults' Activity Engagement and Well-Being." *Journal of Applied Gerontology* 39(3), 323–331. doi:10.1177/0733464819871876.

Smith, Sean M., and Wylie W. Vale. 2006. "The Role of the Hypothalamic-Pituitary-Adrenal Axis in Neuroendocrine Responses to Stress." *Dialogues in Clinical Neuroscience* 8, 383–395.

Sochocka, M., K. Donskow-Lysoniewska, and B.S. et al. Diniz. 2019. "The Gut Microbiome Alterations and Inflammation-Driven Pathogenesis of Alzheimer's Disease-a Critical Review." *Molecular Neurobiology*, 1841–1851. doi.org/10.1007/s12035-018-1188-4.

Song, Yeoungsuk, and Ruth Lindquist. 2015. "Effects of Mindfulness-Based Stress Reduction on Depression, Anxiety, Stress and Mindfulness in Korean Nursing Students." *Nurse Education Today* 35(1), 86–95. doi.org/10.1016/j.nedt.2014.06.010.

Stavrova, Olga, and Daniel Ehlebracht. 2016. "Cynical Beliefs About Human Nature and Income: Longitudinal and Cross-Cultural Analyses." *Journal of Personality and Social Psychology* 110, 116–132.

Stellar, J. E., N. John-Henderson, C. L. Anderson, A. M. Gordon, G. D. McNeil, and D. Keltner. 2015. "Positive Affect and

Markers of Inflammation: Discrete Positive Emotions Predict Lower Levels of Inflammatory Cytokines." *Emotion* 15(2), 129–133. doi.org/10.1037/emo0000033.

Stern, Stephen, L., D. Allen Donahue, Sybil Allison, John P. Hatch, Cynthia L. Lancaster, Trisha A. Benson, Allegro L. Johnson, et al. 2013. "Potential Benefits of Canine Companionship for Military Veterans with Posttraumatic Stress Disorder (PTSD)." *Society & Animals* 21(6), 568–581. doi.org/10.1163/15685306-12341286.

Stoner, Susan A. 2017. "Effects of Marijuana on Mental Health." *Alcohol & Drug Abuse Institute, University of Washington* URL: http://adai.uw.edu/pubs/pdf/2017mjanxiety.pdf.

Stravrova, Olga, and Daniel Ehlebracht. 2018. "The Cynical Genius Illusion: Exploring and Debunking Lay Beliefs About Cynicism and Competence." *Personality and Social Psychology Bulletin* 45, 254–269. doi.org/10.11770/0146167218783195.

Takeuchi, H., Y. Taki, H. Hashizume, and et al. 2016. "Impact of Videogame Play on the Brain's Microstructural Properties: Cross-Sectional and Longitudinal Analyses." *Molecular Psychiatry* 21, 1781–1789. doi.org/10.1038/mp.2015.193.

Tarrasch, Ricardo, Lilach Margalit-Shalom, and Rony Berger. 2017. "Enhancing Visual Perception and Motor Accuracy among School Children through a Mindfulness and Compassion Program." *Frontiers in Psychology* 8(281), 1–10. doi:10.3389/fpsyg.2017.00281.

Teicher, M. H., and J. A. Samson. 2016. "Annual Research Review: Enduring Neurobiological Effects of Childhood Abuse and Neglect." *Journal of Child Psychology and Psychiatry* 57, 241–266.

Todd, Stephanie M., Cilla Zhou, David J. Clarke, Tariq
    W. Chohan, ilara Bahceci, and Jonathon C. Arnold.
    2017. "Interactions Between Cannabidiol and Delta
    9-THC Following Acute and Repeated Dosing: Rebound
    Hyperactivity, Sensorimotor Gating and Epigenetic and
    Neuroadaptive Changes in the Mesolimbic Pathway."
    European Neuropsychopharmacology 27, 132–145.
    doi.org/10.1016/j.euroneuro.2016.12.004.

Toribio-Mateas, M. 2018. "Harnessing the Power of Microbiome
    Assessment Tools as Part of Neuroprotective Nutrition and
    Lifestyle Medicine Interventions ." *Microorganisms* 6(2), 35.
    doi.org/10.3390/microorganisms6020035.

Toussaint, L., G. S. Shields, G. Dorn, and G. M. Slavich. 2016.
    "Effects of Lifetime Stress Exposure on Mental and Physical
    Health in Young Adulthood: How Stress Degrades and
    Forgiveness Protects Health." *Journal of Health Psychology*
    21(6), 1004–1014. doi:10.1177/1359105314544132.

Toyoda, Masahiro, Yuko Yokota, Marni Barnes, and Midori
    Kaneko. 2020. "Potential of a Small Indoor Plant on the Desk
    for Reducing Office Worker's Stress." *Hort Technology* 30(1),
    55–63. doi.org/10.21273/HORTTECH04427-19.

Tripp, Thomas, M., and Robert J. Bies. 2009. *Getting Even:
    The Truth about Workplace Revenge and How to Stop it.*
    San Francisco: John Wiley & Sons, Inc.

Tu, Pei-Ghun, Wen-Chen Cheng, Ping-Cheng Hou, and Yu-Sen
    Chang. 2020 . "Effects of Types of Horticultural Activity
    on the Physical and Mental State of Elderly Individuals."
    *International Journal of Environmental Research and Public
    Health,* 1–13.

Tutu, Desmond M., and Mpho A. Tutu. 2014. *The Book of Forgiving: The Fourfold Path for Healing Ourselves and Our World*. New York: Harper One.

Umberson, Debra. 1987. "Family Status and Health Behaviors: Social Control as a Dimension of Social Integration." *Journal of Health and Social Behavior* 28(3), 306–319.

Vago, David R., and David A. Silbersweig. 2012. "Self-Awareness, Self-Regulation, and Self-Transcendence (S-ART): A Framework for Understanding the Neurobiological Mechanisms of Mindfulness." *Frontiers in Human Neuroscience* 6(296), 1–30. doi:10.3389/fnhum.2012.00296.

van den Berg, A., and M. H. G. Custers. 2011. "Gardening Promotes Neuroendocrine and Affective Restoration from Stress Journal of Health Psychology." *Journal of Health Psychology* 16(1), 3–11.

van den Berg, Magdalena M. H. E., Jolanda Maas, Rianne Muller, Anoek Braun, Wendy Kaandorp, Rene van Lien, Mireille NM. van Poppel, Willem van Mechelen, and Agnes E. van den Berg. 2015. "Autonomous Nervous System Responses to Viewing Green and Built Settings: Differentiating Between Sympathetic and Parasympathetic Activity." *Environmental Research and Public Health* 12, 15860–15874.

Van Lente, Eric, and Michael J. Hogan. 2020. "Understanding the Nature of Oneness Experience in Meditators Using Collective Intelligence Methods." *Frontiers in Psychology* 11(2092), 1–19. doi:10.3389/fpsyg.2020.02092.

van Vugt, Marieke K., and Amishi P. Jha. 2011. "Investigating the Impact of Mindfulness Meditation Training on

Working Memory: A Mathematical Modeling Approach."
Cognitive, Affective, and Behavioral Neuroscience 11, 344–353.
doi:10.3758/s13415-011-0048-8.

Vert, Christina, Mireia Gascon, Otavio Ranzani, Sandra Marquez,
Margarita Triquero-Mas, G. Carrasco-Turigas, Lourdes Arjona,
et al. 2020. "Physical and Mental Health Effects of Repeated
Short Walks in a Blue Space Environment: A Randomised
Crossover Study." *Environmental Research* 188, 109812.
doi:10.1016/j.envres.2020.109812.

Vestergaard-Poulsen, Peter, M. van Beek, J. Skewes, C. R.
Bjarkam, M. Stubberup, J. Bertelsen, and A. Roepstorff. 2009.
"Long-Term Meditation is Associated with Increased Gray
Matter Density in the Brain Stem." *NeuroReport* 20(2),
170–174. doi:10.1097/WNR.0b013e328320012a.

Vickhoff, Bjom, Helge Malmgren, Rickard Astrom, Gunnar
Nyberg, Seth-Reino Ekstrom, Mathias Engwall, Johan
Snygg, Michael Nilsson, and Rebecka Jomsten. 2013.
"Music Structure Determines Heart Rate Variability of
Singers." *Frontiers in Psychology* 4(334), 1–16. doi:10.3389/
fpsyg.2013.00334.

Volker, S., and T. Kistemann. 2011. "The Impact of Blue Space
on Human Health and Well-being-Salutogenetic Health
Effects of Inland Surface Waters: A Review." *International
Journal of Hygiene and Environmental Health* 214(6), 449–460.
doi:10.1016/j.ijheh.2011.05.001.

Wade, N. G., W. T. Hoyt, J. E. M. Kidwell, and E. L.
Worthington. 2014. "Efficacy of Psychotherapeutic
Interventions to Promote Forgiveness: A Meta-analysis."
Journal of Consulting and Clinical Psychology 82(1), 154–170.

Wang, Y., J Chen, and Z. Yue. 2017. "Positive Emotion Facilitates Cognitive Flexibility: An fMRI Study." *Frontiers in Psychology* 8(1832). doi.org/10.3389/fpsyg.2017.01832.

Weinberg, Robert. 2008. "Does Imagery Work? Effects on Performance and Mental Skills." *Journal of Imagery Research in Sport and Physical Activity* 3(1), 1932–0191??. doi:10.2202/1932-0191.1025.

Weir, K. 2017. "Forgiveness Can Improve Mental and Physical Health." *Monitor on Psychology* 48(1), 30.

Weir, Kirsten. 2018. "The Future of Psychobiotics." *Monitor on Psychology*, 43–48.

White, Mathew P., Ian Alcock, James Grellier, Benedict W. Wheeler, Terry Hartig, Sara L. Warber, Angie Bone, Michael H. Depledge, and Lora E. Fleming. 2019. "Spending at Least 120 Minutes a Week in Nature is Associated with Good Health and Wellbeing." *Scientific Reports* 9, 7730. doi.org/10.1038/s41598-019-4497-3.

White, Mathew P., Lewis, R. Elliott, Mireia Gascon, Bethany Roberts, and Lora E. Fleming. 2020. "Blue Space, Health and Well-being: A Narrative Overview and Synthesis of Potential Benefits." *Environmental Research* 191, 1–14. doi.org/10.1016/jenvres.2020.110169.

Williams, Lynda B., and Shelley E. Haydel. 2010. "Evaluation of the Medicinal Use of Clay Minerals as Antibacterial Agents." *International Geology Review* 52(7/8), 745–770. doi:10.1080/00206811003679737.

Wood, A. M., J. Maltby, R. Gillett, P. A. Linley, and S. Joseph. 2008. "The Role of Gratitude in the Development of Social

Support, Stress, and Depression." *Journal of Research in Personality* 42(4), 854–871. doi.org/10.1016/j.jrp.2007.11.003.

Wood, Emma, Alice Harsant, Martin Dallimer, Anna Cronin de Chavez, Rosemary R. C. McEachan, and Christopher. Hassall. 2018. "Not All Green Space is Created Equal: Biodiversity Predicts Psychological Restorative Benefits From Urban Green Space." *Frontiers in Psychology* 9, 2320. doi:10.3389/fpsyg.2018.02320.

Yahyavi, S. T., M. Zarghami, and F. et al. Naghshvar. 2015. "Relationship of Cortisol, Norepinephrine, and Epinephrine Levels with War-Induced Posttraumatic Stress Disorder in Fathers and their Offspring." *Revista Brasileira de Psiquiatria* 37, 93–98.

Yehuda, R., L. M. Bierer, and J. et al. Schneidler. 2000. "Low Cortisol and Risk for PTSD in Adult Offspring of Holocaust Survivors." *American Journal of Psychiatry* 157, 1252–1259.

Yehuda, Rachel, and Amy Lehrner. 2018. "Intergenerational Transmission of Trauma Effects: Putative Role of Epigenetic Mechanisms." *World Psychiatry* 17(3), 243–257.

Young, D. A., T.C. Neylan, L. L. Chao, A. O'Donovan, T. J. Metzler, and S. S. Inslicht. 2019. "Child Abuse Interacts with Hippocampal and Corpus Callosum Volume on Psychophysiological Response to Startling Auditory Stimuli in a Sample of Veterans." *Journal of Psychiatric Research* 111, 16–23, doi:10.1016/j.jpsychires.2019.01.011.

Young, Simon N. 2007. "How to increase serotonin in the human brain without drugs." *Journal of Psychiatry and Neuroscience*, 394–399.

Yue, G., and K.J. Cole. 1992. "Strength Increases from the Motor Program: Comparison of Training with Maximal Voluntary and IMagined Muscle Contractions." *Journal of Neurophysiology* 67(5), 1114–1123. doi.org/10.1152/jn.1992.67.5.1114 .

Yusifov, Rashad, Anja Tippmann, Jochen F. Staiger, Oliver M. Schluter, and Siegrid Lowel. 2021. "Spine Dynamics of OSD-95-deficient Neurons in the Visual Cortex Link Silent Synapses to Structural Cortical Plasticity." *Proceedings of the National Academy of Sciences* 118(10). doi.org/10.1073/pnas.2022701118.

Zeidan, Fadel, and David Vago. 2016. "Mindfulness Meditation-Based Pain Relief: A Mechanistic Account." *Annals of the New York Academy of Sciences* 1373(1), 114–127. doi:10.1111/nyas.13153.